FROM PROSPECT TO PROSPERITY

Wildcatting in Arabia and the Rockies

FROM PROSPECT TO PROSPERITY

Wildcatting in Arabia and the Rockies

By PAUL T. WALTON

UTAH STATE UNIVERSITY PRESS
Logan, Utah — 1994

Printed in the United States of America.
All rights reserved.

A McMurrin–Henriksen Book
For Utah State University Press.
All photographs are from the author's personal collection.

*The paper in this book is acid free and meets the standards for permanence and
durability established by the Committee on Production Guidelines
for Book Longevity of the Council on Library Resources.*

Library of Congress Cataloging-in-Publication Data
Walton, Paul T., 1914–
    From prospect to prosperity: wildcatting in Arabia and the
Rockies/by Paul T. Walton.
        p. cm.
    Includes index.
    ISBN 0-87421-173-5 (cloth) — ISBN 0-87421-174-3 (pbk.)
    1. Walton, Paul T., 1914–   . 2. Petroleum engineers — United
States — Biography. 3. Petroleum — Prospecting — Saudi Arabia.
4. Mines and mineral resources — Utah. I. Title.
TN869.2.W35A3   1994
622′ .338′09 — dc20

Frontispiece: King ibn-Saud, left, and Paul T. Walton, right,
sign the Neutral Zone concession agreement for the Getty oil interests
at the Royal Palace, Riyadh, Saudi Arabia, February 1949.

For My Mother

LENORE WATTS WALTON
June 26, 1887–February 10, 1938

FOREWORD

Robert H. Woody

FOR HIS EFFORTS, PAUL WALTON got a "foreign bonus" of $1,200. His boss, J. Paul Getty, went on to become the richest man in the world.

In early 1949, Walton, representing Getty, had quietly upped the royalty offer to "Lord of the Desert" King Abdul Aziz Ibn Saud of Arabia to an unprecedented 55 cents a barrel in exchange for the operating concession from the Saudi government for its undivided half-interest in the then–"neutral zone" between Saudi Arabia and Kuwait.

It was an appalling and arrogant act as far as the traditional Mideast operators were concerned. They—British, Anglo-American, and Dutch consortia — had long been used to paying 25 cents. But Getty had properly forecast that the price of $1.50 a barrel for Middle Eastern oil was not to stay at that level forever.

Garbed in Arab clothing, and with facial features and a mustache that nearly passed him off as an Arab, Walton watched ibn-Saud affix his signature to the concession agreement.

It was a momentous event, one that would have implications forty-one years later as President Bush assembled American troops south of the former zone in 1990 as prelude to Desert Storm. For most of those years, the petroleum prospect Walton had identified and garnered for Getty was being produced as Kuwait's Wafra oil field. By 1990 it had yielded nearly five billion barrels of oil.

Walton's role in the 1949 negotiation, however, unhearalded at the time, by 1990 was certainly little known or even remembered in his native state of Utah.

For Paul Walton is a quiet and unpresuming being.

And it is only in this chronicle that there is record for the general public. Written first from diary notes and later as recollections, the book deals with Walton's lifelong involvement in petroleum and minerals prospecting.

Although he would certainly not have been conscious of it, Walton comes off a bit like the late William L. Shirer in his diary and the fictional Indiana Jones in his adventures.

Romantic? Not always.

Walton had first gone to the Middle East as the chief of a prospecting team for Standard Oil of California in the late thirties. The diary takes note of the cruel details of nomad life and the rigors of pioneering a new field in a hostile desert.

In 1939, after a close encounter of the worst kind with death — the local crematorium reportedly kept its furnaces stoked in anticipation of his body — Walton headed for home, weakened by rheumatic fever, jobless, and in deep depression. His weary return took him through Europe, a continent on the brink of war that September, where he witnessed the alarming assembly of German armament and troops in Austria.

Public health still had not reached the Middle East in 1949, when Walton returned to negotiate the Saudi–Getty concession in Riyadh. Then, as in 1939, he was plagued with severe bouts of dysentery, cramps, and nausea — an agony, and an inevitability of the time and place, that does not afflict swashbucklers of the cinema.

The volume's latter years are based on records and recollections of Walton's associations, prospecting, and wildcatting around the world, and his discovery of the Clear Creek gas field on Utah's Wasatch Plateau.

In part, that discovery was compelled by the fact that Mountain Fuel Supply Company, then with limited reserves, was not able to provide gas to a home Walton had built in the Salt Lake suburb of Holladay. Clear Creek was to become the basis for Walton's principal wealth. It set him up for life and provided the means to buy his beloved and beautiful ranch in Jackson Hole, Wyoming.

Walton had not enriched himself in his Mideast assignments. Nor, as a geologist–prospector–investor–partner, had he triumphed in other ventures ranging from uranium to iron ore to shale oil to geothermal.

The minerals business is rife with risk. For small independent operators, wildcatters, one discovery or successful claim will be the batting average of a lifetime of tries. And those who score even once are among the very few.

But it is not Walton's wealth and possessions (although these are modest compared with those of J. Paul Getty), but rather his wealth of competence and character that have been most appreciated by intimates and associates. Mind more than money got respect.

In an industry legendary for brashness, boisterousness, and bravado, Walton was the quiet man. He was not necessarily reclusive: He attended professional meetings. He gave and published geological papers. He enjoyed the company of peers.

Says one of Walton's business associates, "He was a scientist who went into the field. He was a promoter with a small 'p.' People listened to him. He had respect. He was not afraid to speak out."

Adds another industry veteran: "He minded his own business and did it very well."

When I joined *The Salt Lake Tribune* as a reporter in 1957, I was assigned part-time to the business page until 1965, when I was named business editor, a post I held to retirement in 1990.

I got to meet and know a lot of "oil patch" people — the genial, the genuine, the geologists, the "oil scouts," the landmen, the operators, the contractors and suppliers, the pretenders and promoters with a big "P," and a few chairmen and presidents, ranging from the Salt Lake City–based Equity Oil to Justheim Petroleum, to El Paso Natural Gas to Northwest Energy, Union Oil of California, Phillips Petroleum, and British Petroleum.

Some of my favorite acquaintances and sources—Dorsey Hager, Glen Ruby, and Red Nevins — are mentioned favorably by Walton in his account.

But I had only a slight awareness of Walton. I should have had more. He simply did not proclaim or assert himself. Though he was associated in ventures with the late Thomas Kearns and with my employer, the Kearns-Tribune Corporation, there was never a nudge or even a suggestion that Walton was to get any special consideration.

There had been a *Tribune* story on Mr. Walton's deal with ibn-Saud in 1949. But it was not among newsroom legends when I got there. Indeed, it was not until 1990, when President Bush marshaled Desert Shield forces in Saudi Arabia that Walton's deal with Saud was recollected.

Utah's petroleum community was by then a fraction of what it had been in its heyday in the late fifties. During those tense days of 1990, his longtime office manager, the late Betty Allen, called to say Walton might have some relevant views on the Middle East crisis.

Indeed. Walton fully understood Bush's intent: It was not the ouster of the bully of Baghdad, Saddam Hussein. It was protection of the Middle East oil reserves so vital to the economies of East and West and to Bush's vision of a "New World Order."

Later, when Desert Storm struck at Baghdad and thundered into Kuwait, the Wafra oil field was the first torched by the fleeing Iraqi army. In the flame and smoke, Walton saw the cruel wasting of the very petroleum resources he had so painfully secured for Getty.

Having missed a date with death when he was twenty-five, Paul Walton took up polo with a passion when he was fifty-five and did not give up mounts and mallets until he was seventy-five.

Just turned eighty as of this writing, Walton spends his time putting plays together from a modest office in the Walker Bank building in downtown Salt Lake City, actively working his ranch in Wyoming, and writing and relaxing at his condominium in Indio, California.

It is good that Walton has been encouraged to remember, record, and be published. He would not have done so on his own.

And Utah would have missed *From Prospect to Prosperity*, a good yarn on and by one of its own.

PREFACE

IT HAS BEEN SAID — PROBABLY WITH SOME JUSTIFICATION — that the average person thinks milk comes from a bottle, oil from a can, and gasoline from a gas station pump. The following collection of episodes in the life of an exploration geologist should acquaint the "average" reader with the problems, successes, and heartbreaks connected with finding the raw materials needed to make that gallon of gasoline flow from the pump or that gas furnace turn on with the flick of a thermostatic switch.

It would be wrong to suggest that the experiences related in these episodes are typical or that they happen to all exploration geologists. They do not. The great bulk of oil and gas exploration is now done in plush offices by men in white shirts shuffling well logs, seismic cross sections, structure maps, and stratigraphic data. I intend no criticism of that modus operandi, but these days much of the downright earthy satisfaction of doing geologic work in the field, putting deals together, and getting wildcat wells or core holes for uranium drilled or pits for iron ore dug is missing from their work. In this day of rule by committee, a lot of personal heartache over failure and elation over success are denied them as well. It is a chancy business which has been compared with the lot of an M.D. who consistently sees nine out of ten patients die. A lot of "patients" die in this book. Some don't.

A good exploration geologist is usually not a prudent man in a business sense. He is akin to the prospector who pans one more gulch or shoots one more round into his hole in the hill before giving up. He must be a perpetual optimist, able to recover from the failures of his pet projects. One of the most successful geologist-geophysicists in the United States became an alcoholic and eventually took his own life because he was convinced he was a failure. He was looking only at his failures, however — not at the dozens of oil fields he had helped to discover. A successful oilman remarked about the wrecked life of another who was successful at exploration: "He just couldn't stand prosperity."

And, the exploration geologist must be lucky! Some I know have found production on their first tries — others after more than sixty dry holes. Faith is also a necessity. Some adhere to the Islamic saying, "If Allah wants me to be a rich man, I will be one without having to do anything."

My grandfather's philosophy, "You can tell what the Lord thinks about money when you see who he gives it to," has helped me in my own attempts to rationalize the failure of an exploration venture.

I hope the following yarns will give the reader an understanding of what goes into exploration: the tedium, the problems of coping with the personalities and vagaries of the people involved, the waiting and the uncertainty that precede the final success or failure of making a discovery of oil and gas or mineral wealth and getting it developed. The problem of keeping one's health when working in foreign countries is a major theme here. In the days before sulfa and penicillin, it was particularly difficult. Of the people I knew in the early days in Saudi Arabia, almost all died prematurely. The constant exposure to disease takes its toll.

This story may seem to relate more failures than successes, but let me assure the reader that I am currently working on several more "plays," one of which is bound to pay! In the view of many oilmen, exploration for oil is not a profession; it is a disease for which there is no permanent cure. And so, on we explorationists will go, to the offshore areas, to the Disturbed Belt, to the inaccessible corners of the earth, to look for oil and gas!

Jackson Hole, Wyoming
March 1994

ACKNOWLEDGMENTS

I WISH TO THANK THE PEOPLE who have encouraged me in this project:

Milton Fisher must take the blame for the book, because it was he who encouraged me to write the first draft back in 1977.

Glenna Sorensen, who first typed the manuscript, dutifully nagged me to keep on writing ("Haven't you got any more yet?").

Betty Allen, my longtime support system, stalwartly encouraged me and moved the project forward. We shared many years of work and many laughs brainstorming the book and chapter titles.

My wife Betty has been both skeptical and curious about this project from the beginning. My three children — Holly Walton-Buchanan, Paul T. Walton, Jr., and Ann Walton Brinton — have been encouraging over the long haul. I hope they all feel it was worth it.

Trudy McMurrin, editor and project director, made the manuscript into a real book, handled all the production decisions, and encouraged me to seek a publisher. Her longtime colleague Donald M. Henriksen, designer and master typographer and one of the last in his tradition, set the type in hot metal. They were ably assisted by Richard Firmage, who designed the jacket and cover, and by Helen Eckersley's typing service. John Alley and the staff of Utah State University Press have given the book a gracious reception.

Together we have made a book that I hope will be enjoyed by students of recent history and energy exploration, as well as by my family and friends.

CONTENTS

Part I
THE PRIZE

PERSIAN GULF AREA
OIL FIELDS, 1938-39

IRAQ

Basra
Abadan

KUWAIT
Neutral Zone
Burgan
Neutral Zone

Bandar Bushehr

IRAN

Persian Gulf

Strait of Hormuz

Ma'gala

Dhahran
Dammam
BAHRAIN
Awali

QATAR

Riyadh

UNITED ARAB EMIRATES

SAUDI ARABIA

Ar-Rub' 'al-Khali

OMAN

YEMEN

Legend
● City
🛢 Oil Field
⬦ Dry Hole
—·— Political Boundary

PERSIAN GULF AREA
OIL FIELDS, 1948-49

IRAQ

Basra
Abadan

KUWAIT

Neutral
Zone

Burgan

Neutral
Zone

Jauf

Abu
Hadriya

Ma'gala

Abqaiq

Qatif

Dammam

Khurais

Riyadh

Al
Gahwar

QATAR

Bandar
Bushehr

IRAN

Persian Gulf

Strait
of
Hormuz

UNITED ARAB EMIRATES

SAUDI ARABIA

Ar-Rub' 'al-Khali

OMAN

YEMEN

Legend

● City
♯ Oil Field
⬡ Dry Hole
–··– Political Boundary

KUWAIT NEUTRAL
ZONE AREA
OIL FIELDS, 1961

Tigris

Euphrates

IRAN

IRAQ

Basra

Abadan

Shatt al-Arab

KUWAIT

Kuwait
City

Burgan

Persian

Gulf

Umm
Gudair

Old Neutral
Zone 1961

Wafra

Neutral Zone
divided, 1991

Kafji

South
Fuwaris

SAUDI ARABIA

Ras
Misha 'ab

Safaniya

Legend

● City

Oil Field

–·–· Political Boundary

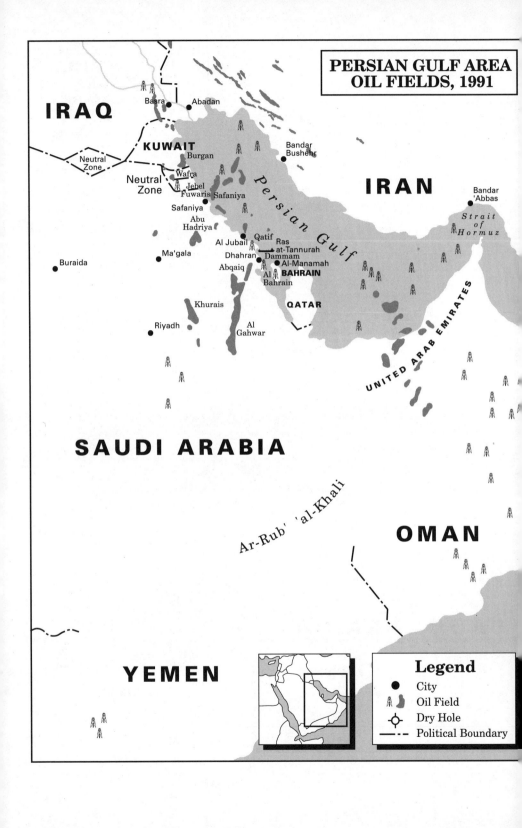

Taking a break during the Cairo negotiations for the Neutral Zone concession agreement, Barney Hadfield, left, and a more comfortable-looking Paul Walton visit the Sphinx and the Pyramids, Giza, Egypt, January 1949.

The major players in the Neutral Zone concession agreement, at the Royal Palace, Riyadh, Saudi Arabia. Left to right, Paul Walton, Barney Hadfield,

Sheikh Abdullah Sulaiman, Ahmed Bey Tewfik, Sheikh Muhammad Surur, Ahmed Fakhri.

Signing the Neutral Zone concession agreement at the Royal Palace, Riyadh, February 1949. Left to right, *seated*, King ibn-Saud, Paul T. Walton, Barney Hadfield, Sheikh Abdullah Sulaiman, Ahmed Bey Tewfik; *standing*, interpreter, Abdullah Tariki, Sheikh Muhammad Surur.

A light moment during the formal signing.

CHAPTER 1

THE GAME

SHEIKH ABDULLAH SULAIMAN beckoned us to follow. We filed into the great marble hall of the king's palace. Garbed in black camel's-hair *abbas* with gold beaded trim and white *gutras* (head cloths) with black, ropelike *agals* wrapped around our heads, Barney Hadfield and I were shown our chairs before the small table. Abdul Aziz Ibn Saud, the king, sat behind. Armed with four copies of the concession agreement, two in English and two in Arabic, bound in black leatherette, we were ready for the signing. We had even bought several gold fountain pens in Cairo for the signing, and they were stashed in our suitcoat pockets under our *abbas.*

After exchanges of *Salaam Alekum*, "Peace to you," the king burst out with "By Allah, these men look more like Arabs than the Arabs do!"

My black hair and mustache probably prompted this remark, for Barney Hadfield's blue eyes and pink Irish complexion wouldn't have. Turning to one of his sergeants-at-arms, the king continued, "Give them each a complete set of clothes for their wives."

"I guess he's going to sign the royal decree," I thought, and shortly a servant appeared with a purple indelible ink pad, which he held until King Ibn Saud had signed the document. The servant placed a big blob of saliva on the signature page, and the king pressed his royal signet ring first on the ink pad and then on the saliva-wet spot.

Sheikh Abdullah Sulaiman then signed the forty-one-page concession agreement as Finance Minister of the Government of the Kingdom of Saudi Arabia. The royal decree empowered him to do so, for in this feudal society, the Saud family owned the oil rights to the whole country, and the government merely administered the king's will.

After much picture-taking by photographers borrowed from ARAMCO and flown over from Dhahran, we gathered up the papers. With soldiers presenting arms and stamping their feet as we went by, we were taken to Sulaiman's quarters, where we were served a lunch of roast lamb, curried rice, and sour milk with sheep's eyes for dessert. Before we left, Barney and I each were handed a bundle covered with grey cloth, tied with string of the same cloth. Inside each was an undergarment of magenta silk, unsewn at the seams, and a black silk outer garment covered with gold sequins.

Sulaiman had more photos taken, and then we were driven back to our quarters at the Badia Palace on the western outskirts of Riyadh. We took off the Arab clothes and relaxed.

"Well, we finally made it," Barney said.

"This breaks the whole damn Middle East open," I added, and time showed this to be true. Soon many small American oil companies were operating in the area, as well as French, German, Japanese, and Italian enterprises. The terms of our concession agreement were generous, and all the other Arab countries began looking at their hole card before granting concessions. First, they insisted that companies meet Pacific Western Oil's terms. Then, after production was found, the Arab ministers insisted that these new contracts provide for fifty–fifty profit sharing. Then even that wasn't enough. So they started the oil boycott in 1974 and quadrupled oil prices. Then they got even more greedy and virtually nationalized the petroleum industry of the Arab world. The oil companies were reduced to service operations, producing, refining, and transporting oil for the Arab owners.

And it all started, in my opinion, with the signing of this concession agreement for oil rights on the undivided Saudi Arabia half of the Kuwait–Saudi Arabia Neutral Zone to the Pacific Western Oil Corporation, a small oil company controlled by J. Paul Getty.

The year was 1949, and for more than thirty years the oil of the area had been pretty well controlled by the Anglo-Persian, Iraq Petroleum, Standard Oil of New York and New Jersey, and the British government oil companies on concessions taken by Gulbenkian, known in Iraq and Iran as Mr. Five Percent. Later, Gulf and British Petroleum went into Kuwait; Standard of California and Texaco got concessions and found oil on Bahrain Island and on the Saudi Arabian mainland. Production was so prolific in Saudi Arabia that Standard of New Jersey and Standard of New York were taken in as partners in Arabian American Oil Company — ARAMCO. Now the companies had so much oil it was running out of their ears, and they were paying the Arabs a royalty of only a shilling a barrel. So, why should a small upstart independent like Pacific Western Oil come in and break the whole Middle East price structure with a royalty of fifty-five cents per barrel? It is an interesting story, and my part in it had begun four months earlier, in November of 1948.

I was division geologist for the Rocky Mountain and Canadian oil exploration program of the Pacific Western Oil Corporation. Skelly Oil Company and Mission Corporation, also controlled by J. Paul Getty, each had a one-third interest in the Pacific Western operation. My job was to discover drilling prospects, that is, areas where oil and gas are likely to be found. In late 1948 we were drilling one or two wildcat wells a year on prospects found by me or by my staff of three geologists attached to our Casper, Wyoming, office.

Standard of California had just made an oil discovery in south-central Utah at a place called Upper Valley, a little east of Bryce Canyon National Park. I thought there might be other oil prospects nearby, so I went to Utah to look over the general area around the discovery. I took my wife Betty and our two little kids along (Tad, three years old, and Ann, just two) and left them with my Aunt Till in Salt Lake City.

I spent a day or two around the Upper Valley area before driving back to Salt Lake City, where I received a message to call Dave Staples, president of the Company, at the head office in Los Angeles. Staples told me that Mr. Getty wanted someone to go to Saudi Arabia to represent him, and since I had been there some years earlier with Standard of California, was I interested in going, and, if so, would I call Mr. Getty in New York City?

I was young, ambitious, and wanted to get ahead in my profession and in the Company, but this presented a real dilemma for me.

The first time I was in Arabia I had contracted a severe case of rheumatic fever and had been sent back to the States with a damaged heart and told I might have only six months to live.

I called Mr. Getty, and he asked if I had worked in the north part of Arabia near the Neutral Zone. I asked him which one, Kuwait or Iraq, and said I had run some gravity surveys and had seen some of the seismic and surface work which had been done just south of the Kuwait Neutral Zone. Mr. Getty said he was interested in negotiating for a concession on that Neutral Zone, and would I go to Arabia to carry on the negotiations?

The temptation was too great not to take on an obvious adventure like this, so I said yes, I would go.

"Do you have a passport?" he asked.

"Just an old one, but I can get it from Casper in a day and apply for a new one here in Salt Lake City."

"Get here as soon as you can!"

I bought a summer suit and two metal Halliburton suitcases, which I could lock effectively to keep out sand and prowlers, made reservations to New York City on United Airlines, and took off on the night flight. I had never flown in a plane bigger than a DC-3, so the DC-4 was quite a thrill. I changed planes to a DC-6 in Chicago and got to La Guardia Field at 5:00 AM on Sunday. I hadn't slept a wink all night. I was worried about Betty driving the 450 miles back to Casper in a snowstorm and the rigors for me of another trip to Saudi Arabia.

The taxi dropped me off at the Pierre at 7:00, and I checked in at the desk. They advised me that Mr. Getty was never called until 8:30, so I walked around Central Park until then.

Mr. Getty had me come up to his suite, and we discussed the negotiations for the concession. He showed me a letter he had written to the Saudi Arabian minister in Washington, Asad al Fagih, saying that he was interested in acquiring the concession and would make an initial bonus bid of eight million dollars. He wanted to discuss how close my work in Arabia had been to the Neutral Zone, and I told him about working on the Abu Hadriya field with the gravity crew and seeing the seismic work compared with our gravity meter surveys. I also mentioned a very large and beautiful anticline northwest of Abu Hadriya near the southwest corner of the Neutral Zone, called El Jauf, which had been drilled and was dry.

I told Mr. Getty I thought the Neutral Zone should be a good place to look for oil since it was so close to the biggest field in the world — Burgan in Kuwait — but before we did any more, it should be determined if there were any anticlines that could be seen on the surface. All the fields in Saudi Arabia were on surface anticlines, so a field examination would be important.

I said, "If there aren't any anticlines in the Neutral Zone, eight million dollars may be too high a bid."

I think this shocked him a little, but we were both oil men, and the uncertainties of wildcatting for oil were uppermost in our minds. He went on to tell me that American Independent Oil Company (AMINCO), composed of several large American independents and headed by Ralph Davies, a former Standard of California man, had made a cash bid of seven and a half million dollars and were giving the Sheikh of Kuwait a two-million-dollar yacht as consideration for the concession on the Kuwait half of the Neutral Zone. The granting of this Kuwait concession had been in *Oil and Gas Journal* recently, but the exact terms were not revealed. Mr. Getty told me to try to get a copy of that concession agreement, which would be helpful in our negotiations. I said I would.

Then he gave me the terms which I could use as a top bid: ten and a half million, a million dollars a year guaranteed royalty prior to production, with a fifty-six cents per barrel royalty after production was begun. He cautioned me not ever to write them down — just to carry the terms in my head and be sure not to reveal them in any conversation with anyone, including my friends in ARAMCO and anyone in the U.S. Embassy. He said American Independent and probably several other U.S. and possibly French, German, or English companies would be after the Saudi Arabian half of the Neutral Zone.

We were selling our oil in Wyoming for $1.35 a barrel, so I was shocked at Mr. Getty's royalty figure of fifty-six cents per barrel. I didn't know how to tell him that I felt it was an awfully high figure, so I said, "Isn't that a pretty large amount to be paying when ARAMCO is only paying a shilling [then about twenty-five cents] per barrel?"

"Oil isn't always going to sell for a dollar thirty-five," he said.

This prediction certainly has been borne out over the years. Oil is currently about twenty dollars a barrel and has been as high as thirty dollars.

Mr. Getty was at that time the largest stockholder in the Tidewater Associated Oil Company, a large independent producer and refiner — much larger than Pacific Western. He picked up the telephone, rang a room, and asked "Billy" to come down. A dignified gentleman in his late sixties entered the room, and Mr. Getty said, "Billy, this is Paul Walton. He's going to Saudi Arabia to negotiate a concession for me. You'd like to have some of that Arabian production, wouldn't you?"

Billy, who I shortly found out was William Humphrey, president of the Tidewater Company, said, "Yes." We exchanged a few pleasantries, and Mr. Humphrey left.

I thought to myself, "It would be helpful to have a well-known company like Tidewater in the deal when I talk to the Arabs." However, as far as I know, they weren't in the deal until after Mr. Getty took control of Tidewater and then put the company's and his own holdings into Getty Oil Company many years later.

Mr. Getty told me to make a plane reservation for Arabia and to go to Washington to see the Saudi minister and get my passport. I was anxious to see if any of the U.S. government agencies had maps of the Neutral Zone.

While I was checking out of the hotel, I asked to see Frank Paget, the manager. Dave Staples had told me that he could be very helpful in making arrangements. I told Paget I was going to Arabia for Mr. Getty and that while I had bought my own ticket to New York City, I couldn't finance my trip forever.

"I need some money," I said. "I don't like to ask Mr. Getty for it, but Dave Staples said you could be helpful."

In typical New Yorker style, Paget narrowed his eyes and acted as if I were trying to rob his hotel. He didn't offer to help in any way. I promptly put him down in my book as a first-class S.O.B. I couldn't finance my trip out of an $800-a-month salary!

The airlines were weathered in at New York City. I had to take the train to Washington and arrived late that night at the Ambassador Hotel. I was sure tired. I hadn't had any sleep for forty-eight hours, and my head was buzzing with all the things I had to do.

Next morning I took a cab out to the Saudi Arabian Embassy and had a pleasant chat with the minister, Asad al Fagih. I told him I was going to Jidda to negotiate for Mr. Getty. He said I should get letters of introduction to the Saudi Arabian minister in Cairo and get my visa and traveling instructions as to how and when to go to Jidda and to whom to talk.

Later that day I got my shots for typhoid and cholera and a smallpox vaccination. I also had to get passport photos and apply for a new passport, as my old one could not be renewed.

I was beginning to run out of money, so I called Mr. Getty. He told me to contact a Mr. Charles Krug in Wilmington, Delaware, an officer of the Company. I did, and Mr. Krug sent his secretary down to Washington with a $1,160 check for a ticket on TWA to Cairo, $1,500 in traveler's checks, and letters of introduction to use at the Saudi Arabian Embassy and our Consulate in Jidda.

I went out to the Army Map Service and talked to the staff about aerial photos and maps of the Neutral Zone. All they had were 1:1,000,000 scale (15.78 miles-per-inch) maps made by the Geographical Section, General Staff, from data furnished by the Survey of India and the British government. I got two — the Bushire, Iran, and Basra, Iraq, quadrangles, each of which covered a portion of the Neutral Zone — thinking: "Oh, my God! Are these the only maps there are of something we are going to pay ten and a half million dollars for?"

To an oil man, and particularly a petroleum geologist, a map is everything. You plot your geology, claim your land ownership, and locate and drill your wells on the basis of maps. Coping without a map is unthinkable, and here all I had was a sketch of the Neutral Zone two inches square.

The old saw about the tramp being asked what he used to work at in his better days illustrates this thought. "Oh, I used to be an oil man, but I lost my map"! So it was with many misgivings that I wondered how I would be able to examine the Neutral Zone, in the field or possibly from an airplane, and know where the hell I was on the map.

Rounding up my visas took time, and I had to go back to New York City to get the Egyptian one. At war with Israel, the Egyptians were being picky about a long stay. I got my smallpox vaccination certified and my immunization chart stamped at the U.S. Health Service. My yellow fever shot would have to be taken in Cairo.

I checked in at La Guardia Airport for TWA's Cairo flight. It was an evening flight twice a week, and the plane was a Lockheed Constellation. This was my first airplane trip across an ocean, and even though I had a pilot's license for single-engine aircraft, the black water and the unknown lying ahead made me nervous, and I slept very little.

The sun came up over the Azores, where we landed for fuel. We didn't leave until 9:30 AM, landing again at Lisbon at 3:00 PM. We had a two-hour layover, so I took a cab tour of downtown Lisbon with a TWA man who was headed for Cairo as well. The poverty and the black clothes with patches on patches were depressing.

We left for Madrid at 5:00 PM and got there well after dark. The refueling stop gave me a chance to stretch my legs and drink a brandy and soda and strike up a conversation with a young man named Briant, who was with the United Nations and on his way to Israel.

The runways of the airport at Rome were still covered with the steel invasion mats. They really made a vibration in the Connie. We fueled up and took off for Athens, where we landed before dawn on more steel mats on the runways. I got off the plane and had some black coffee. It was cold and damp, with no heat in the airport building. We took off in the dawn and flew above the clouds to Cairo. I caught a glimpse of the Pyramids.

The customs people wouldn't let me bring in my Leica or my 8mm Bell and Howell movie camera, so I had to leave them in bond in the smaller of the Halliburton bags. I took the airport bus into town and went to Shepheard's Hotel, where I got a room without a bath. It was nine years since I had been in Cairo, returning from Arabia before the war, and I had forgotten how dirty the buildings and streets were.

The usual crowd of dragomen hung around the front of the hotel, and I picked one named Khodry Samedi to take me to the

Saudi Arabian Embassy. His English was so amusing I often wish I had had a recording of it. Later, when I spent much time in Cairo, I got to know him better. He was very useful, and everyone called him Sam.

The Saudi Arabian minister was very cordial. He had heard from al-Fagih, the Saudi minister in Washington, that I was coming. We had the usual Arab coffee, *gahwa*, scented with cardamom seed and poured with a flourish from a long-necked coffee pot called a *nol* into very small, handleless cups. I much preferred it to the thick, sweet Turkish coffee I would have to drink a barrel of when I returned to Cairo.

The minister told me he was much interested in our bidding for the concession and had made space for me on the Saudi Arabian Airline plane which left the next day — Sunday.

I got up at 4:00 AM, ate breakfast in my room, checked out of Shepheards, and rode the bus to the airport at Heliopolis. The customs people always give the impression that you are the first person who has ever gone through their lines and that everything you need to do to get cleared is not just difficult, it is nearly impossible. I finally got my cameras out of bond and loaded onto the made-over C-47, and we took off at 7:00 AM. We followed the west side of the Gulf of Suez south to the end of the Sinai peninsula and then crossed over the Red Sea.

We flew over the only sizable oil field in Egypt at that time, Ras Ghârib. The anticline was plainly visible in the morning light. Located in the large Red Sea graben fault zone, it represented a different type of geology from any I had ever seen.

As we passed across the Arabian mainland, the many cinder cones and lava flows reminded me of Nevada and Oregon. This igneous terrain persisted from Medina to Jidda. To the north of Medina I could see the thin trace of the Damascus-to-Medina railroad that Lawrence of Arabia blew up repeatedly during World War I, keeping the Turkish army tied up here in the desert. All the rails were gone and most of the wooden crossties, but the road grade was faintly visible still.

We landed on the sand runway at Jidda, a wave of heat hitting me in the face as I disembarked. It was December fifth — should be winter. I went through customs, leaving my passport there for processing, and was wondering what to do next when a battered old Hudson sedan drove up and a young Arab got out, came over to me, and asked if I were Mr. Walton. He said his name was Mustafa, and he would be my driver.

He drove me a short distance to the edge of town and pulled up in front of an old yellow two-story stucco house with six or eight high-ceilinged rooms, no screens on the windows, and lots of flies. The plumbing in the single communal bathroom was archaic, mostly broken. Only one toilet worked, and there was no hot water. My bed was twin-size, with a straw tick mattress, one blanket, and soiled sheets. The door had no lock, so I was glad I had my metal suitcases in which to lock my belongings. The Kandara House was the best hotel in Jidda.

"So, this is my base for carrying on negotiations on a ten-and-a-half-million-dollar deal that could involve *hundreds* of millions of dollars if the concession proves productive," I thought. It seemed more like a base for a field mapping or construction job than for high finance.

Jidda is the port for Mecca, where millions of Muslim faithful, *hajjis*, disembark from the many boats bringing them on their pilgrimages. Many save their whole lives to make the sacred journey, and many come in the advanced stages of fatal illness. Consequently, cholera, typhus, typhoid, and yellow fever are common in the city. I had had only my first shots for these diseases in the U.S., and my first thought on arriving there was to get the necessary second shots to be immunized.

CHAPTER 2

THE NEGOTIATIONS

DECEMBER 6, MONDAY:

Mustafa drove me to the United States Embassy — Wazier Americi to him — and I met Hermann Eilts, a very cordial young man of my age who had been at Harvard working on his Ph.D. at the same time I had been working on mine at the Massachusetts Institute of Technology. Eilts told me of a French physician, Dr. Gonet, who could give me my shots. He also gave me some background on the advisers to the Saudi Arabian finance minister, Sheikh Abdullah Sulaiman.

Mustafa came at 4:00 PM and took me to Sheikh Abdullah Sulaiman's house. I was escorted onto a porch overlooking a small patio and introduced first to Sheikh Muhammad Surur who, Eilts had said, was Sulaiman's chief adviser. I was surprised to see that he was coal black, probably of Sudanese descent. He was a very pleasant-faced man, in contrast to Sulaiman, who had a classic Arab nose, fierce, piercing black eyes, and a short black beard beginning to turn grey — a rather formidable appearance. All were dressed in standard everyday Saudi Arab clothes — red-and-white-checkered *gutra* and black *agal* on their heads and black *abbas* for the outer garment. Close by stood a man who was introduced as Ahmed Bey Tewfik. This was the Egyptian lawyer Hermann Eilts had said would be here. He spoke excellent English and served as interpreter.

After a very short exchange of pleasantries, I said to Sheikh Sulaiman, "I have met you before at Ma'gala in 1939, when you came and visited my gravity meter camp."

[23]

He looked puzzled, and I continued, "I was camped there with Tom Barger and Jerry Harris." He brightened up a bit at Tom Barger's name. Barger was a mining engineer with geologic training who had been working as field assistant to Jerry Harris, doing reconnaissance surface geologic work along the east coast of Saudi Arabia when I first met him in 1938. He was an excellent field man and picked up the Arabic language very quickly. Consequently, he was put into public relations work with the Saudi government and became well known to all the top Saudi government people.

Sulaiman didn't acknowledge anything more, so I tried another tack: "I came from a part of America that is much like Saudi Arabia."

He turned to his advisers and spoke quickly, then asked, "Texas?"

"No," I said, "Utah."

Again the quick chatter to his group and then he continued, "Where's that?"

I explained it was north and west of Texas and had sand deserts and black lava flows like the area around Jidda. This seemed to satisfy him, but I could see he was champing at the bit to get on with business. Abruptly he asked, "What is your interest in the concession?"

I said, "We want to assist in developing oil in the Neutral Zone."

Sulaiman countered by saying he was sure there was oil in the Neutral Zone. We wouldn't have to do any geological or geophysical work, and it was ready to be drilled. I wanted to laugh, remembering several dry holes that had been drilled on beautiful structures farther south, but thought better of it.

So I said, "I respect your judgment, Sheikh Abdullah, but we have a saying in the oil business that you don't have oil until it's in the tank."

This ended the interview; he turned me over to Muhammad Surur, who was very pleasant and wanted to meet with me the next day at 10:00 Arabic time, which I calculated would be 4:00 PM, local time. (Telling time in Jidda was always confusing to me. The Saudi airline ran on Greenwich Mean Time (GMT). Local time was three hours later, but the Arabs set their clocks each day at sunset. So when it was 1:00 PM in London, it was 4:00 PM "local time" in Jidda and 4:00 "Arabic time" — but only during December. As the days grew longer, Arabic time was six or seven hours different.)

That night at the Kandara House I talked with two Palestinians staying there. One, Badr al Fahoum, was working for the Saudi government; the other, Khaladi, an older man, was working for an Arab bank trying to establish a branch here.

Khaladi told me that the secret to winning approval from Sulaiman was to get Muhammad Surur on my side. He said he wanted to advise me on this and would contact me later. I was a little suspicious of his motives and didn't want to use him in the situation at all. I could smell *baksheesh* or some kind of graft on his part, so I watched very carefully what I said to him.

I made arrangements to eat at the Bechtel construction camp mess hall. They were building some port facilities and had about forty or fifty men in residence. Also, they had a recreation room where I could buy an Amstel beer occasionally. Saudi Arabian Airlines was run by TWA, and their pilots and personnel were mostly Americans from the ATS (Army Transport Service) which flew cargo for the war in Europe. They were a nice bunch of fellows, all in their late twenties or early thirties.

DECEMBER 7, TUESDAY:

After going downtown to buy some stationery and sandals, as it was still awfully warm, I returned to find Ahmed Fahkri at Kandara House. He said I should have been at Muhammad Surur's house at 10 AM. I was mortified because I thought I was to be there at 4 PM. Fahkri was from Port Sudan and had had some education as an engineer at Fuad University in Cairo. He was Sulaiman's technical adviser and a very nice man, but he knew little about the oil business. He had spent a lot of time with an elderly American mining geologist by the name of Twitchell, trying to find old gold mines mentioned in ancient Arab writings. He succeeded in finding a large dump which had been mined at least 1,500 years ago. Recently the Saudi Arabian government had given a concession on it to an American mining company associated with the Guggenheim

interests. They were just beginning production and were known as
the SAMS — Saudi Arabian Mining Syndicate — so Fahkri was in
Sulaiman's good graces.

We went to Sulaiman's house again, meeting on the patio with
Surur, Tewfik, and Fahkri. Always in the background were three
or four other men to whom I was never introduced but who, I
found out later, justified their existence with Sulaiman by thinking
up questions to ask people coming to deal with him in his various
duties as minister of finance for the Saudi government.

The first question today was funny. They asked me if the Company's main business wasn't running a railroad. Obviously they
were confusing Pacific Western with Western Pacific Railroad Company. I told them about Pacific Western, Skelly, Mission Corporation, and Mr. Getty's large interest in Tidewater. I thought, "This
will keep them busy for a few days getting the dope on those
companies."

We jumped right into negotiations, with Tewfik interpreting.
He wanted to know what I could bid, and I said I could bid the
following:

> $8½ million bonus
>
> 50¢ per barrel royalty
>
> $1 million per year guaranteed royalty
>
> 25% net profits interest in any refinery built.

This prompted much chattering among them. The advisers all
had their say, including requesting a trade school for the workers.
Then Tewfik said they wanted a "call in kind," that is, an advance
share, of refined products from a refinery to be built in the Neutral
Zone. This was a real monkey wrench in the negotiations, and I
responded that Mr. Getty and I had not discussed this possibility
at all.

Tewfik offered the use of the government wireless system to
contact Mr. Getty on the matter, but I thought it best to use
Mackey Radio, which sent most of Bechtel's messages. Besides,
Sulaiman, *et al.*, would know exactly what I had wired Getty —
and his answer—if the message went out on the government system.

Sulaiman said the American Independent agreement with Kuwait provided for this in-kind call from a refinery to be built. He told me I could see a copy of the agreement which Ahmed Fahkri had in his office. This pleased me very much, because the terms of this agreement were a well-kept secret, and Mr. Getty had asked me to try to get a look at it. I asked Tewfik, "Do you have in mind an agreement with us similar to the one American Independent got with Kuwait?"

Then the other shoe fell. He replied, "We want a much better one. The Sheikh of Kuwait is only the little brother to ibn-Saud, and any deal he gets is fine for him but not for Saud."

I hoped this put American Independent behind the eightball. Saud won't take any deal unless it is better than Kuwait's. American Independent probably can't give Saud a better deal or the Sheikh of Kuwait will raise hell. I thought, "This eliminates AMINCO as competition right now!" If they raise terms to Saud, they will have to raise terms to Kuwait, and then Saud will want his raised ad infinitum! But I was wrong.

Ever since my preliminary conversation with Mr. Getty, I had been wanting to fly over the Neutral Zone to see if I could spot any surface geology. Since I had learned that there were no airplanes in Jidda except those owned by the Saudi Arabian Airline, it appeared impossible to rent one. Tewfik gave me a perfect opportunity to determine whether I could get the use of one of theirs when he asked, "Do you have authority to increase the bid you have given us?"

"I do," I said, "but only if there is geological evidence which makes me believe there is oil there. I feel, as a geologist, that I should fly over the area and, if it appears favorable, I can increase the bid."

This seemed to interest Sulaiman, and he said he would request the use of a plane from the king. He said it would take a few days to get a decision from ibn-Saud.

Tewfik brought up another point, saying the tidelands lying offshore from the Neutral Zone probably would be up for bid. I asked if ARAMCO had been awarded a concession on the tidelands off the eastern shore of Saudi Arabia.

Tewfik conferred with Sulaiman on this point, and I sensed that Sulaiman didn't want to discuss this phase of the Neutral Zone concession. The question of granting a concession on the territorial waters of the Neutral Zone or even if the territorial waters should be included in this concession seemed to bother him. Tewfik said some legal questions on this matter had to be resolved before more discussion could be held.

At this time Texas and Louisiana were fighting the U.S. government concerning whether or not they had rights to their territorial and offshore waters, so I understood how this point could be unresolved for many countries.

DECEMBER 8, WEDNESDAY:

Mustafa drove me downtown to Ahmed Fahkri's office, where Fahkri showed me a copy of American Independent's contract with Kuwait. Up to this point I had been flying blind. The contract gave Kuwait a bonus of seven and a half million dollars and a shilling a barrel royalty. American Independent was required to build a refinery after production exceeded 15,000 tons (about 115,000 barrels, using a figure of 7.61 barrels per ton). The refinery's capacity would have to be in excess of 1,500 tons (about 11,500 barrels) per day, and Kuwait would get an interest equivalent to 15 percent of the net profits of the refinery.

Obviously, I was bidding more than AMINCO, and I discussed this with Fahkri. However, I was still well within the limits Mr. Getty had set for me as to royalty and bonus. But I needed clearance on the refinery situation, so I sent Mr. Getty a wire recommending we obligate ourselves to build a 1,500-ton refinery when production exceeded 10,000 tons per day (76,000 barrels), giving Saudi Arabia a 20 percent net profits interest. I also recommended that we start the first well within a year and then drill 6,000 total feet the second year and 10,000 the third year.

Afterward I hurried to get another yellow fever shot, and Dr. Gonet gave me some Atabrine tablets for malaria and some mosquito repellent oil. He said there was very little malaria around, and I hoped he was right.

DECEMBER 9, THURSDAY:

In the morning I went to Ahmed Fahkri's office, where he told me the okay had been given for the airplane flight over the Kuwait Neutral Zone. He said Tewfik wanted to see me immediately and would send a car for me at the Kandara House. I hurried back to the hotel and then waited nearly all day. At 4 o'clock Tewfik's driver showed up and took me to his villa, where Tewfik proceeded to tell me our terms were too low — that we had our foot in the door and that was all. I couldn't tell if this was just lawyer talk, throwing sand in my eyes, or if we really had strong competition from companies other than American Independent. This all came as a surprise, because Ahmed Fahkri had acted as if I was probably the high bidder so far.

I had established a pretty good rapport with Fahkri. Knowing I was from mining country in Utah, he told me more of his travels in western Arabia searching for the ancient gold workings, of which he had found twenty-three. Some of the sites were probably thousands of years old. The miners had burned wood on the ore face and then thrown water on the hot rock to fracture it so it could be pried loose with hand tools. The logistics of finding wood and water in the desert seemed so difficult that I wondered if some of these workings weren't more than 5,000 years old. At that time, when the glaciers were receding from southern Europe, Arabia was an area of live streams and forests.

DECEMBER 10, FRIDAY:

Ahmed Fahkri came to the Kandara House just before noon and took me to Sheikh Sulaiman. I thanked the Sheikh for making a plane available, and then he brought in a man in his early twenties, Abdullah Tariki, who was the only Saudi Arab graduate geologist in the country. He had a master's degree in geology from the University of Texas and was married to an American.

Sulaiman didn't have much to say, and he kept leaving the room and then returning. When I got a little closer and happened to smell his breath, I realized he was a bathroom drinker and had to have a nip every little while.

Tariki and Fahkri took me to the airport and introduced me to
Colonel Tassa, Saudi Arabia's director of aviation. His bright eyes
and strong grip gave me the feeling he was the only Arab I had
seen so far with whom I would want to fly. Most Arabs had a soft
handshake that seemed sort of like a wet noodle to me.

Colonel Tassa asked me if I had a choice of pilot for the Neutral
Zone flight. At the Bechtel mess hall I had become acquainted with
Captain Coffey, an American from Texas who had been an ATS
pilot in the war. I told the colonel that Coffey was my choice. He
said, "OK."

Our flight plan was to fly over the Iraq Neutral Zone, then the
Kuwait Neutral Zone, and then land at Ras Misha 'ab on the Persian Gulf. We would go to Dhahran for the night. I was surprised
when he told me Tariki and his American wife would be along.

DECEMBER 11, SATURDAY

Tariki picked me up at 4:15 AM and we drove to the airport. It
was dark, but the runway was lighted with kerosene lamps like those
we used on highway construction jobs in the U.S. in the twenties.
They are spherical, about 12 inches in diameter, and have a wick
sticking out of the top.

The Saudi Arabian Airline's C-47 sat near the middle of the
runway, only faintly visible in the flickering yellow lamplight. We
climbed aboard and Captain Coffey greeted me. He had been talking to a short, stocky man dressed in mechanic's overalls. The man
turned and smiled at me, and I was startled to see he had stainless
steel false teeth. I had heard that an expatriate Russian mechanic
was working for the airline. He had defected in Iran. I knew it was
the policy for the mechanics to have to ride occasionally in the
planes they serviced. We took off and flew northeast over the SAMS
gold mine, then east to the town of Buraida, where we encountered
low fog.

Captain Coffey had me take the Saudi Arab copilot's place, and
I tried to navigate using the maps I got in Washington, D.C. We
flew down low under the fog, and I recognized the Anseb oasis. This
gave me a fix, and I navigated us right over the Iraq Neutral Zone.
Mr. Getty was interested in this Neutral Zone as well, since it was

not under concession, so I wanted to take a look at it on the way.

The Iraq Neutral Zone has numerous nearly circular structural domes — some slightly elongate. Similar structures occur in Saudi Arabia to the south, and they had been mapped by ARAMCO geologists at Khurma Karim. None had been drilled, since they were thought to be related to sink holes developed in underlying salt formations.

We flew at about 500 feet directly east and hit Burgan Field in Kuwait right on the nose. The oil well derricks and gas flares were an impressive sight. This was the biggest oil field in the world, and I wanted to see everything I could from the plane to get an idea of the possibilities of anticlinal structure to the south in the Neutral Zone.

I was elated to see some small outcrops on the north end of the field that appeared to be the top of an anticline. "Surface exposure does mean something," I decided. I had been afraid that only seismic work would definitely delineate an anticline in this area — especially on a windblown sand desert with only some small brush cover.

A wind began to blow and visibility got worse, so we dropped down to about 300 feet and made four passes across the Neutral Zone. Sticking up out of the desert near the Zone's center was another set of outcrops that looked like the top of an anticline. This really gave me a thrill, for here, near the biggest oil field in the world, was another anticline. Might it not also be a huge oil field?

I was jarred out of my reverie by Tariki who, unknown to me, was standing just behind Captain Coffey. He too had seen the outcrops. I had wondered why Sulaiman wanted him to come along — now I knew.

We flew out over the tideland and territorial waters and saw definite evidence of shoaling in the water near the southeast corner of the Zone. Such shoals were probably indicative of a structural high there too. I was now determined to try to get the territorial waters as part of the concession, since an oil field might be located there as well.

We had sufficient gas without refueling at Ras Misha 'ab, so we flew directly to Dhahran. On the way we passed over the Abu Hadriya oil field, where I had run gravity surveys nine years earlier.

I was elated to see that this area showed up well as a surface anticline. I also saw the surface structure at Qatif which later became
an oil field.

We all stayed at Bechtel Company's boarding house in Dhahran.
Tariki brought up the subject of geologic structure in the Neutral
Zone, and I responded guardedly. I told him I knew about the
deep dry hole on the El Jauf structure just southwest of the Neutral
Zone. He surprised me by bringing out his master's thesis, a very
general description of the geology of the Arabian Peninsula. In his
thesis he had the location of the El Jauf well and its depth, 3,658
meters. I knew it was a surface structure, and a seismograph survey
had confirmed the structure at depth. Lack of oil shows in the
El Jauf well cast a little gloom on that part of the Arabian coastal
area, and I began to have some second thoughts about oil in the
anticline I had seen in the Neutral Zone.

DECEMBER 12, SUNDAY:

At Dhahran, which is headquarters for ARAMCO, I wanted to
talk to some of my old friends who were still with the company to
see what work, if any, they might have done in the Neutral Zone.

I found Dick Kerr, who had run one of the Geophysical Service,
Inc. (GSI), seismic crews when I was there nine years earlier.
(GSI was the parent company of Texas Instruments.) You covered
a lot of ground when you talked to Dick. He reminded me of the
radio broadcaster of many years ago — Floyd Gibbons: He talked
like a machine gun fires and thought just as fast. According to Dick,
ARAMCO definitely had done no gravity, seismic, or surface work
in the Neutral Zone and, as far as he knew, they were so busy
developing their concession in Saudi Arabia they were not interested
in it. He confirmed that the El Jauf structure was a big one, had
good structural closure both on the surface and seismically, and had
no significant shows.

Dick offered this advice: "The most important things in Arabia
are keeping the Saudi Arabian government happy and keeping the
ARAMCO personnel happy." He introduced me to Gary Owen,
who was in charge of company relations with the Saudi Arabian
government, and Owen told me the same thing.

I was glad Dick Kerr didn't ask me about the details of my negotiations on the Neutral Zone. But he would have known I couldn't talk about them and, being the gentleman he was, would never have asked.

We took off for Jidda at 1:30 PM and had a full plane, mostly friends of Sulaiman who had business in Dhahran. Captain Coffey asked me to fly copilot again. We landed at Riyadh for fuel and took off again at 4:30 PM. It soon got dark, but the moon was full. It takes a week to drive from Dhahran to Jidda, so I really was getting a good look at the country much more easily than I could have from the ground.

Halfway to Jidda, Coffey had to go to the restroom at the back of the plane, so I flew it briefly. When he came back to the cockpit he was laughing. One of the sheikhs in the passenger compartment had asked him excitedly what he was doing back there. Was the plane flying itself?

Coffey pointed out a spot below us. He said he had had to make a forced landing there and had spent several days getting the engines repaired. A Bedouin sheikh came to visit him, and Coffey's Arab copilot acted as interpreter. Coffey asked the Bedouin if he had ever seen a plane before, and the Bedouin said no. Coffey asked, "Don't you think it is wonderful a big piece of machinery like this can fly?" The Bedouin replied, "What's so wonderful about it? It was built to fly, wasn't it?" Such lack of appreciation for machinery and equipment was obvious at every turn — cars were treated with less care than donkeys. A string of broken-down cars stretched from Riyadh to Jidda — more than 400 miles.

We circled Jidda twice while the kerosene lamps along the runway were lighted so we could land. I was glad there wasn't a wind to blow the flares out.

DECEMBER 13, MONDAY:

Sulaiman sent his driver to pick me up right after breakfast. I guessed he wanted to know what I saw on the flight. Tewfik and Surur were there, and so was Tariki. I guessed they had been quizzing him about what he saw. They asked me if I had seen anything interesting, and I told them there was some indication of oil structure but that I couldn't see too much. However, what I saw was interesting enough to raise the bid to nine million dollars and fifty-three cents per barrel royalty. This seemed to please Sulaiman, but Tewfik wanted to play it tough.

He said, "One million dollars per year is not enough guaranteed royalty."

I countered, "It amounts to royalty on 6,000 barrels per day, which is quite a lot of production.'

Tewfik wouldn't indicate whether my bids so far were adequate to get the concession, and, since I still had no word from Mr. Getty concerning approval to build a refinery in the Zone, we agreed to postpone further negotiations until that point could be resolved.

I checked in at the U.S. Embassy for my mail, and Hermann Eilts asked me how things were going. I told him we were stalemated at present, and he said I should remember that the Saudi Arabian government would extract the last drop of blood from the deal all the way down the line. I could see he was right.

DECEMBER 14, TUESDAY

Eilts had me over for lunch at the Consulate. We couldn't discuss my negotiations, since he had another guest, a Frenchman from the Indochina Bank who had lived in China for fourteen years, and Getty had still sent no word on the refinery issue.

The French visitor told us of the great floods on the Yangtze and Yellow rivers, where a million people were drowned every year, and of living in Tientsin, where the Chinese used to freeze to death outside his door and were left on the sidewalk for days before being removed. He said China could never be consolidated because the Cantonese are as different from the other Chinese as Norwegians are from Italians. But he said it looked like all Asia would go "red" nevertheless.

DECEMBER 15, WEDNESDAY:

I was uncertain as to how I should inform Mr. Getty of the apparent anticlinal structure in the middle of the Neutral Zone and its significance with respect to the Burgan Field and anticline. I felt strongly now that an oil field or two probably existed in the Zone.

I decided to send him a personal, handwritten letter, which would probably not be opened by the Saudi Arabian postal service, and he should have it in a week. This I did, and then I sent the following cable:

> Cabled you a week ago via Arabian minister Washington stop Negotiations stopped pending your answer stop Made aerial reconnaissance area which increased my interest.

I knew he would understand the significance of the aerial reconnaissance, since we had discussed the desirability of my doing it in New York. Also, the letter telling him of the anticline in the Neutral Zone should be there soon.

DECEMBER 16, THURSDAY:

I checked at the Consulate for mail or cable. None. Checked Mackay Radio. None. I was beginning to wonder if someone in the Saudi government was holding his reply so a competitor could slide under me. I sent a cable to Getty via Mackay Radio, asking him to wire an answer via them.

DECEMBER 17, FRIDAY:

Friday is the Muslim Sabbath. Still no wire. I went fishing on the Red Sea with Rollie Onstad and Bill Barrett, Bechtel engineers. I caught a thirty-pound jack fish, a twenty-five-pound red snapper, and a twenty-pound barracuda on a hand line. It got rough and Barrett got very seasick.

Back at the Kandara House, I talked to Badr al Fahoum, the Palestinian working for the Saudi government, who volunteered that the concession deal was now between two companies, Pacific Western and another whose name he would not tell me. He said the Saudi Arabian government was not concerned about Getty's delay in answering concerning building the refinery. It was pretty hard to keep a secret in the Saudi Arabian government, so maybe he was right.

DECEMBER 18, SATURDAY:

Ahmed Fahkri picked me up at 9:00, saying Sulaiman wanted to see me. Sulaiman had a cable for me from Mr. Getty which had been sent in Arabic via the Saudi Arabian minister in Washington. In substance, the cable — which suffered from being translated into Arabic to be sent to Jidda, then retranslated into English — apparently okayed all my recommendations and indicated that Getty wanted the territorial waters included. Of course I wanted them too since my aerial reconnaissance, because I had seen an offshore shoaling which was probably an anticline. Tewfik was to retranslate the cable, and we would meet again that afternoon.

At this meeting negotiations really started in earnest. Tewfik insisted that I make my highest possible bid so he could submit it to the king. My stop was ten million and fifty-six cents per barrel royalty, but I thought I would not show all my hand now. I said I would go to nine and a half million and fifty-five cents as the absolute high royalty if he would guarantee that the concession would be granted. Otherwise, I would fall back to the former bid of nine million and fifty-three cents. He didn't like this approach.

Tewfik said he had to wait until American Independent's representatives came on December twentieth, and, if we were higher than they, he would grant the concession right away. I asked for preferential rights on the territorial waters, but he declined.

Sulaiman entered the negotiations and asked for 100,000 gallons of gas and 50,000 gallons of kerosene in cans to be given to the Bedouin annually. I countered with putting the gas in a 100,000-gallon tank at either Jidda or Riyadh. I could just see us having to find 100,000 one-gallon cans every year to haul from the refinery in the Neutral Zone.

Then one of the several advisers whispered in Sulaiman's ear and out came another request: to build a dispensary and hospital for the workmen in the Zone. ARAMCO had done this already in Dhahran, so I thought it best to agree to it.

Sulaiman wanted all this put in writing in a letter from Mr. Getty to the Saudi Arabian minister in Washington, so I went to Fahkri's office to compose a cable recommending this to Mr. Getty. Before sending it I went back to show it to Tewfik and Sulaiman, who made a few suggestions and changes. I remembered that they wanted a trade school for the workers, so I had already put that in.

Sulaiman had an old Imperial typewriter, and I had started to bang out the cable when, out of the blue, Sulaiman said he would give us the rights to the territorial waters and islands. I was very surprised and pleased at this.

The cable I sent proved to be the basis for the whole concession agreement:

J. Paul Getty
Spartan Aircraft Company
Tulsa, Oklahoma

Finance minister Sheikh Sulaiman pledges Saudi Arabian Government will grant company concession its part Kuwait Neutral Zone land territorial waters and islands within which same area under American Independent agreement and government will reject all subsequent offers from rival companies if we meet following terms which I have offered stop Bonus 9½ million stop Royalty 55 cents per U.S. barrel stop Net interest 25 percent guaranteed royalty one million per year in advance all monies U.S. currency stop Refinery to be built when production reaches 75,000 barrels per day capacity 12,000 barrels per day net carried interest 20 percent stop Free in kind 100,000 gallons gasoline and 50,000 gallons kerosene or gasoline optional government per year delivered Jidda and Riyadh stop Company agree hire Arab labor where possible and provide necessary medical care all company workers by erecting adequate dispensary and hospital stop Company will build trade school adequate to train Saudi Arabian nationals for jobs they are fitted within three years after oil is discovered in commercial quantities such terms in Kuwait American Independent agreement stop Recommend strongly you accept these terms and submit Saudi Arabian minister at Washington fully executed written bid okayed by U.S. State Department after which government written acceptance will be delivered stop Final drafting left to legal advisors of parties stop Please cable when bid delivered.

WALTON

I thought, "This gets us down to the final wire, I hope." But much more was still to come.

DECEMBER 19, SUNDAY:

Sulaiman sent his driver for me. He had a cable for me from Getty asking for clarification of the net profits interest in the oil from the wells and the profits from the refinery. I worked out a cable with Tewfik's help and sent it off. The awkward language was put in at his insistence. Sometimes I thought his legal training in Napoleonic law in the French language made it difficult for him to write comprehensible legal English.

> J. Paul Getty
> Spartan Aircraft Company
> Tulsa, Oklahoma
>
> Retel delete work carried [*sic*] stop 25 percent refers to interest in net profits derived from sale of products from wellheads stop 20 percent refers interest in net profits derived from sale products of refinery stop One barrel pays one single rate no possible accumulation stop After acceptance of your written bid Saudi Arabian government assures me preparation contract mere formality main points agreed upon no subsequent difficulty being completely to your satisfaction stop In addition terms already agreed upon the contract will contain usual arbitration forfeiture and force majeur clauses similar concession agreements stop No corporate taxes in Saudi Arabia now stop Government agrees not levy corporation tax unless any foreign country subsequently does and allows deduction for Saudi Arabian tax stop No double corporation taxation possible stop Exemption from custom duties for requirements and products stop Government shares of 25 or 20 percent of net profits not to suffer any foreign taxation.
>
> WALTON

Tewfik wanted to go to the States to draw up the final legal documents, and I thought this was a great idea.

DECEMBER 20, MONDAY:

A wire from Getty came in at breakfast inquiring if the tidelands were included as territorial waters and islands. I tried unsuccessfully to find Tewfik and Fahkri to work out an answer, so I sent the following:

> J. Paul Getty
> Spartan Aircraft Company
> Tulsa, Oklahoma
>
> Retel regarding property description stop Is mutual understanding here that concession covers land area plus all territorial

waters tidelands submerged areas and islands adjoining coast Neutral Zone over which government now has or may hereafter have sovereignty stop Suggest you word written bid similarly.

WALTON

DECEMBER 21, TUESDAY

Tewfik sent for me. He had a copy of the cable I had sent to Getty the day before. I was afraid the Saudi Arabian government had access to Mackay Radio messages. He said, "We will not give the continental shelf high seas area in the concession. You can only have the territorial waters"!

Of course I was glad to get the territorial waters, for that was where I thought I could see another structure. I reminded him, "ARAMCO has the continental shelf and high seas."

"Yes," he said, "but we are not going to give them in this concession!"

DECEMBER 22, WEDNESDAY:

The following cable arrived:

My previous letter offered much less and I understood it to include the government's share in the Neutral Zone embracing all territory in the Neutral Zone over which the government now has or might hereafter acquire sovereignty if the government proclaims that its sovereignty in the Neutral Zone includes the continental shelf we believe it only fair that we should have it rather than our competitors we understand that our interest in the continental shelf will exist only if as and when the government may proclaim its sovereignty thereover and that there is no representation on the government's part to us that they will ever do so.

J. PAUL GETTY

I went to talk to Sulaiman and Surur. It appeared we were at an impasse. I decided to lay my cards on the table. I told them I had understood that the shelf and high seas were excluded from the very beginning and appreciated Sulaiman's giving us the territorial waters. But since Mr. Getty was so adamant about the shelf, could they stretch a point and include that also?

That request got a pretty cold reception. They just wouldn't budge an inch. So afterward I sent the following cable to Getty:

> Consulted legal advisor government feel further clarification for yesterday's cable stop Government wishes give oil rights exclusively Saudi Kuwait Neutral Zone consisting land territorial water and islands within using legal sense of words stop Your previous letter delivered Saudi minister Washington does not cover high sea area stop Negotiations same stop Careful written bid expected excludes high seas continental shelves and sea subsoils to avoid international conflicts stop Still recommend acceptance.
>
> WALTON

That night Hermann Eilts and his wife Helen took me to the English "locust camp" thirty miles north of Jidda. The group was studying methods for eradicating locusts throughout the Middle East. They served us a dinner of gazelle, turkey, and warm beer.

DECEMBER 23, THURSDAY:

I received two cables:

> Reluctantly conforming bid to exclude continental shelf.
>
> GETTY

> Terms as clarified appear satisfactory preparing written bid for prompt submission to minister and State Department along lines indicated stop Will cable when submitted stop Walker in New York just received cable setting forth details your latest offer and stating he will be given refusal of our bid when submitted please verify discreetly.
>
> GETTY

I thought Ahmed Fahkri could handle this request best, so I went to see him. He went to Sheikh Surur's house to talk to him. Then they went together to see Sulaiman. Fahkri came back saying, "The finance minister says he has accepted your bid and denies that Walker has any right of refusal." So I sent the following cable:

> J. Paul Getty
> Spartan Aircraft Company
> Tulsa, Oklahoma
> Finance minister confirms mutual agreement here and denies Walker has any right of refusal stop If written bid submitted promptly we have concession but urge immediate action.
>
> WALTON

Well, did I or didn't I have the concession? I thought Walker represented a large investment firm probably acting for themselves and "others unknown." Fahkri told me the Syrian representing American Independent was in town and was a friend of Badr al Fahoum, whom I saw every night at the Kandara House.

When I questioned al-Fahoum later, he said he knew many Syrians but none who were dealing for American Independent.

A U.S. Navy plane had come in, and Eilts invited me to a cocktail party for the arriving brass. They were three admirals — Des Flowers, Miles, and Radford — and a civilian who turned out to be Senator Robertson from Wyoming. He was flabbergasted to see someone from Wyoming this far from home. We had a nice talk about people we both knew in Casper and Cody.

Captain Coffey was there, and I asked him if Saudi Arabia had any potential chief pilots for the C-47's.

He answered, "We haven't had a chance to train very many, but I know one who could sure make it."

"How come?" I asked.

"One of the king's younger brothers talked to me about it once. He speaks some English and wanted to sit in the cockpit. He asked me to start up the two engines, which I did. After I shut them off, the prince said, 'I'll bet you five Egyptian pounds I can start them again.' I didn't think he could do it because it took me days to memorize the checklist, so I bet him."

"Did he do it?" I asked.

"Hell, yes," Coffey said, "without a bobble! He was smart."

Thirty-seven years later I heard this teenager's name again — Khalid. He became king after Faisal's death in 1975.

DECEMBER 24, FRIDAY:

On Christmas Eve I received two wires:

Submitting bid as agreed to minister tomorrow or Monday.

GETTY

Secured State Department approval of bid today submitting same to minister tomorrow or Saturday.

GETTY

So all I had to do was wait to see if the bid was submitted and accepted.

December 25, Saturday, Christmas Day:

I went down to Ahmed Fahkri's office to tell him about the cables. He seemed very pleased and said he would tell Sheikh Sulaiman.

Hermann and Helen Eilts took me to U.S. Minister Childs' dinner. A big crowd was there. My stomach was pretty queasy, and I guess I was upset at having heard from Betty that Tad was sick.

December 26, Sunday:

Abdullah Tariki and his wife moved into the Kandara House. I loaned them the car and driver to go downtown and move their things, and they really appreciated it. Mrs. Tariki had lived in New York City and Texas most of her life and was having a rough time adapting. Tariki was insisting that she dress with a veil, as the Arab women do. Of course he was under pressure to be an Arab now rather than an American school boy. One of the king's brothers had given him a real dressing down the day before for wearing his leather jacket instead of Arab dress.

December 27, Monday:

I was still waiting for word that the bid had been submitted to the Saudi Arabian minister in Washington but received no wire or mail.

December 28, Tuesday:

I checked in at Mackay Radio. No cables had come in and I was getting worried.

I went to Ahmed Fahkri's office. He called Surur, who said no cable had come yet from the minister in Washington. He said another group had offered a bid higher in some respects than ours, but he wouldn't divulge who they were. So I cabled the following:

J. Paul Getty
Spartan Aircraft Company
Tulsa, Oklahoma
Please advise when bid is to be submitted Saudi Minister stop
We are dangerously near losing deal due to delay and competi-

tive bids stop Strongly recommend immediate action to acquire concession from geologic standpoint.

WALTON

Maybe I was getting jumpy, but Fahkri seemed pretty honest. Voluntarily, he said, "The American Independent man told me that Getty is discussing the negotiations with his company and that Getty is planning to do nothing at all!"

I went to a party given by Muhammad Alireza, a wealthy young Arab in his late thirties who spoke excellent English. It was rumored that one of his four wives was an American. I found out later that it was his brother Ali who had the American wife, Marianne Alireza. When she wrote a book about her trials and tribulations in the marriage, *At the Drop of a Veil: The True Story of An American Woman's Years in a Saudi Arabian Harem* (published in 1971 and reprinted in 1991 by Houghton Mifflin), she had to flee for her life — first to Switzerland and then to the U.S.

DECEMBER 29, WEDNESDAY:

At breakfast, Long of Mackay Radio gave me a cable which had arrived late the night before:

Formal bid containing terms agreed on and approved by State Department was personally handed to Minister at Washington December 27 stop He promised to cable it immediately to finance minister.

GETTY

I took the cable to Fahkri's office, and he called Sulaiman, who said he wanted to see me in the afternoon. I went back to the Kandara House to wait.

Hermann Eilts came over early in the afternoon, wanting to know if I had heard anything from Fahoum or Khaladi about the Saudi Arabian government canceling its banking agreements with the Dutch bank because of the Dutch-Muslim trouble in Indochina. I hadn't heard any mention of this and realized that he really had a lot to keep track of for the Consulate.

Fahkri didn't show up until 6:15 PM. Sulaiman was entertaining one of the king's sons, a light-skinned man of about twenty.

Everyone else always took off his shoes on entering Sulaiman's house, but this prince didn't. I guessed he had some right to his arrogance.

We talked through Tewfik, who was tired and troublesome. Sulaiman said he was giving the other negotiators the brush-off, but for me to keep it confidential. Tewfik had an Arabic version of Getty's written bid, which of course I had not seen, and started to question me about it.

"Why does Mr. Getty want this concession to run sixty years or as long as oil is produced? That's much too long."

"Our government and states give oil leases with those terms," I replied. "They always honor a lease as long as oil is being produced from it. It is the custom of the industry."

I could see Tewfik didn't believe me.

"Mr. Getty wants the right to cancel the concession agreement at any time. The Saudi Arabian government should have the same right."

"We are putting up nine and a half million and a million dollars a year guaranteed royalty," I said. "This is in effect a performance bond, and we have shown our good faith. The Saudi Arabian government wanting to cancel does not indicate their good faith. Of course, you have the right to cancel if we don't perform."

This stopped him for a while. He said a copy of Getty's letter was coming on TWA from Washington, and he wanted to put off further negotiations until it arrived.

DECEMBER 30, THURSDAY:

At the Eilts' cocktail party, I met the Syrian minister and Kim Philby, an Englishman who in later years would be the subject of an English diplomatic scandal by defecting to Soviet Russia after having been a double agent inside English intelligence.

The Tarikis had guests at the Kandara House that day as well. One was an interpreter for the king — an old friend of Tariki from the desert village in the Nejd where he was raised. I was really surprised to hear that he was an admirer of the Russians. He said he hoped the Communists would have more influence in Arabia.

DECEMBER 31, FRIDAY:

Fahkri took me to see Sulaiman in the morning. As finance minister, Sulaiman wanted to discuss the handling of the payments for the concession. Before I had a chance to suggest anything, Sulaiman, Tewfik, and Surur argued long and loud among themselves for more than twenty minutes. I was both embarrassed and amused.

We finally came to the agreement that Getty would deposit the bonus and the guaranteed royalty, a total of ten and a half million dollars, in the Guaranty Trust Company Bank in New York City on account for the Saudi Arabian government. The contract was then to be drawn up in Cairo. Fahkri took me down to his office and sent the following cable, which Tewfik, as Saudi Arabian government legal adviser, and I had worked out:

J. Paul Getty
Spartan Aircraft Company
Tulsa, Oklahoma

Negotiations with other companies stopped definitely stop Financial terms your written bid acceptable Saudi Arab Government stop Saudi Arab Government desires you deposit ten and one-half million Guaranty Trust Company New York on account payable to government if formal agreement is signed by both parties within two months stop Further negotiations necessary for other terms of bid and final closure of concessional agreement stop Such negotiations to take place in Cairo with your attorneys and me as company representatives with full power to negotiate stop Legal advisor of government there by Sunday stop Please advise when money deposited and date of arrival of your attorneys in Cairo stop Understood secrecy concessional negotiations still being strictly observed.

WALTON

I hoped this would wrap the deal up, but little did I know what was still to be resolved. I went back to the Kandara House and sat around all evening talking the politics of capitalism and communism with the Tarikis. A hell of a way to celebrate New Year's Eve!

JANUARY 1, 1949, SATURDAY:

A sandstorm had come up during the night and covered everything with sand — my hair, clothes, bed, the whole house.

After cleaning up, I went over to the TWA party. Theirs were the only commercial planes serving Jidda, and they were doing their best to please everyone. Everybody at the party was having such a good time that I thought their humor might be forced. I was tired of Arabia and homesick for my family and Wyoming, and I received no word from Getty that day as to the deposit or the arrival of attorneys.

JANUARY 2, SUNDAY:

I received two cables from Getty; the first asked about a circular lava crater and lava flows in the Neutral Zone. I didn't know who could have told him about them, but I wired that there was no crater or lava flow in the Zone; it was all sedimentary rocks. This first cable also said that his attorney, Barnabas Hadfield, would be in Cairo about Tuesday and would meet me at Shepheard's Hotel.

Getty's second cable said ten and a half million would be deposited in the Guaranty Trust Company Bank in New York City on Monday. What a relief!

Emir Faisal, second-oldest son of King Abdul-Aziz ibn Saud, was coming to Jidda from Riyadh. Some of his party were staying across the road from the Kandara House, and their servants came and took the only mirror in the building off the wall and the lock off the bathroom door.

JANUARY 3, MONDAY:

Emir Faisal was met at the airport by a big crowd. All our Embassy and Legation representatives were there.

I took my passport to Fahkri to get it visa'ed for exit and return, and also got a one-month Egyptian visa. When I returned to the hotel, Mrs. Tariki was waiting for me in the lobby. "Have you seen Abdullah?" she asked.

"No, not all day."

She was obviously distraught and needed someone to talk to, so I listened.

"Abdullah wants a son. I have been trying to get pregnant. He says all I do is sit on the nest and nothing hatches. He has been staying out late at night, and I think he may be planning to divorce me or to marry an Arab woman. If he divorces me, I have no place to go."

"You could go back to the States," I said. "Don't your folks live in New York?"

"Yes," she said, "but I was born in Germany and went to the States as a small child. I'm not an American citizen."

She went on to tell me how Tariki had been born in a small village in the Nejd Province in east-central Saudi Arabia. He had been a bright student and had been sponsored by Emir Faisal to attend Fuad University in Cairo and later the University of Texas, where they had met. While Faisal had been Saudi Arabian representative to the United Nations, Tariki had visited him in New York City.

Now that Tariki had graduated as the first Saudi Arabian geologist, Faisal was particularly pleased with him, and he could work into a good position in the government. In some ways this worried her, because with this success would come more pressure for her to be a typical Arab wife, and she didn't fit in at all. She spoke no Arabic and did not want to have to wear a veil and dress in Arab clothes.

I didn't know how to advise her, so I tried to placate her by saying I thought it would all work out all right. "East is East and West is West and never the twain shall meet" kept going through my head, but I didn't say anything. I really felt sorry for her.

JANUARY 4, TUESDAY:

Hermann Eilts had me over for lunch, and I told him I was going to Cairo to write the concession agreement. I saw Ambassador Childs for a few minutes and reported our progress.

"What are you going to do when you get the concession signed?" he asked.

"I'm going back to Wyoming," I said. He was thunderstruck.

"Wyoming!" he snorted. "You're in the bigtime here; why go back there?"

"That's where I want to be."

Fahkri finally got my passport visa. As Emir Faisal is a great favorite of the people, everything was in a hubbub because of his visit. Faisal was Saudi Arabia's representative to the United Nations and consequently a world figure, and he was next in line for the throne after Crown Prince Saud.

In the evening Fahkri took me to see Sulaiman, who was sick in bed. Gary Owen of ARAMCO was there too. I told Sulaiman I thought everything in framing up the contract would be okay. Through Fahkri, Sulaiman said, "I like the frank way you have negotiated."

We exchanged mutual compliments, after which he told me Tewfik could be reached at the Saudi Arabian Embassy in Cairo. He said he would be glad to see me when we came back to sign the contract.

That night Fahkri came to the Kandara House and brought me a wristwatch, Arab headdress (white wool *gutra* and black *agal*), and brown Arab cloak (*abba*) from Sulaiman. I was very surprised. I tried to find out from Fahkri what to bring Sulaiman when I came back from Cairo, but he wouldn't say. I knew that the exchanging of gifts for the occasion is very important, so I quizzed Tariki later. He suggested pen and pencil sets and several gold pens for the signing, to be given away at that time.

JANUARY 5, WEDNESDAY:

Tariki went with me to the airport after an early breakfast. We had coffee with Emir Abdullah, brother of King ibn-Saud, and Emir Monsour, one of the king's sons. Abdullah was a rough-looking Bedouin type, and he had an old powder-blue Rolls Royce that he drove like he probably rode a camel — hell-bent down the rough road, dust and sand flying.

Captain Bartlett, the pilot of the C-47, asked me to sit in the copilot's seat, and I enjoyed the better view. We flew along the west side of the Red Sea, right over the Ras Ghârib oil field, and the anticline showed beautifully in the morning light, going right out into the water.

Landing at Cairo, I had to leave my camera in bond as before. I went up to Shepheard's Hotel and got a room, and while I was showering, Mr. Getty's attorney, Barnabas Hadfield, whom I hadn't met, came to my room.

Barney had the map of Ireland on his florid freckled face. He was about forty and just a little on the plump side. His black suit and homburg and his steel-blue eyes labeled him a man of the law at first glance. He was a little gruff at first, like most New Yorkers, and I had the feeling he really didn't approve of a geologist from Wyoming handling such a big deal. This attitude would change as we got further into the negotiations and he discovered that I knew a lot more about the oil business than he did. It even got to the point where Tewfik turned to me for advice on the way the industry operated, calling me his "petroleum adviser."

Hadfield and I went down to the famous Shepheards Hotel bar, where the Scotch drink called the "Suffering Bastard" was invented. We had a few drinks while we sparred around, trying to figure each other out. I wanted to be sure I understood him, because I knew we would be a long time here in Cairo negotiating with Ahmed Bey Tewfik.

At this time Shepheards Hotel was the crossroads of the Middle East. Through its revolving doors came people from all over the Arab world. Red tarbooshes (fezzes) of the African world mixed with the Bedouin Arab headdress. A sprinkling of Greeks, local Jews, English, French, and Americans made the dining room look like the United Nations. With its French cuisine and the dinner music played every night, this was one of the most-frequented spots in Cairo. It was great to be back in civilization. The only trouble was that I was suffering from amoebic dysentery, and my health was rapidly going downhill.

CHAPTER 3

THE CONCESSION AGREEMENT

JANUARY 6, THURSDAY:

Barney Hadfield and I went out to the Saudi Arab Legation, where Sulaiman had told me to locate Tewfik. I got Tewfik's home and office numbers and called him. He sounded glad to hear from me but couldn't see us until late that afternoon.

We went over to the United States Consulate to check in, but they were closed. Back at the hotel, the dragoman Samedi saw me and called me by name, so I had him take us on a tour of the city to visit the graves of the Mamelukes, the mosques of Sultan Hassan and Muhammad Ali, and the Coronation Mosques. This was Hadfield's first trip to Cairo, and he enjoyed seeing the sights.

We met Tewfik at 4:30 PM and had tea with him at Groppis, a sidewalk cafe and confectionary. Tewfik was in good spirits and looked so different in his Western clothes I hardly knew him. He still wore his fez, however, always. I brought him up to date on my meeting with Sulaiman and the last word from Getty.

Hadfield and I had discussed what we thought should go into the concession agreement, and we thought we knew how to proceed in drawing it up. Barney, I am sure, had envisioned writing the agreement in a couple of days, getting it printed, and then going to Saudi Arabia to get it signed. He was really thunderstruck when Tewfik announced, "It will be at least a fortnight before the agreement can be finished."

I thought to myself, "That will be pretty good time!"

We all agreed that Hadfield would start writing up the agreement, putting in all the financial terms and the necessary clauses so we could explore, drill, produce, and refine.

Hadfield put in a call for Getty that evening, and we sat around for three hours waiting for him to return it. He didn't. So, disgusted, we decided to go out for a drink at the Badia Palace, a nightclub of sorts, featuring Egyptian belly dancers on a stage. The star of the show was really a terrific wiggler and, after a few drinks, we agreed we should cable Getty to book her at his Pierre Hotel Supper Club. But then we figured his wrath might be aroused, considering the other important business we had at hand.

JANUARY 7, FRIDAY:

Starting early Barney began writing the agreement in longhand. I found a typewriter I could rent. It was a French make, and the A, Q, M, and W were in different places from an American machine. It took me a long time to get used to it.

I typed all Barney had written and then went out for a walk. There was a student demonstration in the Opera Square, and I was warned to stay away. This was the beginning of the riots which would lead to the eventual fall of the monarchy and the exile of King Farouk.

JANUARY 8, SATURDAY:

We met Tewfik at 10:00 AM and went to his office on the third floor of an old, ratty building without any heat. There was no elevator signal button, so when you wanted the elevator, one of the men stationed on each floor would clap his hands, and the operator would hear him and bring the elevator to the right floor. I felt sorry for the men, who had to dress in business suits but made less than a pound ($2.50) a day. Their poverty was demoralizing.

Since Tewfik's office was so dirty and smelly, Barney and I often speculated on what kind of place he lived in. Although we saw him nearly every day for six weeks, he never took us to his home or showed us where he lived. All we knew was that he had an apartment somewhere in Cairo.

We started to talk, and I could see that Barney was really taken aback. Tewfik insisted that King Saud and the Saudi Arabian government have no responsibility to secure or guarantee our full rights to explore, exploit, and export oil. He also insisted that the Saudi

Arabian government have the right to take oil in kind at a big discount. He wanted a definite date for our starting the geologic work, which was all right. But then the real curve came when he insisted that the Saudi Arabian government have a right to repurchase the concession at cost if and when it proved productive.

This wasn't all. He wanted some type of proration to spread the oil production over six years. He also wanted us to accept the same termination dates that the American Independent Company had on the Kuwait half.

Then, to cap it all, he showed us a letter in Arabic from AMINCO in which, he said, they offered to take our deal on the same terms!

I reminded Tewfik that he had given his word that we had the deal. This made him wince, but he was out to chisel everything he could, and it was a way of life in this part of the world to deal that way. Clearly, the advisers to Sulaiman and the king had dreamed up a lot of these new demands in order to continue to justify their existence.

Hadfield was beginning to see what I had been up against these past weeks and now realized it would be a long siege before we broke these crippling demands down. He tried again to call Mr. Getty but failed to reach him. I had the feeling he would tell Getty it was impossible to deal with these people and to call the whole thing off. I hated to see this happen, because I thought we could eventually get what we wanted. I figured Sulaiman was going to get something out of the deal if it went through and that he would be pulling for it. Only time would tell.

JANUARY 9, SUNDAY:

We revised and rewrote parts of the agreement, with me sitting at the typewriter all day. We would discuss a clause, and Barney would write it out in longhand. I would type it up, and then we would tear it apart.

We went over to the Tabarin nightclub after dinner for a drink. They had a Spanish dancer named Cecelia who came and sat at our table. Barney danced with her — did the rhumba, samba, tango, even the jitterbug. I asked him where he learned to dance like that.

He said, "Some people play golf for a hobby or fish, but I dance."

Cecelia was ecstatic. She said she would like to go around the world on a dance tour with Barney. She also invited him over to her hotel — the National.

Barney asked me what sort of place it was. I told him John Ryan of TWA had described it as a "fairly clean hotel where the room clerk wouldn't even look up if you came in leading a camel."

JANUARY 10, MONDAY:

We met Tewfik at 10:00 AM, and he proceeded to throw us a few more curves. He said, "If you drill and find oil and the Neutral Zone becomes a very rich and valuable property, Russia may want to come down and take it over. We think your company should pay for soldiers, fortifications, and equipment to protect it from this threat."

My reaction was, "You'll fortify it to death. There won't be any income from the property."

Apparently this idea was very important to someone in the government, for we didn't get the fortification point resolved for many weeks; it took a cable from the U.S. State Department, signed by Secretary of State Dean Acheson, saying no American company could get involved in such a plan.

Tewfik then brought up the problem of radio communication, airplanes, airports, roads, and railroads. He insisted that all these be owned and operated by the government and leased to the Company. We argued hot and heavy about the difficulties of trying to develop a desert wasteland into producing oil fields, refineries, etc., without having the right to build our own roads, fly our own planes, communicate by radio with our field crews, and so forth. These points were going to have to be negotiated long and hard.

Tewfik inquired about the right he had requested to repurchase at cost. I paraphrased an argument I had heard from Fred Goodstein, a very successful oil man in Casper, Wyoming: "Look, why go to all the trouble to explore, drill, and find oil and then just get my money back. Hell, I've got my money now!"

While my argument seemed to head this demand off for good, another one popped to the surface. Tewfik wanted an Arab on the

Company's board of directors. He wouldn't take no for an answer, so we let the matter drop. Then Tewfik threw in another real monkey wrench — the government's demand to be able to limit production if they desired.

We spent the rest of the afternoon arguing about roads and airplanes and railroads but didn't seem to get anywhere with Tewfik. So we went back to Shepheards and cabled Getty, reporting the status of the negotiations and our refusal to allow a repurchase agreement and an Arab on the board.

JANUARY 11, TUESDAY:

We met Tewfik at noon, after receiving a cable from Getty stating that he would not consider a repurchase agreement or an Arab on the board or a limit on production. He also wanted the minimum royalty payments limited to only three consecutive years before he could relinquish the concession in the event of disappointing production.

Getty said in his cable that his information was that AMINCO had not offered to match our bid, having bid to Saudi Arabia only what they gave Kuwait. I didn't know where he got his information, but I felt that Tewfik's letter represented a genuine bid — maybe not an official one, but a feeler Saudi Arabia could take if they desired. Getty also agreed to give the government a right to buy 20 percent of the products at a 5 percent discount, but that was all.

We really got under Tewfik's skin when we reported Getty's answers. He blew and blew, but I felt he would accept these terms.

Then Tewfik brought up what I called the social features of the agreement. He wanted free housing for the workers, pension plans, and the right to quarantine airports and villages if necessary. After twelve years of Franklin Roosevelt at home, this didn't seem very much out of line because we were going to have to do these things anyway. I felt we might just as well put them in the contract now and gain some good will, so we cabled Getty for his approval.

JANUARY 12, WEDNESDAY:

We worked on the arbitration clause most of the day. This was really important, since it could resolve the conflicts which I felt would undoubtedly arise over interpretation of this agreement. I was prophetic in this thought, for the Company and the Saudi Arabian government went to arbitration several times.

No word came from Getty on the recommended social features of the agreement.

JANUARY 13, THURSDAY:

After another conference with Tewfik, I believed we were making progress with him. He seemed less demanding and acted as though he really wanted the deal to go through.

JANUARY 14, FRIDAY:

After working on the clause relating to customs officials, the post office, and soldiers domiciled in the Neutral Zone, we met Tewfik at 5:00 and he approved our language. We took him to dinner at Shepheards, and he condescended to drink some wine with his dinner. We were breaking through his tough Muslim shell!

Getty called while we were eating, giving approval for the social features of the agreement and for compensating Saudi Arabian representatives in the Company's operations.

JANUARY 15, SATURDAY:

Tewfik had insisted that an Arabic version of the concession agreement must be the governing language, but we got him to agree that it would have no more than equal weight with the English version. Nevertheless, we were worried about who we could get to translate our English version into Arabic.

We went out to the United States Legation and talked to their press section. They steered us to Dr. Harold Glidden, a Princeton graduate in Arabic language and literature, who in turn sent us to the American University to see Dr. Butrus Abd al-Malik, who had been a classmate of his at Princeton.

Dr. al-Malik was a Presbyterian minister, and we felt we would like to have him do the translation. It was terribly important, because a poor translation could be no end of trouble in future operations.

We met Tewfik at 5:00. There were no public stenos or any qualified clerical help in Cairo, and we had discussed with him several times getting a good stenographer to retype the agreement.

While we waited in Tewfik's office, his garageman brought in one he had found. She was a teacher of English literature at a girls' school in Heliopolis (a suburb of Cairo), an Arab, and a Christian. This surprised me for a minute, until I remembered that no Muslim girls were trained for this in the Egypt of 1949. Her name was Aida, and we took her home in Tewfik's car — with the concession agreement manuscript. We didn't want to risk her losing it on the bus, since it would have taken more than a week to produce another one on my French typewriter.

Afterward, Tewfik drove us over to see the Pyramids in the light of the full moon. It was a very inspiring and awesome sight. This ancient land and its antiquities like the Pyramids have a feeling about them that I had never experienced anywhere before. I seemed such a small grain of sand compared with the totality of life that had been in this spot.

JANUARY 16, SUNDAY:

I slept late, but after I waited down in the lobby for an hour, Hadfield hadn't shown up. This worried me because he had suffered a very serious heart attack only a year earlier. He was all right, however, and after breakfast we took a cab out to the Pyramids again.

We walked over to the Sphinx and had our pictures taken riding camels. After that I went on an excursion into the Great Pyramid. It was really a climb, and I was glad Barney hadn't come. The king's entire chamber is lined with Aswan granite, and it has a hole to let in fresh air from the outside. It was really an interesting trip, but I had horrible cramps and dysentery all night.

JANUARY 17, MONDAY:

I was very sick with dysentery during the morning. We went to Tewfik's office at 5:00 PM and waited until 7:15, when Aida arrived with the typed manuscript. It looked pretty good.

JANUARY 18, TUESDAY:

The pattern continued, with my being sick again all morning and going to Tewfik's at 5:00 PM. He was throwing us new curves and had no doubt been getting instructions from Sulaiman's advisers.

Now they wanted to bring up the proration of production again — to be at their discretion, of course. We thought we had beaten this proposal down earlier. It could hamstring the Company if we weren't allowed to produce enough oil to pay for our employees, contractors, etc. We argued until 8:30 PM.

JANUARY 19, WEDNESDAY:

Tewfik agreed to meet at 10:00 AM instead of his usual 5:00 PM. Perhaps he felt we needed to start making more progress. Now he wanted the concession to be forfeited if sixty days of idleness occurred during operations. He wanted two strings of tools operating. (He pronounced it "stringess of tools." Sounds funny, but it wasn't.) And he brought up the oil proration again. We were really peeved at these added demands popping up *again.*

We met Tewfik again at 5:30, waiting an hour in his cold, dingy, smelly office. Barney got sick after a while, and we had to close off the talks. Every time we met we were subjected to a serving of thick, sweet Turkish coffee. It was taking its toll.

JANUARY 20, THURSDAY:

After editing part of the typed version of the contract, we met Tewfik at 11 AM. Now he wanted the Company to have a continuing liability even if we abandoned the concession; that is, to keep paying the million-dollar minimum royalty annually, keep the Saudi Arabian workers on salary, etc.

We took along some additional articles of the concession which I had typed up, and Aida came to the office and got them.

JANUARY 21, FRIDAY:

We went out to the United States Consulate to meet the new petroleum attaché, Dick Funkhouser. He was young, a former Air Force pilot in Southeast Asia during the war, and he had had a little experience in oil in the U.S.

We discussed our deal with him, and he seemed surprised that Getty could do business on the fifty-five cents per barrel royalty. We didn't press the point.

JANUARY 22, SATURDAY:

I took a cab out to Heliopolis to pick up more typing from Aida's mother. Barney and I reread and smoothed out some of the language.

We met Tewfik at 4:30 and went through the whole contract with him. It now had more than forty articles and was more than thirty-five pages in small type. Our completion date of a fortnight had long since passed, but we thought that now our only stumbling block was the fortification issue.

Getty had wired a definite *no* on proration and on the two strings of tools. We showed the cable to Tewfik, and it seemed to satisfy him. I think he just wanted to see if we had the authority to say no — wanted to get the no from the horse's mouth, so to speak.

JANUARY 23, SUNDAY:

I sat out on the Shepheards' east-side terrace in the sun for an hour in the morning, then retyped some of the articles of the agreement.

We met Tewfik at 5:00, but he had a headache and didn't want to discuss business.

JANUARY 24, MONDAY:

Barney had been sick all night with dysentery. I gave him some of my sulfa pills.

We met with Dick Funkhouser at the American Legation to discuss the Saudi demand that we fortify the Neutral Zone. He said, "The State Department doesn't want anything like that in contracts."

We met Tewfik at 11:00 and went through the fifty-four articles, making only minor changes. It looked like we were in agreement on everything now. We told him the U.S. State Department in Cairo had said no on the fortifications issue.

Dr. Butrus Abd al-Malik came to the hotel, and we showed him what his translation job would be.

Later we received a cable from Getty saying he wanted a drilling deal on the Sinai Peninsula.

JANUARY 25, TUESDAY:

Barney and I were both sick from dysentery in the morning. We went out to talk to Funkhouser about Getty wanting a deal in the Sinai. He showed us a map of the concessions in the Red Sea–Sinai area, and they covered every place there were sedimentary rocks. It didn't look like we could get any sort of concession for Getty in this area.

I had lunch with Dr. Butrus, as we called him, and asked him to translate the agreement that ibn-Saud had made with the Sheikh of Kuwait in December of 1922, when the Neutral Zone was set up. I had tried unsuccessfully to get my hands on one in Saudi Arabia, but Funkhouser had one in his office. We had to show the exact geographical description of the Zone for our agreement.

In the evening we showed Tewfik Getty's cable about drilling rights in the Sinai. Tewfik jumped on this and wanted to make a big deal out of it — more legal work representing Getty to the Egyption government.

Barney and I decided that only preliminary studies and contracts could be made with the Egyptian government now, and we cabled Getty an answer in this respect. After all, Egypt was at war with Israel now, and field operations in the Sinai would be difficult and hazardous.

JANUARY 26, WEDNESDAY:

Our stenographer Aida was not making much progress in typing, so we were waiting for her. We had Tewfik and Funkhouser for dinner at Shepheards. Tewfik said he had a wire from the government to hurry up the contract, and I could see he was a little annoyed.

JANUARY 27, THURSDAY:

We got some typing from the stenographer and spent the day checking it and correcting typing errors.

JANUARY 28, FRIDAY:

The balance of the agreement was now typed, and I took it out to Dr. Butrus so he could start translating.

Tewfik brought up the matter of fortifications again. Obviously we were going to have to get official word directly from the U.S. State Department in Washington to lay this issue to rest.

Tewfik told us Shell Oil had been in touch with the Saudi Arabian government and had made a bid. I said, "I'll bet it isn't as high as ours." He didn't answer.

Dr. Butrus brought his brother and a friend to see us at Shepheards. They both asked for jobs. One worked as a clerk for Shell and the other was in the library. Neither had potential as an employee, in my opinion. Tewfik had told us we should have an interpreter of our own when it was time to go back to Saudi Arabia, however.

I don't know how the news got out, but we were besieged by people wanting jobs. The number of unemployed in Egypt must have been astronomical — a perpetual 1932-type depression! However, we were going to need some good people in Saudi Arabia when we got the concession, so we should start looking for possible employees.

JANUARY 29, SATURDAY:

Butrus's brother came to see me at 9:30 and said he had been talking to some people who had been in Jidda. He said he did not want to go to Saudi Arabia as our interpreter because of religious prejudice toward Christian Arabs. I realized that this might make it difficult to obtain a good man.

John Ryan of TWA, who had been in Saudi Arabia for a time, introduced me to an Arab by the name of Kasamal. He seemed quite intelligent and might be someone we could take to Jidda.

I asked John if Kasamal was Muslim or Christian. He said he didn't know but would find out for me. Kasamal was in the hotel later that day, and Ryan collared him, asking, "Did you enjoy your stay in Jidda?"

Kasamal said, "Yes."

"Were you able to go up to Mecca while you were there?"

When Kasamal said "Yes," I knew. He was a Muslim, and we had found out without having to ask him outright.

JANUARY 30, SUNDAY:

While waiting for Dr. Butrus's translation of the contract, we had Samedi (Sam) take us out to Saqqara and Memphis. We saw the statue of Ramses II at Memphis — a huge thing of polished Aswan granite, lying on its back. We saw the step pyramid (Third Dynasty) at Saqqara, which is older than the Fourth Dynasty pyramids at Giza. Sam's description of the rise and fall of the various dynasties was priceless, reminding me of the Uncle Remus stories, complete with dialect.

We had lunch at the Mena House at Giza, named after King Mena (Menes) of the First Dynasty. Although it was a windy, nasty day, we decided to go to the horse races at the Heliopolis Sporting Club. The horses are all Arabians and smaller than Thoroughbreds. It was Barney's lucky day. He won a 30-to-1 longshot in the second race on a little grey horse named Burgh.

I bought a *Time* magazine to read at night, but most of the Middle East news had been snipped out with scissors — government censors!

JANUARY 31, MONDAY:

I met John Ryan of TWA, who took me to the Saudi Arabian Airlines offices to see Major Mahmoud. We needed exit visas as well as extensions of our Egyptian visas, and with the country at war, it was difficult to obtain them.

Tewfik was checking Dr. Butrus's Arabic translation and said it appeared all right so far.

We went to see Dr. Butrus, who had managed to finish only four pages of the contract. He said it was difficult to translate. At this rate, it would be weeks before we were ready to go back to Saudi Arabia.

FEBRUARY 1, TUESDAY:

Major Mahmoud came to the hotel to see me. I guessed that he wanted to leave Saudi Arabian Airlines. He told me he had an

M.D. degree from the University of London but had lost his physician's license because of an abortion he performed in which the patient died. He seemed to be a very intelligent man, and I felt sorry for him.

Dick Funkhouser invited us to his home for cocktails. We met two other Embassy people there, someone named Betts and Judd Polk, an economist. Barney got pretty wild and did an Irish jig that really brought the house down.

We had been hearing for some time about a place called the Club Scarabiah, so we had a taxi take us out there. It was a not very impressive looking place in the old part of north Cairo. They had a black pianist and a European orchestra. Both were good.

Along about midnight, I noticed a couple of Mafia-type gorillas come in and case the place. Their guns showed very plainly under their coats. A dark-haired singer was in front of the orchestra singing a song in French. I saw her pause and speak to someone in the audience. It was a pudgy man with a fair complexion, smoking a big cigar. I looked at Barney and silently formed the word "Farouk." It was the Egyptian king on one of his nightly forays. He was still there when we left, and the singer was having a drink at his table. They obviously knew each other. Within a year and a half, civil war would break out in Cairo, and Farouk would be forced to abdicate in 1952. His self-indulgence and dissipated appearance no doubt helped to turn his countrymen against him. And then, of course, he wasn't really an Egyptian but the last of the line founded by the Turk Mehemet Ali in 1805.

FEBRUARY 2, WEDNESDAY:

Dick Funkhouser at the U.S. Legation had an official cable for us from the State Department saying fortifications in the Saudi Arabian Neutral Zone were out. It was signed by Dean Acheson, the Secretary of State. We paraphrased the cable and took it over to Tewfik. He was now resigned to there being no fortifications and could get ibn-Saud's or Sulaiman's adviser off his back — whichever had been pushing for this provision.

FEBRUARY 3, THURSDAY:

Going over the latest pages of the translation with Dr. Butrus, I found that he was still having trouble putting English legal phrases into Arabic.

Later I saw the movie *Red River* with John Wayne. It really made me homesick for the West. I swore that if I ever got through with this deal, I was going back to the West to stay!

FEBRUARY 4, FRIDAY:

My dysentery was bad again, and my kidneys ached like the devil, but I had breakfast with Butrus, who needed more guidance on the translation.

Jack Keegan, the manager of TWA, had us out to lunch at his home in Gezira, an island in the Nile. He had houseguests — one of them the wife of a famous English polo player. Keegan was having trouble with his hearing. He had been in the King David Hotel in Jerusalem when it was blown up recently and was still suffering from the concussion.

I wrote Betty a nasty letter asking why she hadn't answered any of mine. My poor health was beginning to depress me terribly. And then today was my thirty-fifth birthday, which didn't help either.

FEBRUARY 5, SATURDAY:

I went out to the Embassy to see Dick Funkhouser, although I was feeling very ill. Apparently he had been instructed to keep pretty close tabs on the progress of this concession agreement. We were still waiting for the translation.

Barney and I went out to the Heliopolis races again. Jack Body, a Saudi Arabian Airlines pilot, went along with us, but we didn't pick a winner.

FEBRUARY 6, SUNDAY:

With not much to do, we went out to Khan al Khalili bazaar — the big *suk* or market of Cairo — where I bought some copper and silver boxes and a pair of coral earrings for Betty.

Barney wanted to go to the races again, so we did. I lost three more Egyptian pounds, even though I did pick some winners.

FEBRUARY 7, MONDAY:

The morning blues hit hard, and I was feeling terrible. Out at the Embassy, the new typist Dick Funkhouser got for us had finished the English version of the concession agreement and made mimeograph copies of it.

Tewfik was glad to get the copies and said he would check them through for any mistakes.

Several letters from Betty arrived. She and the kids were okay. It had been weeks since I had heard from her, and the mail censors had held some of the letters all that time. I sent a cable telling her not to open my nasty letter of the fourth.

FEBRUARY 8, TUESDAY:

Up all night with cramps and dysentery and nausea. I took some sulfa pills and later some enterovioform.

Funkhouser had the Polks and Tewfik out for cocktails. (Tewfik didn't have any with alcohol.) Then, since I was feeling a little better, we took them to dinner at Shepheards, where we had grilled prawns, beef Chateaubriand, crêpes suzette, Champagne, and white and red wines.

Polk and Tewfik got into an argument about what Saudi Arabia was going to do with all their oil income. Polk was a little drunk and rattled on and on. Tewfik sat with the look of the Sphinx on his face and listened. Polk made some good points, like the desirability of hiring a good economist to advise the Saudi Arabian government. I had the feeling that Tewfik believed the money would be Saudi Arabia's to do with as they pleased, when they pleased, and resented any outside advice.

FEBRUARY 9, WEDNESDAY:

After having dysentery all night, I saw Jack Keegan of TWA, who made arrangements for Barney and me to have our stools examined for amoebic dysentery. I went for a walk and bought Barney a tarboosh. He wore it, so I guess he liked it.

We were still waiting for the Arabic translation.

FEBRUARY 10, THURSDAY:

I had bad cramps all night. In the morning I took a stool sample to Dr. John Weir at the Rockefeller Foundation offices. He came to the hotel in the afternoon to tell me I had amoebic dysentery; he had found many cysts. He prescribed a treatment for me — ten days of carbarsone capsules. They are an arsenic compound, and he told me I was bound to have some reaction from them. February 10 is always a bad day for me. This was the eleventh anniversary of my mother's death.

We finally got our exit visas from Egypt and a Saudi Arabian visa for Barney.

FEBRUARY 11, FRIDAY:

Barney took his stool sample in. He didn't have amoeba, which was very lucky, since he was having enough trouble recuperating from his heart attack. I started the carbarsone treatment.

We had no word from Butrus on the translation.

FEBRUARY 12, SATURDAY:

I was up with terrible cramps from 4 to 6 AM. I got a bismuth-carbonate-paregoric mix from the apothecary across the street. It helped the pain, but I was passing gobs of bloody mucous.

Butrus came to the hotel and said he was almost finished with the translation. Barney had drawn up an affidavit for him to sign which declared his translation to be a proper and true translation. When Butrus refused to sign it, Hadfield got pretty sore at him. We got to the bottom of his refusal, however.

Tewfik had told Butrus that he might be legally liable if anything went wrong with the concession agreement. This had Butrus scared, and he wanted to talk to Dr. Glidden about the problem. Of course the affidavit was necessary for us, since equal weight would be given the Arabic text of the agreement in the event we had to go to arbitration over any dispute.

It now appeared that we would have the completed Arabic text done by tomorrow.

FEBRUARY 13, SUNDAY:

One of the facts of life in the Middle East is the ceremonial giving of gifts. It is an ancient custom, and we had been conferring with Tewfik on what would be expected of us when we returned to Saudi Arabia for the signing of the agreement. At his suggestion, we ordered boxes of candies, nuts, and dried fruits from Groppis. We planned to take these boxes with us to Saudi Arabia the next day. The gift list included:

2 boxes	Sheikh Sulaiman	Finance Minister
1 box	Muhammad Surur	Sulaiman's adviser
1 box	Sulaiman Hamad	Son of Sulaiman
1 box	Hammad Sulaiman	Brother of Sulaiman
1 box	Ahmad Mosula	Sulaiman's adviser
1 box	Ahmed Fahkri	Engineer adviser to Sulaiman
1 box	Sheikh Yusuf Yussain	Assistant to Sulaiman and real power in the government
1 box	Hermann Eilts	Economic Section, American Legation, Jidda

We also had a box made up for Tewfik and presented it to him.

We met with Dr. Butrus in Dr. Glidden's office in the American Embassy, and Glidden pretty well allayed his fears about signing the affidavit. So Butrus signed, much to my relief. The fear most Christian Egyptians had for their lives and well being, particularly during wartime, was very real. Tewfik, working for the Egyptian government as he did, really had Butrus scared. I felt sorry for him.

Butrus brought the Arabic translation to the hotel, and we sat up until 2:00 AM going over it word for word. We had Butrus translate into English from the Arabic version — checking it carefully against the English version. We found only two mistakes, and we changed those with pen and ink.

CHAPTER 4

THE SIGNING

FEBRUARY 14, MONDAY:

Up at 5:45 AM after three hours of sleep, I had breakfast in my room and left for the airport at 6:45. After customs, we took off at 9:00, landed for gas at Medina, and arrived in Jidda at 3:15 PM. Tewfik was wearing his Arab clothes and Barney hardly recognized him. Tewfik had wired ahead, and we were met at the airport by Surur, Mosula, Tariki, and Tasson — pretty much the red-carpet treatment.

They had put a car and driver at our disposal, so we drove down to the American Legation to pay our respects to Hermann Eilts. It was a short meeting, and he invited us back in the evening for cocktails, when he would have a chap there by the name of Rassim who might serve as our interpreter at Riyadh.

In the meantime, we had the gifts delivered. Then Tewfik took us to Sulaiman's home for a brief social call.

We met with Muhammad Rassim, who seemed to speak English well enough to be our interpreter. We were going to need someone to represent us in Jidda to receive and transmit messages from the government to the Company and Mr. Getty. We hoped Rassim would be suitable for that as well.

FEBRUARY 15, TUESDAY:

Tewfik came to our rooms at the Kandara House and told us there were certain protocols we should observe. We must wire King ibn-Saud our respects, so, we went down and got Rassim to type one in Arabic. At the same time, we cabled Getty, telling him of our whereabouts.

In the afternoon, Tewfik and Fahkri picked us up, with Rassim, and took us to the Palace to meet Emir Faisal, viceroy of the province of Hejaz where Jidda, Medina, and Mecca are located. Faisal met us in the so-called Green Room, a large marble-floored room with green walls and drapes and green-upholstered furniture.

Rassim interpreted. This was really just a social visit during which we assured him of our desire to develop oil in the Neutral Zone, etc. Tewfik guided the conversation pretty well. Hadfield was introduced as vice president of the Company and I as assistant secretary. I didn't care for the title, but we had to have someone to attest to Hadfield's signature on the concession agreement and imprint the Company seal. So, I was it.

We ended the interview by saying we hoped there would be good will and cooperation between the Company and Saudi Arabia. Rassim interpreted this as good will between the country of Saudi Arabia and the USA. Tewfik corrected him, and Rassim went crimson. I was sure Faisal understood English, but he spoke in Arabic only.

FEBRUARY 16, WEDNESDAY:

Tewfik picked us up in the morning and took us to the Embassy, where we had a nice visit with Ambassador J. Rives Childs. The Ambassador stressed that if we used complete candor in our dealings with the Arabs, we would get along all right. By all means we must meet Sheikh Yusuf Yussain, the Assistant Minister of Foreign Affairs. He was a real power in the Saudi Arabian government and leader of a clique opposing Sheikh Sulaiman, the Minister of Finance. Childs made an appointment for us to see Yussain.

Gary Owen, ARAMCO's representative in Jidda, was at the Embassy, and we discussed the advisability of cooperating rather than playing against each other — bidding for labor or the favor of the Saudi Arabian government. I brought up the possibility that it might be desirable for us to be able to use ARAMCO's port facilities at Ras Misha 'ab, and Owen said he thought they could be made available to us. That would be a big step forward in our operations in the Neutral Zone, because at the time there was no port between Kuwait and Ras Misha 'ab, and we also wanted to avoid Kuwaiti customs and import duties.

Owen declared that if Tewfik's demands became outrageous, he would take the matter up directly with Sulaiman, who was much more practical and lenient.

Tewfik took us to our appointment with Sheikh Yussain, a pleasant black-bearded chap, very strong and intelligent. I could see why he was a power in the government.

FEBRUARY 17, THURSDAY:

Eilts took us to the only bank in Jidda, the IndoChina Bank, where we made arrangements for a company account. Eilts told us that $200 per month would be more than adequate for a part-time employee for a few months until we could find a permanent representative for Jidda.

We asked Rassim how much he would need to work part time for a few months, and he said he wanted $500 per month. I told him we had in mind about $200, and he reddened up and was obviously hurt. He said he would let us know the next morning.

Ambassador Childs gave a cocktail party, where we met Ed Locke of the Chase Bank of New York and were surprised to see Dick Funkhouser, the petroleum attaché from Cairo. Dick was on a tour of Saudi Arabia with two Navy air attachés. He was a pilot in World War II, flying men and materiél over the "Hump" into China, and he had told me he swore that if he ever got through that tour of duty alive, he would stay away from airplanes for the rest of his life. So I asked him why he was flying again, and he said he was just too interested in the geology of the Arabian Peninsula to miss what he could see on this trip.

FEBRUARY 18, FRIDAY:

Rassim informed me that he would not go to Riyadh with us. This was very embarrassing, since we should have our own interpreter. I went to see Gary Owen, who said his interpreter, Saber Mouir, was going to Riyadh with Ed Locke and we could utilize him. This might work out all right.

Tewfik came by to report that we would be leaving for Riyadh in the morning and not to worry, because he would fix us up with an interpreter. This was a relief, since it was Tewfik who had been insisting all along that we needed our own.

Abdullah Tariki, the young Saudi Arabian geologist who accompanied me on the aerial reconnaissance to the Neutral Zone, was now living with his American wife at the Kandara House. He told me he would like very much to go to Riyadh with us and would I ask Tewfik if he could go? I went to the apartment Tewfik maintained in town and talked to him about taking Tariki along. Tewfik was adamant; he didn't want him to go.

Tariki was bitterly disappointed. He said, "Here I am, the only graduate geologist in the country and the only Saudi Arab educated in petroleum, and they won't let me be in on the signing. Why did they send me to school to study these things if they won't let me use the knowledge?"

I had to agree with him, but I gave him a long lecture on the necessity of patience in these matters and told him that he should spend a lot of time observing the ARAMCO operations and familiarizing himself with all they did from exploration and drilling to refining, and that his day would come if he persevered. He did and it did.

FEBRUARY 19, SATURDAY:

I was up at 3:30 AM preparing to leave for Riyadh to see the king!

Tewfik picked us up at 4:30. Captain Coffey was our pilot. We taxied out to take off and stopped. There was much scurrying of feet, and mechanics rushed out in a pickup. We had an airlock in the fuel line. By the time it was fixed, it was grey in the east and we didn't need the kerosene flares that lighted the runway. I was thinking, "I hope this isn't the way this whole damn signing ceremony is going to work out." But it was.

Sulaiman looked a little bleary-eyed and hung over. I could smell wine on his breath. Sheikh Surur, the black minister, was taciturn but friendly. Ahmed Fahkri looked tired and harried. Tewfik, the Egyptian, looked like the Sphinx. They had all had their field day with me and later with Barney. Now it was coming up their turn. They had to justify their approval of the concession agreement to King ibn-Saud and his advisers in Riyadh.

We landed at Riyadh on the single sand strip and were met by several cars, mostly Studebakers. Our driver took us to a guesthouse on the west side of town called the Badia Palace. (*Badia* means a place where green and growing things are present. It was the same name as the belly-dancer club in Cairo!) Sulaiman and company were taken to a wing of the king's palace.

After a lunch of chicken, including a dish of giblets with asparagus and a cabbage and tomato stew, a driver came to take us to have coffee with Sulaiman. Ed Locke of the Chase Bank was there too. Sulaiman had Arab clothes for us to put on and told us we were to make a social call on the king. This was a surprise. Locke came along and brought the ARAMCO interpreter, Saber Mouir.

We filed into the throne room and were introduced to the king. Ibn-Saud, the Lord of the Desert, as he was known, looked tired and old. He didn't seem to want to talk much, so we left after a few minutes.

Sulaiman took us back to his quarters, where he started to quiz us about beginning operations in the Neutral Zone. He assumed that I was going to stay in Riyadh and run the show, but I had other ideas. Yussuf Yussain, the Minister of Foreign Affairs, came to this meeting, as well as a cabinet minister, Fuad Hamza, a blond, blue-eyed Lebanese who looked enough like Barney Hadfield to be his brother!

I had been apprehensive about some of these advisers throwing a monkey wrench into the proceedings but, apparently, all were in agreement about going ahead with the signing.

While we were meeting, a severe dust storm blew up. We had expected the ARAMCO plane from Dhahran, bringing their photographer to take pictures of the signing. The plane didn't come in, and we were worried all afternoon that it might be down someplace between Riyadh and Dhahran, on the east coast of Saudi Arabia. Word finally came by wire that they had started out but had to turn back because of the storm.

We went back to the Badia Palace and tried to keep warm as the temperature dropped below freezing. The whole building reeked of kerosene smoke and fumes.

I discovered that my room had a guest register. I was interested to see that Anthony Eden, later to be Prime Minister of England, had stayed in the room two years earlier.

It really wasn't much of a room, about fourteen by fourteen feet, with metal office-type furniture—practical, though, because nothing was ever maintained in the Arab world. I was glad to have an English-type water closet with a pull chain instead of the Arab floor-type found in the king's palace. (On those you just squat down to do your job. Usually a smooth, glossy-type toilet paper was provided, but sometimes not. In a corner of the king's palace I had seen a pile of dung on the marble floor where someone had relieved himself without using toilet paper.)

FEBRUARY 20, SUNDAY:

The dust storm subsided during the night. It wasn't the usual *shimal* blowing out of the north that might last for days. I was awakened by a loud, squeaky noise, and I couldn't think what might be making the sound. Looking out the window, I saw a small donkey hitched to a wooden water wheel that lifted water from a shallow well into a flume and ditch arrangement that watered the date palm trees. I could hear others in the Badia Palace gardens. They started near daylight every day, and the sound was both distinctive and weird.

Ahmed Fahkri came at 10:00 AM and told us His Majesty was ready for us to sign. We put on our Arab clothes and rushed down to Sulaiman's house, the damned driver nearly turning the car over on a curve. We looked over the concession agreement and found that Tewfik had not made the typographical changes on the Arabic copies that we had discussed Saturday. Then Barney discovered he had left the corporation seal in his suitcase at the Badia Palace.

So while Barney and Tewfik made the changes, I had the crazy driver take me back for the seal. "If we ever get this damned thing signed," I thought, "it will be a miracle."

Sulaiman, Barney, and I signed all four copies, two in English and two in Arabic, and then went to the palace to see the king. Sulaiman led the way, and we found ibn-Saud seated at a small table. Sulaiman arranged the chairs so he sat on one side of Barney, and I sat next to the king.

We had bought two gold pens in Cairo for the signing and gave them to Sulaiman to use. Ibn-Saud signed the decree. A man brought in a purple indelible ink pad on which the king rubbed his ring, then pressed it on the agreement — his royal seal. Barney wanted one of the pens back, as a keepsake, I guess, but Sulaiman wouldn't give it to him. It was amusing to see Sulaiman's pettiness.

We left with Sulaiman for a lunch at his home. We were served curried lamb and some sheep's eyes as a delicacy. They turned my stomach, but Barney seemed to get along all right on the eyes and sour milk.

Tewfik let us have a car and driver to see the sights around Riyadh. We drove around the palace grounds, taking pictures, then down to the market or *suq*. We had made the mistake of leaving our Arab clothes at Sulaiman's, and as we walked around the *suq*, a crowd gathered around us. They weren't used to seeing people in European dress, and they began hissing and jeering. We decided we had better leave.

But before we left I saw something that really got to me. One small vendor had a series of metal trays or large pans on a table. Myriads of black flies buzzed around, and he was moving a small tree branch back and forth to scare them off. I looked closely, and whatever was in the pans was so black with flies I couldn't identify it. Then he waved his stick over the pans and, as the flies took off, I could see that it was fresh meat. Every time afterward that we had meat at the Badia Palace, I wondered if it had come from a place like this. It had, of course.

The filth and unsanitary conditions within a few hundred yards of the king's palace were unbelievable. I couldn't help but reflect that the daily income from their oil royalties was already more than a million dollars and wonder why such disease-ridden conditions would be allowed or tolerated in the very shadow of the palace. Still, it was a country just beginning to enter the twentieth century. Maybe soon some public health projects would change all of this.

Back at Sulaiman's home, he presented Barney with a little gold sword and me with a gold-mounted Movada wristwatch with the Saud royal seal on the dial. We were both pleased. Barney preferred the sword, and I preferred the watch, so it worked out very well.

Sulaiman had received word that the ARAMCO plane still could not get to Riyadh because of the high winds and low visibility, so we returned to the Badia Palace for the night.

FEBRUARY 21, MONDAY:

Fahkri arrived at 10:30 AM, saying the king wanted to see us again. We put on our Arab clothes and drove to Sulaiman's house and then to the palace and the king. The ARAMCO photographers from Dhahran had arrived and set up their equipment. They took several shots of the group. Emir Faisal was there, and he spoke to us. Cabinet members, advisers, and general palace guard people were there as well, all hoping to get in on the celebration.

The ARAMCO people had their own interpreter. He came over and spoke to me in Arabic. When I answered in English, he acted surprised and said, "I thought you were an Arab."

"I guess I've been here too long. I must look like I belong here."

Saud was in a good mood and, after telling us we looked more like Arabs than the Arabs, he ordered Arab outfits for us to take home to our wives.

Sulaiman took us back to his home for more picture-taking, with our Arab clothes on and then our European suits. He seemed very relieved that everything had gone so well. I believe many of the king's advisers had been against giving the concession to a small company, and he had been getting a lot of flak from them because of his desire to deal with us.

A happy Ed Locke joined us at Sulaiman's; he had been granted a concession to build a cement plant at Dhahran.

As part of the protocol, Tewfik advised us that we must now pay a courtesy call on the Emir of Kuwait, and ibn-Saud would make the plane available to take us to see him. The king was sending a letter with us introducing us to the Emir and asking for his help in furthering the operation in the Neutral Zone.

Tewfik and Fahkri took us to the airport, and we waited two hours before they could get the plane ready to fly. It was nearly dark when we arrived in Kuwait, where we were met by the Saudi Arabian agent, Nefessy. He called Dr. William Morris of American Independent, who came and took us to the company quarters.

Dr. Morris found rooms for us and, after dinner, we had a long talk about our coming joint operations. Of course, we were now obliged to become partners in any operations in the Neutral Zone. American Independent Oil Company owned the oil rights to the undivided Kuwaiti half of the Zone, and we now had a concession on the undivided Saudi Arabian half.

Morris had been in the Gulf seismograph party that first shot out the Burgan anticline. He had done gravity work on the area as well and said the field was a strong gravity maximum, indicating that it isn't associated with salt intrusives, as are some of the Saudi Arabian fields to the south.

FEBRUARY 22, TUESDAY:

The Emir of Kuwait's secretary, Izzat Jaffar, came for us at 8:30 AM. Morris, Barney, and I were shown into a long rectangular room mostly devoid of furniture, but with a large davenport against one wall. Emir al-Sabah was sitting when we entered the room but rose to greet us. He was about fifty, a little on the stout side, but had a pleasant square face. His hair was greying, and he had a small grey beard. Our interpreter, on loan from ibn-Saud, had to sit between Barney and me. I don't believe al-Sabah understood any English.

The Emir, who ibn-Saud regarded as his little brother, was a very wealthy man and the ruler of Kuwait, despite not being called king. The Burgan field was the most productive oil field in the world at this time and was operated by Kuwait Oil Company, a consortium of Gulf Oil, British Petroleum, and Anglo Iranian Oil. The Sheikh's royalties must have run to millions of dollars a day.

Barney did most of the talking, and the tenor of the meeting had apparently been set by the letter we brought from ibn-Saud. We pledged our mutual support and cooperation with American Independent, which had the concession on the Sheikh's part of the Neutral Zone.

The Emir called in a secretary, and he and his advisers drafted a reply to ibn-Saud to be delivered by personal courier.

After our audience with the Emir, Dr. Morris took us around the Burgan field. I was particularly interested in seeing the small

outcropping called Jebel Burgan, and we drove over to it. This was
the principal topographic expression of the large Burgan anticline or
dome, and it had heavy oil staining in its sandstone outcroppings.
These oil and tar stains on the surface were typical of the large oil
fields to the north, such as Kirkuk and Mosul in Iraq. None of the
fields I knew of to the south in Saudi Arabia had these surface
hydrocarbon showings.

I was very anxious now to have a look at the outcrop in the
Neutral Zone to see if it showed oil stains.

We took off after lunch, landing at the Ras Misha 'ab airport
just across the line in Saudi Arabia. Kuwait and Ras Misha 'ab had
oiled runways, and Captain Coffey at the controls of the C-47 said
he was glad to be out of the sand and dirt for a while.

We came unannounced into Ras Misha 'ab, the staging area for
the construction of the TransArabian pipeline known as Tapline.
ARAMCO had built an ingenious unloading device they called Sky-
hook to lift the large oil pipeline joints from the ships onto the storage dock at the port. Tapline was then under construction and
would soon pick up oil from the Saudi Arabian fields and pipe it
across the country to Syria and Lebanon on the Mediterranean. It
was a tremendous undertaking, and the trucks and tractors for
building the line dwarfed all other equipment I had seen.

A Bechtel construction man met the plane and took us to the
ARAMCO office. Bill Chandler, whom I had known years earlier
during my first sojourn in Saudi Arabia, showed us around the port
facilities. His boss, Mr. Hall, the chief engineer, arrived from the
field in a Navion — an early four-place low-wing aircraft built by
North American — and was very cordial. He said they would make
their facilities available to us when we got into operation. Barney
and I were beginning to feel like VIP's!

We flew into Dhahran that evening. I remembered the Dammam field there with the few early wells as having gas flares burning
at many of them, but I was not prepared for the sight as we approached from the north. The whole sky was lit up with burning
gas from the Qatif field on the north to Dammam and Abqaiq on
the south. There must have been hundreds of millions of cubic feet
of gas being wasted here every day. Coming from Wyoming, where

we nurtured every little gas well and ran a pipeline to it so the gas could be used to heat homes, this sight appalled me. Here it could have been injected into some dry anticline and saved. Even after hearing all the reasons for flaring — no market, no need to reinject because the fields have a good water drive, etc.—it still, after twenty-seven years of operations here, haunted me to see this waste of natural resources.

We were met at the Dhahran airport by the commandant of the Saudi Arabian Air Force and taken to the international rest house. I was surprised to see the Tarikis there. Abdullah told me he had asked Emir Faisal to let him see the ARAMCO operations first-hand, as I had suggested, and had been sent over here for a while. I hoped he would get along all right. He wasn't very humble in light of his limited technical knowledge at this point, but maybe he wouldn't ruffle too many feathers among the operating personnel here.

FEBRUARY 23, WEDNESDAY:

After an early breakfast at Bechtel's boarding house, we found a phone to call MacPherson, the manager of operations for ARAMCO. He picked us up and took us on a tour of the camp — the hospital facilities, etc. A likeable Englishman, he had as his assistant Floyd Oliger, who had been manager of the original operating company when I was here in 1938. We had a nice talk, and I outlined my plan for operating in the Neutral Zone.

Tom Barger, whom I had worked with as a junior geologist doing surface work at Abu Hadriya and Ma'gala, came and took us to dinner. It was old home week for me, catching up on the whereabouts of the fellows I knew here years ago. I had wanted to see Max Steineke, who was my boss then, but he and the chief paleontologist, Dick Bramkamp, were gone. They were in the Ar-Rub' 'al-Khali desert doing field work. Dick Kerr was also in the field. Despite the absence of some friends, I believed this public relations trip to ARAMCO headquarters was well worth the effort.

FEBRUARY 24, THURSDAY:

We were up at 3:30 AM to catch the TWA DC-4 flight to Cairo via Basra. We had to get visas for Iraq even to be in transit to

Cairo. Flying over the northern part of the Saudi Arabian desert, I saw many structural features which could be mapped by aerial photography. Aerial photo work was all the rage in the U.S. now, and I thought it would soon extend worldwide.

I had to leave bags in bond again at the Cairo airport. We got in late at Shepheards, where they had only a very dirty suite for us.

We cabled Getty, saying the concession agreement was signed and we were coming home!

CHAPTER 5
THE OPERATIONS

February 25, Friday:

I woke up in the night with terrible cramps and was sick to my stomach. During the day I took a stool sample to Dr. Weir at the Rockefeller Foundation, who said I was reacting to the arsenic in the carbarsone tablets I was taking.

In the morning I had received a cable:

Paul Walton
Shepheards Hotel
Cairo

Would appreciate it if you would remain in Saudi Arabia for a few weeks to do geological work and locate first well.

JEAN PAUL GETTY

Since I was beginning to really worry about the state of my health, I decided to try to call Mr. Getty on the new radio telephone the hotel advertised. It took several hours to get the call through, but it finally came, and I told him how I felt. He said I should be able to get some help at one of the Cairo hospitals. Dr. Weir had already warned me to stay out of the hospitals, saying, "If you aren't sick when you go in, you will be before you get out."

I told Mr. Getty I would have to think about staying, because I knew it entailed going back to Kuwait and doing field work in the desert under the usual adverse conditions. Then I got a call from Dave Staples, President of Pacific Western Oil Corporation, asking me to stay. They sure work a willing horse to death.

So I consented to stay and cabled Betty, telling her I would be delayed for several weeks. She had gone to her parents' home in

Iowa with the two children in anticipation of meeting me on my return to New York City.

The phone was really busy. Barney got a call from his law partner in New York City, Dave Hecht, giving him hell for signing the concession agreement without Mr. Getty's approval. Barney was so mad he said he was going to resign from the firm. We were both very peeved at this turn of events, having just gone through the ordeal of Jidda and Riyadh.

FEBRUARY 26, SATURDAY:

Barney was up all night with dysentery. I had a terrible headache. We sorted out our belongings in the bags in hand, and Barney checked them all through to New York City on his TWA ticket.

If we were to drill a well on a possible extension of the Burgan anticline axis where it projects south into the Neutral Zone, we had to be sure we made the location in the Neutral Zone and not in Kuwait. This might require a cadastral survey to delineate the border, which was ill-defined. The problem of where to drill the first well was in my bailiwick. I was the only one in the Company who had any firsthand knowledge of the area or had seen it from either the ground or the air.

I had lunch with Dr. Butrus, and he brought me a copy of the translation I had requested of the geographical description of the Neutral Zone which the American Embassy had in their treaty files. Dick Funkhouser got me a translation made by their people, and the two were not quite the same.

I had two definite ideas as to where to drill. The first was to try for a possible extension of the Burgan axis where it must jut southward into the Neutral Zone. The other was to drill near the outcrop which I had seen on my original aerial reconnaissance of the Zone in December. I was much intrigued with the indication of a structural high under this outcropping, for it resembled remarkably the surface exposures on the top of the Burgan structure. However, the odds in wildcatting for new fields are about one chance in five on an extension to an old field, in contrast to one chance in ten on a new structure at a distance from current production.

In my phone conversation with Mr. Getty, I had indicated that I favored the Burgan extension for the first well but would like eventually to drill on the surface feature farther south and west, shown on the Army Map Service map as Jebel Fuwaris. For this reason I thought it imperative that I go into the field for a further look.

I wanted to get these two ideas across to Mr. Getty clearly and convincingly, so I wrote a letter to Dave Staples, President of the Company, describing the conditions and possibilities in the Neutral Zone. I hoped Staples would have the opportunity to discuss this with Mr. Getty at their next committee meeting.

When I talked to Dr. Morris in Kuwait, I got the impression American Independent wasn't in any great hurry to drill. Now that I had agreed to stay until the first well location was made, I sent the following telegram to try to get them off center:

American Independent Oil Company
c/o Dr. William Morris
Kuwait

Company desires make location for well immediately stop I have urged drilling a possible extension Burgan with location made near border stop Will your company agree location made by mere projection axis or will it require geophysical work please advise stop If the latter can we use your present gravity meter for making survey on extension and what date can work begin stop Have you necessary surveying equipment geodetic data to make reasonably accurate boundary survey and well location for Burgan extension stop Have you room so I can come Kuwait and assist.

                                            PAUL WALTON

FEBRUARY 27, SUNDAY:

While waiting for word from Morris, I went to see Dr. Abu Zeid, Director of Mines for Egypt. We planned to get together soon and talk further about a possible drilling deal for Mr. Getty in Egypt.

A cable arrived from Kuwait in the evening:

Dr. Paul Walton
Cairo

Your cable of twenty-sixth stop Have requested instructions from San Francisco regarding well location and starting date stop Necessary surveying equipment here stop Different type gravity meter needed for terrestrial survey stop Will advise answer to other questions later stop Best regards.

WILLIAM LIND MORRIS

At least now I had them thinking about going ahead with the exploration work.

FEBRUARY 28, MONDAY:

I put Barney on the early TWA plane for New York City. I hated to see him go. We had worked pretty well as a team for the past two months. I chuckled to recall that Barney thought at first we could write the contract and get it signed in a week or ten days! And our troubles were at an end just like those of newlyweds — the front end! We still had all the iron to move, the wells to drill!

I thought I had better advise Getty of the answer I got from Morris of American Independent so he could appreciate the reason for my delay in going there:

J. Paul Getty
1060 Subway Terminal Building
Los Angeles, California
Have been in contact Independent man Kuwait stop Has referred questions of well location boundary survey geophysical geological surveys and my obtaining accommodations company house Kuwait all to San Francisco stop To further clarify our telephone conversation please take cognizance that there are no accommodations Kuwait or Ras Mishā 'ab and our moving into Neutral Zone to drill well involves same logistics of invading desert island stop No oil well supply stores in Middle East which necessitates our setting up warehouses, repair shops, etc., etc., for all equipment including transportation stop Will advise when further word comes from Independent stop Still in bad health plan being Cairo several more days.   PAUL WALTON

After sending the cable, I thought of what my friend Ray Chorney always used to say: "Go to the head man!" So I sent the following:

J. Paul Getty
1060 Subway Terminal Building
Los Angeles, California
Believe Independent representative Kuwait carries little weight suggest you contact Davies for better company cooperation.

PAUL WALTON

I didn't know what weight Morris carried, but if Getty contacted Ralph Davies, President of American Independent, surely things ought to happen faster.

MARCH 2, WEDNESDAY:

When I went to Kuwait, I'd have to pass through or stop in Iraq, so I needed a visa. I went out to the Iraq Legation for it, and they told me I needed photos and a letter saying I was not a Jew. Mr. Low of TWA got the letter for me. Apparently, to sell tickets from Cairo to Basra they had to do this all the time.

Tewfik came to Shepheard's to have dinner with me. His work done, he was resting. I hoped his fee from Saudi Arabia was substantial. When I mentioned that Mr. Getty had told me on the phone that his son George would be coming to Kuwait to take over as manager, Tewfik really pricked up his ears. By all means, he wanted to see George before he went to Kuwait, so I sent the following cable:

J. Paul Getty
1060 Subway Terminal Building
Los Angeles, California

Saudi legal advisor wants meet George before he goes Kuwait stop Accommodations for Kuwait not yet available so suggest George meet me here for introduction please advise.

WALTON

I didn't know what Tewfik had in mind, but I kept remembering Dick Kerr's advice: "Your biggest job is keeping the Saudi Arabian government happy" — so we had better have George come here first.

The answer arrived in the morning.

Dr. Paul Walton
Cairo

Davies and Getty conferring now on questions raised your cable stop Regard your coming Kuwait you are welcome stop Space is limited but will arrange accommodations stop Regards

WILLIAM LIND MORRIS

MARCH 3, THURSDAY:

The red tape and stamping of papers which goes on to get any-thing done here is so time-consuming. I was out at the Iraqi Lega-tion finally getting my visa. To paraphrase Kipling, "East of Suez where the best seems like the worst" is so true! I was waiting for George Getty to show up .

MARCH 4, FRIDAY:

During this interlude I continued to have the dysentery and cramps that Dr. Weir said were caused by the arsenic in the car-barsone. Friday and Saturday were spent with dysentery and cramps and waiting for George.

MARCH 6, SUNDAY:

I was awakened by a bomb blast. The bomb went off in the police station on the west side of Shepheards, knocking out windows in the hotel. People said it was the Ikhwan, the Brotherhood — an anti-Farouk group.

I had tea on the hotel terrace while a demonstration by street people was in progress outside — a horrible thing to see and hear. The dull rumble of the voices and the noise of breaking glass in windows and parked cars was frightening. The mob tried to come up on the terrace, but police held them off. Two years later this world-famous hotel would be sacked and burned to the ground by such a mob.

My dysentery was not improved by the excitement, and I was still waiting for George.

MARCH 7, MONDAY:

When I stopped off to see Tewfik at his office, he took me to lunch at the Semiramis Hotel and then to the trade fair exposition on Gezira Island. It was quite well done and a pleasant diversion from the two main themes of my life: the inevitable dysentery and cramps — which I was treating with enterovioform, paregoric, and bismuth — and, of course, waiting for George.

I received a cable from Ray Chorney, my assistant in Casper, telling me that I should write to my immediate boss in California,

Emil Kluth, the Swiss geologist who was Vice President of the Company. I hadn't written to him for about three months, so I sent him a brief letter.

During the next week Dr. Weir told me I had food poisoning! Dr. Abbas, an Egyptian, said I still had the amoebic dysentery, too, and gave me a prescription for glucose, powdered charcoal, and stovarsal with arsenic compound.

On Thursday the tenth, Dick Funkhouser, oil attaché at the American Legation, took me to lunch at the Semiramis. He was anxious to know when we would start our operations in the Neutral Zone.

Later I went out to the Egyptian tennis tournament at the Gezira Club, where I saw Frank Parker beat Puncec of Yugoslavia and Drobny and Cernak of Czechoslovakia beat Budge Patty and Henri Cochet of France. Parker, an American, Drobny, and Patty would each ultimately win the singles title at Wimbledon within a few years. On Saturday I saw the famous German tennis player Baron von Cramm, and on Sunday Frank Parker beat Budge Patty in three straight sets for the Egyptian title.

MARCH 16, WEDNESDAY:

Dr. Abbas had taken me off stovarsal, saying the arsenic was causing my pain. He gave me a prescription for B-1 shots, and I took the first one today. I was getting pretty weak, with a sore throat and a bronchial infection, and hoped the shots would do me some good.

After so much waiting for George, I sent the following cable:

J. Paul Getty
1060 Subway Terminal Building
Los Angeles, California

Please advise when George Getty will arrive Cairo stop If he is delayed would like to proceed Kuwait and get work finished so I can return home.

PAUL WALTON

MARCH 17, THURSDAY:

The dysentery and cramps hadn't let up. I bought a 20,000-unit vial of penicillin from a drugstore and started taking shots twice a day.

Dr. Abu Zeid, Minister of Mines and Quarries, invited me to dinner at his home in Ma'adi. His wife is American, from Missoula, Montana, and he worked for a time for the Marland Oil Company in the States. A very nice man, he had only one arm, and I didn't have the gall to ask him how he lost the other.

I received an answer to yesterday's cable:

Proceed to Kuwait George meeting you there next week.

J. PAUL GETTY

On Friday and Saturday I was sick all day. I hated the thought of going to Kuwait but wired Morris that I was coming.

MARCH 20, SUNDAY:

I was up at 5:00 AM, but the plane was delayed until ten o'clock. I arrived in Basra at 5:00 PM and stayed at the airport hotel.

MARCH 21, MONDAY:

I left Basra at 10:00 AM on an Iraqi Airlines two-motor Viking. We landed in Kuwait twenty-five minutes later, where Dr. Morris and Allen Weymouth met me. Weymouth was chief geologist for American Independent and had been in Saudi Arabia and Bahrain about fifteen years earlier. They took me to their quarters, which were very crowded, with three men to the room.

MARCH 22, TUESDAY:

Morris and Weymouth took me out to the gravity meter camp at Jebel Gurain, a party of the Gravity Meter Exploration Company, where I saw some small surface evidence of extension to the south of the Burgan anticline. Weymouth thought it continued a long way into the Zone, but I didn't believe it went very far. We discussed a well location, and I agreed that the first one probably should be on the possible south extension of Burgan.

MARCH 23, WEDNESDAY:

I sent my boss a cable:

J. Paul Getty
1060 Subway Terminal Building
Los Angeles, California
American Independent gravity and engineering work started on Burgan extension which will within a month provide data for

making exact well location stop After making geological reconnaissance we are in mutual agreement here as to general area
for location but problem of exact delineation of boundary probably requires international agreement so do not believe we
should plan now on drilling direct offset to boundary stop
Mutually believe here that gravity data after two months will
reveal desirability of making well location in area adjacent to
boundary but not subject to dispute stop Recommend we await
gravity data stop Would like return home during interim please
advise stop American Independent people are in doubt as to
whether we are partners in geophysical and drilling operations so would appreciate your clarifying this issue with them
immediately.

PAUL WALTON

March 24, Thursday:

Lloyd Miller, AMINCO's chief engineer, Weymouth, and I
went out to Wadi es Shugg, the western boundary of the Neutral
Zone. The east side showed up fairly plainly, but a bad sandstorm
came up before we got back. We saw some gravity meter stations —
probably ARAMCO coming up from the south with their surveys.

Looking at the modern Kuwait City of skyscrapers and super-
markets, it is hard to believe that in 1949 it was a small town completely encircled by a wall with a gate on the south side. Soldiers
manned this gate twenty-four hours a day, and no vehicle could
enter or leave without being subject to a checking of papers, etc.

This day the sand was blowing so hard that we could scarcely
find the gate, but finally we did and were admitted by the soldier
on duty. Inside the gate the sand didn't blow so hard, so we easily
found our way to the American Independent compound, where I
spent Friday and Saturday waiting around the office all day for
Getty's answer to my Wednesday cable.

On Saturday my roommate was sick all night. On Sunday I
took my passport down for an Iraqi visa and then drove out south
of Jebel Gurain with Weymouth and Miller. On Monday we drove
out to a circular crater-like outcrop I had seen on the air reconnaissance of the Zone I had made in December. It looked rather
impressive to me as the top of an anticline sticking up out of the
sand. Morris said the local name for the hill was Jebel Fuwaris.

Weymouth and Morris didn't think much of it as evidence of folding. They were geophysicists, and as a geologist who had done much surface work, I was naturally more impressed with this evidence. I was wondering now if this shouldn't be the spot for the first test well.

MARCH 29, TUESDAY:

Marking time around the compound all day, I sent a cable to Dave Staples, President of Pacific Western:

> D. T. Staples
> 1060 Subway Terminal Building
> Los Angeles, California

> Wired Getty six days ago but no reply stop Recommend we await gravity data for making well location since Burgan is well defined gravity high stop Another month required for completion gravity work stop Geodetic work for location boundary requires another month stop Impossible have drilling rig camp etcetera set up here before three months so do not see necessity making exact location now stop American Independent people still in doubt as to our being partners in operations so would appreciate your clarifying this with them stop Strongly recommend we agree participate with American Independent fifty-fifty basis immediately stop My waiting here another month for completion gravity and geodetic work seems great waste of time stop Still having dysentery and feel am getting raw deal having stay here four months instead of two weeks as promised please advise stop Where in hell is George.   PAUL WALTON

I heard later that when Staples received this wire he told the operating committee of Pacific Western that I wasn't a good corporate man. I had lost my health and gone the last mile for the Company. I wonder what else I could have done?

MARCH 30, WEDNESDAY:

Receiving a cable from Staples saying come home, I eagerly got on the Iraq Airlines DH-Dove for Basra. At the airport Shatt al Arab Hotel, I was put in a room with another American, an oil man representing Byron Jackson Company out of Long Beach, California. We knew a lot of people in common. Oil men certainly have worldwide connections and acquaintances.

MARCH 31, THURSDAY:

I took the early TWA DC-4 to Cairo, intending to go on through to Rome and New York. When we landed in Cairo, I ran into Clark Sypher of the American Legation, who said George Getty was in town and trying to find me! I thought it best to see him before I went home, so I persuaded TWA to get me an overnight visa to stay in Cairo.

I had a lot of trouble getting a room at Shepheards, where I thought George would be staying, but he wasn't there. I saw Jack Keegan of TWA, and he located George at the Semiramis.

I called George, and we had dinner together at the Semiramis. He was a pleasant young man in his late twenties who seemed very anxious to do something constructive in his father's business. He told me he wanted to make Pacific Western a real oil company — a major if possible. "The problem," he said, "is that if a project needs a dollar, Father will put up a dime."

George told me he thought Dave Staples was way overpaid (he was getting $25,000 a year as President of the Company) and that Emil Kluth, my boss, should be retired in two years. I guess he thought this made me feel good, but it didn't.

APRIL 1, FRIDAY:

George met me at 8 AM, and we went to the airport. I had to leave since I had only a one-day visa. At the airport we met Mr. Hull, President of the TransArabia Pipeline Company — Tapline. A gruff Texan, he treated us like dirt. George said, "Hull reminds me of a lot of Texans who have five or six million dollars and think they have money!" In comparison with his father's fortune that really wasn't much!

The TWA DC-4 flew all day and all night, landing at Rome, Madrid, and the Azores.

APRIL 2, SATURDAY:

We landed at La Guardia in New York City. Betty met me at the airport. She couldn't understand why Getty wasn't there to meet me — or at least his representative.

APRIL 3, SUNDAY:

Resting up from the flight at Getty's hotel, the Pierre, I continued to have bad dysentery and a sore throat.

APRIL 4, MONDAY:

Doctors' Information Service referred me to a Dr. Marcovicci, an Austrian physician who did a lot of medical work for guests of the Pierre. He came over to the hotel to see me and immediately sent me to the Regent Hospital at 115 East Sixty-first Street, where they kept me until Thursday evening.

I had dysentery, but the hospital couldn't find any amoeba. Dr. Marcovicci came to the hospital with a whole valise full of vials of medicine. He gave me at least fifteen injections of his own concocted medicine, which included vitamins B and C, penicillin, sodium salicylate, and chlorophyll. I had never seen such an array of shots. The next day he gave me more shots and I was feeling much better.

APRIL 8, FRIDAY:

Resting at the hotel, I got more shots from Marcovicci. Betty and I had decided to buy a car and drive home. Barney Hadfield called, inviting us to his home in Stamford, Connecticut, for the weekend.

APRIL 9, SATURDAY:

Barney met us at the train. He looked a lot better than he had when he left Cairo. He acted shocked at my appearance and said he could see I had been very sick.

APRIL 10, SUNDAY:

Barney and his wife took us for a drive around Stamford and to dinner in New Canaan. Barney had to leave for Texas, so we drove into New York City and put him on a plane at La Guardia. Then his wife dropped us off at the Pierre.

APRIL 11, MONDAY:

We picked up a car, a two-door 1949 Buick, in Yonkers and brought it down to the Pierre in rush-hour traffic. I hadn't driven a car in six months, so it was a chore. I stopped and wired our insurance agent in Casper before I dared drive very far. Heading home to Casper, we picked up the children in Malvern, Iowa, and were home on April 18.

The Casper *Tribune* wanted a story, and they printed a picture of me next to King Saud at the signing of the concession agreement.

APRIL 19, TUESDAY:

From the office in Casper I sent a letter telling Mr. Getty that I was back.

APRIL 22, FRIDAY:

Mr. Getty called me about the possibility of a boundary dispute between Kuwait and Saudi Arabia. I told him I would write him a letter setting out all the data I had. He said, "You did pretty well!"

APRIL 23, SATURDAY:

I finished and mailed what would be my last report on the Neutral Zone, including the original 1922 agreement creating the Zone and the geographical description used in siting the first wells.

April 23, 1949
Casper, Wyoming

MEMORANDUM

TO: J. PAUL GETTY
FROM: P. T. WALTON   RE: Boundary Problems
                             Kuwait Neutral Zone

During my stay in Kuwait I discussed with the American Independent people the problem of accurately determining the boundary of our joint concession. Since our concessional contract with the Saudi Arabian government refers the problem of the boundary to the agreement concluded between King Ibn Saud and Sheikh Jabir As-Sabah of Kuwait, dated December 2, 1922, our problem was to come to the correct interpretation of what the latter agreement intended to outline as the actual boundaries of the Neutral Zone. From a bound volume printed in Arabic containing all of the treaties entered into by the Saudi Arabian government, which was furnished by Ahmad Bey Tew-

fik, the Saudi Arabian legal advisor, Professor Butrus Abd al
Malek, professor of Semitic languages of the American University in Cairo, made an English translation of the above said
agreement dated December 2, 1922. A copy of Dr. Butrus's
translation is attached hereto. In addition, Mr. R. B. Funkhauser, Petroleum Attaché at our Cairo Embassy, furnished me
a copy of another translation which he had had made by an
Embassy interpreter of the same agreement dated December 2,
1922, and a copy of this translation is also attached hereto.

As described in these translations attached hereto, the southern boundary of the Neutral Zone should give us little or no trouble to accurately delineate on the ground, since it consists of a
straight east–west line running through Ain El Abd, a large, hot
sulphur water spring whose source can be accurately found on
the ground. Although both interpretations refer to the western
boundary as a low, mountainous ridge called Shaq, actually
Shaq is not a ridge at all, but is a broad, sand filled stream valley
and is called Wadi Es Shaq or Es Shugg. In some places Shaq
is a rather prominent topographic low about two to five miles in
width, but in others I was unable to discern its location with any
certainty. No doubt we will have to come to a mutual agreement with the Arabian American Oil Company in order to
accurately locate our western boundary in the exact middle of
this stream valley. At the present time, however, this is of little
importance.

The main area of potential disagreement, and by far the most
important boundary of the Neutral Zone at the present time, is
the northern boundary which separates the Zone from Kuwait
and which no doubt cuts through a portion of the largest oil
field in the world — the Burgan field. It will be noted that on
both translations of the Kuwait–Saudi Arabian Agreement of
December 2, 1922, attached hereto, that the northern boundary
is called a red semi-circle, referred to in the fifth article of the
Anglo-Turkish Agreement of July, 1913 or 1918. I rather believe that the correct date is 1913, since this agreement was
made prior to World War I, and was never ratified because of
the war. In a footnote occurring in the bound volume of Saudi
Arabian treaties, it states that the center of this semi-circle is the
heart of the town of Kuwait, and the radius is 40 miles. This
was represented to us by Ahmad Bey Tewfik, the Saudian Arabian legal advisor, as being a correct copy of the original treaty
which of course was made in Arabic, and Mr. Hadfield and I
accepted his explanation that the circle had a radius of 40 miles.
However, upon discussing this matter with the American Inde-

pendent people, I found that they had an entirely different interpretation. Their research department had procured a copy of the Anglo-Turkish Agreement of July 29, 1913, and had made an English paraphrase translation from the original Arabic, and nowhere in the fifth article of this said agreement was there any mention that the radius of this circle was 40 miles. Instead, their paraphrase stated that this circle had its center in the town of Kuwait, passed on the south through a point called Krain, and on the north through the mouth of Khor Zubair, a swamp or marsh emptying into the Persian Gulf. The word "Krain" is probably "Grain" which is shown on the Asia 1:1,000,000 map as a prominent hill or jebel. I have been on this point on the ground, and it is a prominent topographic feature lying about 41 miles south of the center of the town of Kuwait. Unfortunately, five and one-half miles to the south of Grain is a series of old water wells called Ain Grain. These are abandoned at the present time, but may have been in existence in 1913 at the time of the Anglo-Turkish Agreement. If this were the "Krain" spoken of in the fifth article in this agreement, then the radius of the circle would be in the order of 46 miles, and at least 5 miles of the Burgan field, where it appears to extend southward into the Neutral Zone, would belong to the Kuwait Oil Company. Khor Zubair, according to our maps, is just about 40 miles to the north of the heart of the town of Kuwait, and therefore, could not lie on the same circle as either Jebel Grain or Ain Grain. We therefore have three possibilities as to the correct location of the semi-circle. One, that it goes through Khor Zubair; two, that it goes through Jebel Krain; three, that it goes through Ain Krain.

Mr. Weymouth, Chief Geologist of American Independent Oil Company, is an old friend of Mr. Jordan, manager of the Kuwait Oil Company, and they had an informal discussion of the problem completely off the record. Mr. Weymouth told me in detail of the discussion, and stated that Jordan's personal opinion was that the boundary should go through Jebel Grain, but that the official Kuwait Oil Company's stand would be that it go through Ain Grain. Naturally, the Kuwait Oil Company is going to attempt to push the boundary as far south as possible in order to include as much of the Burgan field in its concession as they can. Since it is to our interest to keep the boundary as far north as possible, I strongly recommend that we solicit all the aid possible from King Ibn Saud to come to a mutual agreement with the Sheikh of Kuwait as to the correct location of this northern boundary. The Saudi Arabian government people have stated that they feel that Ibn Saud has a good deal more strength and prestige than the Sheikh of Kuwait, and I believe this is an excellent opportunity to get them to attempt to assert all of this authority and prestige they have been bragging about. It would take a little delicate handling in order to get them into that frame of mind, but I feel that it can be done. Of course the English government is vitally interested since it is a major stock holder of the Anglo-Iranian Oil Company, a fifty percent partner in the Kuwait Oil Company, and that they will exert all possible pressure to push the boundary as far south as possible, even possibly to the extent of using very strong pressure on the Sheikh of Kuwait himself.

A semi-circle through Jebel Grain is three and one-half miles southeast of the present farthest south drilling well in the Burgan field. We were unable to get any information whatsoever as to the structural elevations of the wells on the south end of Burgan, but Mr. Jordan did tell Mr. Weymouth that the new deep test, which they are contemplating drilling, would be in the extreme south end of the Burgan field which naturally would lead one to believe that the structurally high spot of the field is in the south end. Further, the regional dip is to the northeast, and going to the south, one should get higher structural elevations for some distance south of the present southern extremity of the Burgan field. The domal structure near the west center of the Neutral Zone was examined in detail in the field by myself, and it appears to be on a direct prolongation of the Burgan axis. I strongly suspect that it is a separate closure on the Burgan line of folding and may even be structurally higher than the Burgan field itself.

My own personal belief is that we will eventually have to agree that the boundary goes through Jebel Grain, and that we should drill our first well along the Burgan axis, a quarter mile or more south of the semi-circle passing through Jebel Grain. I do not feel that the Kuwait Oil Company will be successful in their attempt to push the boundary as far south as Ain Grain. This same thought was held by the American Independent people at Kuwait, and when I left we had mutually agreed that the first well should be just south of the semi-circle passing through Jebel Grain on an extension of the Burgan axis. In another few weeks the gravity work should be nearing completion on that portion of the concession, and since the Burgan field is a very strong positive anomaly, its extension to the south should show up very plainly so that the gravity work would be of considerable help in correctly locating our first well. I trust we will join in 50–50 on the gravity work for I believe that the American Independent crew is doing a good, accurate job.

Signed: P. T. WALTON

PTW:vr

cc: D. T. Staples
Emil Kluth

THE FRONTIERS AGREEMENT BETWEEN NAJD AND AL-KUWAIT

The frontiers between Najd and Al-Kuwait begin in the West from the junction of the Wadi Al-'Awjah (The valley of Al-'Awjah) with the Batin (Al-Batin), (Leaving) Al-Raq'l to Najd from this point extending in a straight line until it joins latitude 29° and the (Red)[1] semi-circle referred to in the fifth Article of the Anglo-Turkish Agreement of July 29th, 1918. This line continues along the side of the Red semi-circle until it reaches a point terminating on the coast south of Ras (Al-Qali'ah) which is the undisputable southern frontier of Al-Kuwait territory.

The area of territory bounded on the North by this line and which is bounded on the West by a ridge of land called (Al-Shaqq) and on the East by the sea and on the South by a line passing from West to East from Al-Shaqq to 'Ayn al-'Abd and thence to the coast north of Ras (Al-Mish'ab). This territory is considered common between the two governments of Najd and Al-Kuwait. They will have it in equal rights until another agreement is entered in between Najd and Al-Kuwait concerning it (the territory) with the approval of the British Government. It is understood that the map on which the frontiers are pointed out (Asia) 1:1,000,000 has been made by the Royal Geographical Society under the supervision of the Military Geographical Department and was printed in the Ministry of War in the year 1918.

This was written in the town of Al-'Aqri and was agreed upon by the representatives of the Governments of the two parties on December 2nd, 1922 corresponding to Babi' II, 1341.

THE HIGH COMMISSIONER IN AL-KUWAIT	THE REPRESENTATIVE OF HIS HIGHNESS THE SULTAN OF NAJD
(Signed) Jessey Moore	(Signed) 'Abdullah Sa'id Al-Damluji

I attest to the contents of this Agreement.

| THE GOVERNOR OF | THE SULTAN OF NAJD AND |
| AL-KUWAIT | ANNEXED TERRITORIES |

Ahmad Al-Jabir Al-Sabbah   'Abd-Al-Aziz
                                'Abd-Al-Rahman Al-Saud
    (The Seal)   (The Royal Seal)

1. This is a circle whose center is the heart of the town of Al-
   Kuwait and whose radius is forty miles.

Translated by Professor Butrus Abd al Malek, Professor of
Semitic Languages, American University, Cairo, Egypt.

[Geographical Description of the Neutral Zone Furnished
by R. E. Funkhauser, Petroleum Attaché, American Embassy,
Cairo, Egypt]

The frontier between Najd and Kuwait begins in the West
from junction of the Wadi al Aujah (W. al Audja) with the
Batin (El Batin), leaving Raq'l (Rikal) to Najd; from this
point it continues in a straight line until it joins latitude 29° and
the red semi-circle referred to in Article 5 of the Anglo-Turkish
Agreement of 29th July 1913. The line then follows the side
of the red semi-circle until it reaches a point terminating [*sic*]
on the coast south of Ras Al-Qali'ah (Ras el Kaliyah) and this
is the undisputable southern frontier of Kuwait territory. The
portion of Territory bounded on the north by this line and
which is bounded on the West by a low mountainous ridge
called Shaq (Esh Shakk) and on the East by the sea and on the
South by a line passing from West to East from Shaq (Shakk)
to 'Ain al 'Abd (Ain el Abd) and thence to the coast north of
Ras al Mish'ab (Ras Mishaab), in this territory the Governments of Najd and Kuwait will share equal rights until through
the good offices of the Government of Great Britain a further
agreement is made between Najd and Kuwait concerning it.

APRIL 24 TO MAY 31:

In the Casper office I was getting caught up on petroleum activities in the Rocky Mountains during the past five months. Our drilling on the Lake Creek structure in the Big Horn Basin had proved
up over thirty million barrels of oil. Our drilling in the adjoining
Murphy Dome structure had resulted in an oil discovery. I made
out a list of plays I had made in the Rocky Mountain area during

the past five years and the reserves of oil we had discovered and sent them to my boss, Emil Kluth. His response was to write that we were going to have some reduction in staff and operating funds.

I remembered asking Barney Hadfield once what his firm was charging Getty for Barney's work on the concession agreement, and he said from fifty to a hundred thousand dollars. My $800-a-month salary for four months certainly was a bargain for my company.

Having been back now for more than three weeks, I had expected at least a call from Kluth or Staples saying welcome home, or something, but none came. I wrote Staples a letter inquiring about my status in the company and wondering what was going to happen to me now. I reminded him of the difference between Hadfield's remuneration and mine. He answered in a condescending manner, saying Hadfield's firm had risked their own money while I had risked nothing, etc. But they did have in mind giving me something for my overseas service. And they did. It was a check for $1,200, which didn't even pay my medical bills for the next three years while I struggled to get rid of the amoebic dysentery I had contracted in their behalf.

Reluctantly, I came to the conclusion that life was too short to work for a company like that, so on May 31 I called Emil Kluth and told him I was quitting. He wished me luck, but I felt he was insincere.

So ended my part in the story of the Saudi Arabia Neutral Zone.

EPILOGUE

I called Mr. Getty when I was in London in January of 1961, and he invited me out to tea at Sutton Place, his sixteenth-century palace. He was very cordial and took me on a tour of the great hall, which was very impressive. We reminisced on the negotiations for the Neutral Zone thirteen years earlier, and he surprised me by asking "How did you get to Washington from New York City after our meeting?"

The airlines were weathered in, and I had taken the train. His keen memory was certainly in evidence.

Mr. Getty brought me up to date on developments in the Neutral Zone. He said they had drilled five dry holes on seismic prospects trying for an extension to the Burgan anticline. Then, at his suggestion, they drilled near the surface anticline feature I had first seen and reported on my original aerial reconnaissance. The wildcat well found a large field, which they named Wafra. He said the firm DeGolyer-McNaughton had estimated proved reserves of nine billion barrels for the field. A field capable of producing 100 million barrels is considered a major field; the Neutral Zone Wafra field would be a giant! In fact, this field contributed greatly to the economic size of Getty's empire, as its biggest single asset. By 1990 the Neutral Zone had produced nearly five billion barrels of oil.

Mr. Getty wanted to know what I was doing, and I told him about work in Libya (see Chapter 13). I suggested that he consider trying to get an oil concession there. He said he wasn't interested because he didn't think Libyan production would be as prolific as the Saudi Arabian, but more like production in Texas and Louisiana. I had to concur in this assessment, but Libya currently produces more than a million barrels a day from a few fields, and at current prices, production there is remarkably remunerative. I have always regretted that I couldn't persuade him to try for a Libyan concession.

I followed with interest later developments in the lives of the people who figured in the Neutral Zone affair. Mac MacPherson of ARAMCO became Mr. Getty's manager in the Neutral Zone. Tom Barger, my geologist friend in ARAMCO, became that company's president. After his retirement he returned to the States.

Abdullah Tariki, the young geologist, became Petroleum Minister for Saudi Arabia. He was displaced after a few years and moved to Beirut, where he set up a prestigious consulting firm. With Pérez of Venezuela, Tariki was a founding father in 1960 of OPEC, the Organization of Petroleum Exporting Countries, which later took control of oil production rates and prices throughout the world.

Hermann Eilts, the helpful and accommodating young man in charge of economics at the American Legation in Jidda, became Ambassador to Egypt in 1976 and later Ambassador to Saudi Arabia and is now retired.

Ibn-Saud died in 1953 and his oldest son, Muhammad, became

king. Emir Faisal displaced him as king in 1962 and was assassinated in 1975. Khalid, the bright young prince, became king, to be succeeded by his half-brother Fahd when his own health failed.

George Getty helped his father take over Tidewater Oil Company. They merged Pacific Western Oil Corporation and other Getty companies into it, naming the new entity Getty Oil Company. George became president. When he died in 1974, the newspapers reported his death as a probable suicide.

George was a remarkable young man who would have been an industrial giant like his father if he had lived. He shared his father's keen memory, telling me once on the phone how he had kept track of my activities, particularly the gas discovery at Clear Creek (see Chapter 11). I felt he might be overly complimentary when he said I had too much ability to remain working for someone else's company.

I had called George (at the request of Professor Robert Shrock, my mentor at MIT) to ask if he thought his father would be interested in talking to President Killian of Massachusetts Institute of Technology about giving the school some money. George said his father's philosophy was not to make endowments or give to charity but to build refineries and find oil fields to give people jobs — jobs, not charity. George himself had given some money to the MIT geology department, however, but he said he didn't think he got back anything worthwhile.

Barney Hadfield died of a heart attack in 1952, only three years after we signed the concession.

In his 1963 autobiography, *My Life and Fortunes*, J. Paul Getty spoke of me as "one of the finest geologists I have ever known." Mr. Getty died in 1976, shortly after publishing *As I See It*. It too was autobiographical, and he mentioned me in his chapter on the Neutral Zone as "always having excellent judgment."

The Neutral Zone was explored pretty thoroughly, and other fields were found along the coast north of Ras Misha 'ab, where I had seen the shoaling — further evidence that surface geology was effective in exploration there.

The Wafra field was one of the first to have its wells set on fire by Saddam Hussein in the Gulf War of 1991. However, a lot of these wells did not flow and had pumping units on them, so the fires were easily extinguished. The Kuwait Burgan field had a high gas-to-oil ratio, and a strong water drive, so its wells were the raging infernos seen in the television coverage.

Kuwait and Saudi Arabia came to an agreement during the 1980's to divide the Neutral Zone. Texaco bought the Getty Oil Company and took over the operations at Wafra.

The recent book by Daniel Yergin, *The Prize: The Epic Quest for Oil, Money and Power* (Simon and Schuster, 1990), speaks of my work in the Neutral Zone and of how the Wafra field made J. Paul Getty the richest man in the world.

Part II

"ALLAH WAS AN OILMAN"

—Contemporary Proverb

Not quite like a horse! A confident Paul Walton astride a camel with leftish leanings at Qatif, Saudi Arabia, where a large oil field is now located, January 1939.

Top: Paul Walton outside the California Arabian Standard Oil Company (CASOC) headquarters, after surviving the fever — and the cure — Dhahran, Saudi Arabia, January 1939. *Bottom:* The town well at Jubail, Saudi Arabia, with Paul in the foreground, January 1939. Jubail is now the site of one of the largest petrochemical complexes in the world.

Camel caravans on the main camel route from the Persian Gulf to the Red
Sea. *Top:* Watering the animals at open wells at Ma'gala, sixty miles west of
Jubail, Saudi Arabia, February 1939. *Bottom:* Filling goatskin bags with water
at Ma'gala, March 1939.

Getting the hang of a new saddle. Paul Walton at Qatif, Saudi Arabia, 1939.

CHAPTER 6

SAUDI ARABIA — THE FIRST
TIME OUT

I LAY DYING IN THE BRITISH HOSPITAL on Bahrain Island in the Persian Gulf. It was Christmas Eve 1938. I had been there two weeks, getting weaker every day. It had started with a bad cold and sore throat, followed by a high temperature. Dr. Dame, an American, had first thought I had Malta fever (brucellosis), then decided it was rheumatic fever. First my right knee, then my right wrist and elbow, became so inflamed I couldn't move them. Then pernicious anemia set in, and I became so weak I couldn't turn over in bed without help.

Talk about being in Hell with your back broke! I was twelve thousand miles from home and almost dead.

Along about 8:00 PM I heard some talk in the hall and saw a grey-bearded man go by in the habit of a Greek Orthodox priest. In a few minutes he came into my room and asked, "How are you, son?"

"Pretty sick," I whispered, with all the strength I had.

"You are going to get well," he said. He took hold of my left wrist and squeezed it. "You are going to be all right." And with that, he smiled and left the room to make some more calls.

One was to the next room, where a young Englishman was seriously ill. He was an oilfield worker with the Bahrain Petroleum Company who worked on Bahrain Island. The company had flown his wife down from London on Imperial Airways to see him. He died within a few days of her arrival and was cremated by the local undertaking establishment in Al-Manamah. I heard later that they had delayed his cremation because they thought they would have me in a day or two and didn't want to heat up the furnace twice.

[107]

I got no better the next few days, and then one of my nurses, Molly Brogan, an Irish girl who later married my good friend Jerry Harris, told me the doctors were planning a new treatment for me. Sulfa drugs had just been invented at this time, but penicillin was still unknown.

Dr. Dame came in to see me on his morning rounds and said he and his English associate were going to try an induced-fever method to attempt to rid my system of the rheumatic fever. He said it might take several treatments, and they would be rough, but he thought I could stand it.

That afternoon the English doctor came to my room, turned me over on my stomach, and shot me with 15 cc. of boiled goat's milk. Within a few minutes my teeth started to chatter, I got the chills and shakes, and they had to bring extra blankets to keep me warm. My temperature went up to 104° F., at which point all my aches and pains vanished. I could move my knee and elbow without pain. It seemed like a miracle!

As the fever wore off, some of my aches and stiffness gradually returned, but by the next morning I could get out of bed to go to the bathroom. I gained strength the next week, but then my knee and elbow got sore again. So Dr. Dame decided to try the induced fever once more.

This time my temperature shot up to 105° F., and I started to have heart palpitations and black out. Molly Brogan couldn't locate the doctors, so she stayed with me all night, giving me smelling salts to keep me conscious until the fever wore off.

I really felt wrung out after that treatment, but most of my aches had left for good. I was up and around within a few days, but they kept me in the hospital for several more weeks before letting me go back to Dhahran and join my gravity meter party.

No doctor I have mentioned this treatment to has ever heard of it. I consider it a miracle to have been cured in this manner. The old Greek Orthodox priest was right!

I was twenty-four years old in 1938 and just starting a lifelong career of geological and geophysical exploration work. The steps leading to this job, my first in the oil industry, I had taken many years earlier.

My parents were Paul and Margaret Lenore Watts Walton. They were raised on adjoining farms in the southeast part of the Salt Lake Valley. Dad was from a large family — ten boys and three girls — and his father was a prominent lawyer and politician in Salt Lake City. Mother's mother was twice a widow and had married her second husband in polygamy. She had two full brothers, one sister, and a half brother and sister.

Mother had gone to the University of Utah to get her teacher's certificate. She taught school all her life. Dad had a business-college education but was never able to find and hold a permanent job. Consequently, our family life was based on a meager income, but the three of us were never really destitute during the Great Depression since Mother was always able to keep her job.

At one point during the Depression, however, the Granite School District, for which Mother taught, passed a ruling that married teachers were to be dismissed. My parents decided that Dad, who was out of work, would leave home and go to stay on his brother's ranch, where he worked for his board and room. On his frequent visits to our home near Forty-sixth South on Wander Lane, he was careful not to be seen so as not to jeopardize Mother's job.

After I had been at L.D.S. High School for only two years, I discovered that I had enough credits to enter the University of Utah, which I did in the fall of 1930. I was just sixteen. The physics, chemistry, and math I had taken in high school allowed me to enter the School of Mines and Engineering, from which I graduated as a geological engineer in 1935.

The mining industry was still depressed, and no jobs were available. The oil industry was even worse; oil in the Big Horn Basin of Wyoming was thirty-five cents a barrel. The New Deal was getting under way with the Civilian Conservation Corps (CCC) camps being established in the West, however, and the government needed technical service employees. With my engineering background, I was able to get a job with the Soil Conservation Service in Utah as a junior engineer at $150 a month — $1,800 a year. I could live at the CCC camp, where room and board were about $25 a month.

Most of my work was surveying, laying out roads, erosion control terraces, etc. This gave me a good working knowledge of transits, levels, and plane tables which I have used all the rest of my life.

I was stationed first at Price, then at Gunlock, in the southwest part of the state, and later at Mt. Pleasant, near the center. In later years these three areas of Utah would be very important in my own geological explorations.

In 1938 one of my boyhood friends, Olie Graham, was operating a Standard of California service station in Salt Lake City. Standard had just recently found some oil production in Saudi Arabia and was starting to explore the whole country. Olie was told they needed geologists and relayed this information to me. At about this time I also heard that Lynn Madsen, a classmate of mine at the University of Utah, had been sent to Saudi Arabia by Standard to work in their civil engineering department. This all really sounded interesting. Then Olie called and said he had to go to Standard's Los Angeles office on business. "Why don't you drive me down and talk to the Standard people?"

I asked for the two weeks' annual leave I had coming, and we drove to Los Angeles. The people in the service station department directed me to Herschel Driver, chief geologist for the Southern California area. We had a nice talk, and he was interested in my surveying experience. He said they needed people with that background in Saudi Arabia and I should go to San Francisco to see their chief geologist, G. C. Gester.

I left Olie in Los Angeles and drove to San Francisco. After I talked with Mr. Gester a little while, he turned me over to his assistant, George Cunningham, whom I liked immediately. Before the afternoon was over, Mr. Cunningham had offered me a job as chief of a gravity meter party in Saudi Arabia. The salary would be $325 per month on a three-year contract.

Mr. Cunningham sent me to their medical department for a checkover, which I passed, and told me to report back to 225 Bush Street in San Francisco as soon as I could. They gave me typhoid shots and a smallpox vaccination and sent me on my way. I was elated but a little sad too. I didn't know how to break the news to Dad. Mother had died earlier in the year, and he was still in a depressed state. I was too, for she had been the mainstay of our small family.

I drove back to Salt Lake City and resigned from the Soil Conservation Service. I sold my nearly-new car for $500, which really
hurt, gathered up my belongings in a suitcase and footlocker, and
left for San Francisco on the evening train. It took twenty-four
hours for the Western Pacific to get to Berkeley, where I had to
transfer to the ferry to cross to San Francisco. I took a cab to the
Chancellor Hotel, where Mr. Cunningham had said I could get a
good, clean room for little money — $2.50 per day.

When I went down to 225 Bush Street the next morning, Mr.
Cunningham opened the files on Arabia and said, "Read all these
reports and you'll know something about Arabia." The reports
started with the earliest surface reconnaissance. Later ones covered
the Dammam Dome, where oil had already been found. I copied a
description of the stratigraphic section to take with me.

In 1938 "gravity work" was just beginning to be used in the
United States on the Gulf Coast, where it was successful in locating
salt domes, many of which have oil and gas fields associated with
them. Salt, being less dense than the surrounding rock, has a smaller
pull of gravity, which shows up on gravity meter measurements.
Standard was using Mott-Smith gravity meters that measured gravity
with a quartz pendulum which was kept at a constant temperature
by a highly sensitive thermostat. This accurate temperature control
was the essential part of the meter. The Mott-Smith meters were
supposed to be accurate to one-millionth of the total pull of gravity
and, of course, were subject to daily or diurnal gravity changes due
to the cycle of the moon and tides. A daily drift curve was made to
correct for these diurnal variations.

Mr. Cunningham said Standard had an active gravity program
going in Mississippi, and it would be a good idea for me to go there
and find out how they operated. He said the bottleneck in gravity
work was the surveying. The stations were placed in mile centers and
had to be exactly located with plane table and alidade for horizontal
control and by dumpy level for vertical control, but the surveying
always lagged behind the gravity meter. I gathered that this was why
they had hired me, a geologist with considerable surveying experience.

Before I left for Mississippi, Mr. Cunningham gave me a fatherly
lecture. He said to learn all I could about the gravity work, the

seismograph work, and also all about the surface geological and core drilling work being done. He said to spend some time around the drilling rigs to find out how they work and why. I was really walking on air when I left that day.

Mr. Cunningham sent me first to Standard's Houston office. He wanted me to meet the district geophysicist, Ken Crandall. Then I was to go to Natchez to spend some time with Neil Smith, Standard's local geophysicist, looking after the Mott-Smith party.

I left San Francisco on the evening Southern Pacific train. I especially enjoyed the trip across West Texas. There was a two-hour watering stop at El Paso, and I had never been in a Spanish-speaking city before. The train arrived in Houston in the evening, and at Mr. Cunningham's suggestion I went to the Ben Milam Hotel.

The next morning I reported to Ken Crandall. He told me more about the gravity program and had me go to the Mott-Smith office as well. Crandall had only a small office and staff, but during the next few years he found lots of oil for Standard's operating company in the Gulf Coast, The California Company. Eventually he became its president. Neil Smith met me at McComb, Mississippi, the nearest railhead to his headquarters at Natchez. He was a very serious, intense person, and I felt I could learn a lot from him about gravity work.

We drove to Natchez on the historic sunken roads, and I entered a whole new world. An active lease play was going on, and I had never been around oil activity before. It was exciting. Neil sent me out with his surveyor and gravity crew to see how they operated. Then he showed me how they calculated the gravity readings and corrected them for elevation, latitude, and daily fluctuations. He showed me the maps with their gravity contours added. Methods to determine the residual or local gravity picture which might be related to geologic structure were just beginning to be employed. Neil was using a regional gravity chart which he laid over the gravity map to calculate the local or residual gravity values. This was pretty rough when contrasted to today's work, but it was a valuable step in the direction of finding buried geologic structure.

Neil's gravity crew had located a prominent gravity high near McComb, and he had stereo aerial photos of the area. Our stereo-

scope was a primitive double-mirror reflective type with no mag-
nification. The resulting three-dimensional image showed a topographic high near the gravity high. California Company leased the
area and later found a good-sized oilfield there.

It was September and still pretty hot and awfully humid. We
went to work at 4 AM and worked until noon. Then we went back
home, took a cold bath, and tried to stay near a fan to keep cool.
I was staying at the Eola Hotel, where each room had a great big
fan right over the bed. I kept mine on all the time.

The gravity stations were marked on Tobin aerial mosaics of
the area. They were quite accurate, and this saved plane tabling the
locations. I wished then we had aerial photos of Arabia. It would
save a lot of work. Running the station elevations was quite a job,
however, due to the narrow, winding sunken roads. The whole area
was covered with a thick layer of windblown silt, called loess, which
erodes easily. Water running down the roadways gradually washes
the silt away, leaving a deeper and deeper set of ruts, until finally
the whole road ends up many feet lower than the adjoining ground.
Thus, all the older roads of Mississippi, including the famous Natchez
Trace, are ten to thirty feet below the ground surface. Running a
level survey on these roads was tedious and slow.

CHAPTER 7

ARABIA BOUND

I LEFT NATCHEZ ON SEPTEMBER 16, 1938. Neil took me to the train at McComb. I was to sail on the twenty-first from New York City. The train took me to Memphis, St. Louis, and Chicago, where I changed to the Pennsylvania Railroad, arriving in New York City at 7:30 AM on the eighteenth.

I used the next three days sightseeing in the city. This was my first trip to New York City, and I wanted to see all I could. I got up early and went to bed late. I saw *Tobacco Road* on the stage and the Eddy Duchin, Duke Ellington, and Charlie Barnett shows. I visited Chinatown, Push Cart Alley, Grant's Tomb, Columbia University, and the American Museum of Natural History. A country boy can get a lot done in three days, and I walked a great part of the way.

I had reservations at the Governor Clinton Hotel, made by the Company. Three other fellows going to Arabia were there as well — two machinists, Harry Clegg and Clarence Quinn, and their boss, John Box, who would be in charge of the machine shop in Dhahran. We sailed at midnight, September 21, on Hamburg American line's S.S. *New York*, a medium-sized ocean liner, about 30,000 tons, with three classes: first, tourist, and third.

The ship was German-owned and operated by a German crew. A German band played military music and Strauss waltzes for two hours before we sailed. We were delayed two hours and used the delay to sit around drinking beer from large steins until the ship left the dock. Although it was off-season, many of the people in first class were in tuxedos and rather stuffy, I thought. In tourist class, however, there seemed to be a lot of young people having a good time.

Between all the beer and the motion of the ship, I woke up with a terrible headache. Going up to breakfast, I found I was earlier than the others. The German waiter recognized my symptoms and suggested a stein of beer as an eye-opener for breakfast. It really did the job, and I was soon out on deck to see the ocean. This was my first trip on anything larger than a ferry boat, and I was very impressed.

John Box had been on the water before, so he guided us in getting deck chairs, playing shuffleboard, and the other things we should do. He had come to the United States from England as a young boy and had made several trips back to see his relatives.

I kept watching the group of young people in tourist, and we decided to go down that evening for a drink. It turned out that they were college students on their way to Munich to take their junior year abroad. Most were from the East Coast — New York and Virginia. Since I was only twenty-four, I was just a few years older than they, so they accepted me in their group right away.

Within a few days I knew all the group and had developed quite a crush on Rosalie Dillard, a blonde girl from Lynchburg, Virginia.

Before we sailed, the newspapers had been full of stories about an imminent war between England and Germany. Neville Chamberlain was Prime Minister of England, and he thought he could deal with Adolph Hitler. Every morning a brief summary of Reuters' news appeared on the ship's bulletin board, picked up by the wireless operator during the night. The seriousness of the war situation was apparent in the news. Then we heard that Hitler was going to give a speech to the German people. Other than the American college students and we four on our way to Saudi Arabia, the passengers were German nationals going home. The dining hall filled for Hitler's radio speech. He ranted and raved and everyone looked glum. I could tell something was up.

The S.S. *New York* was on an easterly course. After the speech, I went out on deck. It was early evening and I could see the North Star and the Big Dipper on our port side. Then I noted the ship slowly starting to turn toward the north. It kept turning until we were headed just a little to the east of the North Star. I went down to the bulletin board, where a big map of the Atlantic Ocean showed the ship's position each day. The map was gone! The news bulletin was gone as well.

When I went down to my stateroom, I noticed the drapes on all the windows and portholes were closed. I had a small world map in my suitcase, and on it I plotted where we had last been shown to be on the ship's map, a few hundred miles southwest of Ireland. I could see that if we maintained our new course, we would end up in Iceland or head for a port in Norway. I figured that Germany and England must be at war.

I joined the college group in tourist class and they, all German language majors, had found out a little from the ship's crew. They too were afraid it was war, which meant they would not be able to go to Munich to school, so they were all very worried. Except for Rosalie. She showed up dragging her fur coat, a cigarette in her mouth and a martini glass in her hand. She said, "Let's have a party," which we did.

We continued on our northerly course all day and the next night, until the North Star was at least 70° above the horizon. I figured we were close to Iceland. Then we went into a fog bank and were in fog until the next morning. As soon as it was light, I went up on deck. The fog was clearing and there, on either side of us, were British cruisers! We were being escorted to an English port, I guessed. The cruisers stayed with us all day, and we swung east first, around Scotland, and then southeast down through the North Sea.

We had been scheduled to land at Cherbourg, France. Now we didn't know what would happen. That evening we were told we would land at Cuxhaven and transfer to the S.S. *Hamburg*, which would take us to Cherbourg. War had been averted!

During the last few days Neville Chamberlain had been to Munich to talk to Hitler. In humiliation, he had come home to Britain to announce that there would be "peace in our time," and World War II was delayed for a year.

The truce wasn't without merit for the group on the S.S. *New York*. They were all able to take their junior year in Munich, and I was able to get to Arabia. I had to; I didn't have a job in the United States.

The S.S. *Hamburg* didn't berth at Cherbourg. They sent a lighter out to pick us up with our trunks. It was dark, and as we headed toward the docks a small meteorite fell into the sea in front of us. It cast an eerie greenish glare over the harbor installation. Little did we know that within a year artillery shells and aerial bombs would be doing the same thing and, before the Normandy invasion six years later, the whole port would be destroyed.

The last train had left for Paris, but we were met by an American Express man who had hotel rooms for us. Events of the last two days were still so fresh in my mind that I couldn't think of going to bed, so we went to the tavern adjoining the hotel for a drink. The four of us sat at a table drinking beer, and everyone seemed to be speaking French except two girls at an adjoining table. We bought them a drink and learned that they were leaving on a ship the next day for Caracas, Venezuela. They were English Communist Party workers who had been in Russia all summer getting their training to work in Venezuela. They were both school teachers and fairly intelligent. This was my first contact with anyone who was actively working to overthrow the United States government and destroy the capitalistic system, and I spent half the night arguing the merits of free enterprise with them. John, Harry, and Clarence went to bed before midnight — since we had to catch the train to Paris at 6:30 AM — but not I. I was fascinated listening to these girls speak English — the King's English.

The bellman knocked on the door at 6 o'clock. It was still dark outside. He had a continental breakfast, black coffee and rolls, ready for us in the dining room. We got to the train on time, and I could hardly keep my eyes open on the way to Paris.

Again, an American Express man met us at the Gare du Nord. We had expected to be put on the Orient Express for Istanbul, but he told us that bad storms had washed out several bridges on the rail line through Yugoslavia, and the trains were not running. They only ran once a week anyway. This would give us several days in Paris while the bridges were being replaced. Hardly a bitter pill to swallow! We were taken to the Ambassador Hotel, where we would stay until further notice.

I didn't want to miss anything, so we joined an American Express tour of the city and went to the Louvre, Napoleon's Tomb, Notre Dame, and all the rest. Clarence and Harry were anxious to see the nightlife, so we took an evening night club tour. There were other Americans along — a lady from Atlanta with two daughters and their girlfriend who were spending the winter in Europe. They had just arrived from England and were enrolled in a French cooking school. They too were relieved the war hadn't broken out; in fact, the tension had been so great in this regard that a certain camaraderie had broken out among Americans in Europe. They automatically spoke to each other and were friendly, which isn't the case any more.

During the post–World War I era, Paris was considered by the returning doughboys as the ultimate place to have a leave or vacation. By my college days, Paris had become one of the major stops on the "Grand Tour" every college graduate dreamed of taking to further his education, cultural and otherwise. Now with the imminence of World War II, everyone felt Paris had become the place to kick up your heels before the lights went out all over Europe. They were having practice blackouts, and cabbies were practicing driving with their lights on dim. The coming conflagration was uppermost in everyone's mind.

"There is no tomorrow, only today," was the philosophy of many. It took many forms. One that amused me and horrified the French was the response of a middle-aged American staying at our hotel. He had become so disgusted with the perpetual extended hand and cries of "Service, M'sieur" from all quarters that he had papered the outside of his suitcase with French banknotes. His contempt for the French monetary system and for the continental solicitation of tips from every segment of French society he encountered was plain for all to see.

The next few days were idyllic. We wandered around town sightseeing and drinking Champagne at sidewalk cafes. We met the girls from Atlanta almost every afternoon and explored the city with them. Finally, Clarence said he owed a debt to Lafayette and left us for an evening with a French girl. But all good things eventually end and, after nine days, the bridges were fixed and we boarded the Orient Express. At 10:15 PM on a Tuesday night it pulled out, headed for Istanbul. I shared a compartment with a dark-haired gentleman who spoke no English and got off at Sofia, Bulgaria.

The Orient Express was a classic train running a scenic route through France, Switzerland, Italy, Yugoslavia, Bulgaria, and Turkey. We arrived in Istanbul late Friday afternoon. The change in country and culture from Paris to the Bosporus was an education in itself.

The club car proved a good place to get acquainted with the other passengers. At least half a dozen Englishmen in their late twenties or early thirties were headed for Iran to work in the oilfields. They had left friends and family behind for two years to go and make a stake for themselves. They called Iraq and Iran the Near East then. One Englishman said, "Iran may be the Near East, but it's too damn far for me." Anything with a skirt on was fair game for these fellows. When we stopped at Sofia, two of them followed a good-looking blonde Bulgarian off the train. Their leader went searching for them without success and got back just as the train pulled out. I have always wondered what happened to them, since they had neither Bulgarian visas nor baggage.

A nice-looking middle-aged woman with coal-black eyes and hair was traveling in our car, and we saw her in the dining room and club car. She was Turkish and spoke excellent English. One evening she spent several hours telling us about the way Ataturk, then President of Turkey, had taken over their country and modernized it. She said that without these reforms she, as a Muslim woman, would be wearing a veil and wouldn't be allowed out of the house — much less be able to make a trip alone to England. She whetted my curiosity about Istanbul. It had been Constantinople until recently; in fact, in grade school we had sung a song called "Con-stan-tin-opel." Our schedule showed that we would have three hours in Istanbul, enough time to take a taxi to see the famous St. Sophia mosque and the Blue Mosque. But alas, we arrived very late and were hustled off the Orient Express onto a waiting ferry and across the Bosporus to Haider Pasa, where we boarded the Taurus Express. It was nearly dark, but the many mosques on the skyline of Istanbul made an unforgettable sight. I vowed to return someday to see them.

We had noticed as we progressed from France and Switzerland into the Balkan countries and Turkey that the quality of the food, service, and cleanliness even aboard the Orient Express had gradually deteriorated. Now, on the Taurus Express, the deterioration became more pronounced. The bedding was dusty, the water muddy, the drinks without ice, and the food poorly prepared. In particular, the toilets were filthy — always a sign to me of lessening culture or civilization.

It got dark as we left the Bosporus, and I hated to miss seeing what was called Asia Minor when I was in grade school. When it got light the next day, we were in country that could have been northern Nevada — junipers and piñon-type pine growing out of bare limestone mountains. We were in the northern foothills of the Taurus Mountains. For the next few hours we went through that mountain range in a series of tunnels that would make the Swiss railroader envious. Harry Clegg reminded me that this part of the railroad had been built by the Germans before World War I, when they had visions of a Berlin-to-Baghdad rail line tying an empire together.

The train left the mountains abruptly as we entered Syria just north of Adana. Here the real desert began as we traveled east. Finally, out in the middle of a big sandy plain, at a place called Tel Kocheck (now Tall Kushik) on the Iraqi border, the rail line ended abruptly. Only a few mud huts comprised the small village, but we were met by a fleet of taxicabs. Everyone's bags and trunks were unloaded from the train and put in the cabs. Then the drivers headed out in the early evening for Mosul, about thirty miles to the east, on ungraded roads or tire tracks which they variously followed. Sometimes there were taxis in front, behind, to the right, to the left — all at the same time — and the resulting dust was stifling. It was pitch dark when we pulled up at the white stucco resthouse at Mosul on the Euphrates River, near the site of the ancient city of Nineveh. Flares from the oil wells in the Mosul oilfield lighted up the sky. The next morning we hired a horse-drawn cab to take us across the river to see Nineveh, where only a few building blocks remained of the once-proud city.

Loading our belongings onto a British-built bus, we rode south down the river valley to Kirkuk, the location of one of the world's largest oilfields and the northern terminus of the Iraqi National Railroad. We had dinner at a resthouse and loaded ourselves onto the train. It was a compartment train with sleepers, and we traveled all night.

When we arrived in Baghdad at 7 AM, taxis took everyone to town. We were taken to the Claridge Hotel, but because of the delay before we left Paris, we were arriving nearly ten days late for our reservations. There was no space for us, so they put cots on the flat roof of the hotel, and we slept there under mosquito netting. Although it was the eighteenth of October, it was as warm as summer at home.

The hotel overlooked the Tigris River. Since it was harvest time for the large melon crop and there was no highway bridge across the river, the loads of melons were being taken from one side to the other in circular boats that looked like big bowls being poled across.

The American Express representative told us our boat wouldn't leave Basra for Bahrain Island in the Persian Gulf until October 22, so we were to stay until October 21. This gave us three days to look around Baghdad. What an interesting city! It was really something right out of the Arabian Nights stories. The shops, the bazaar, the beggars were a sight to see. I had been entranced by the movie *Kismet*, starring Otis Skinner, when I was in grade school, and here was the movie in real life! The story concerned the fortunes of a Baghdad beggar who attains riches and then loses them, returning to his rags. Everywhere I looked I saw candidates for this role.

The night we left by train for Basra, a big sandstorm came up. I shared a compartment with an English RAF officer on his way to Tehran. He had a little wooden suitcase that he opened after we had talked a while. It held a bottle of Johnny Walker scotch and a bottle of Schweppes soda. No ice, of course. It was the first scotch and soda I had ever tasted. I really felt worldly; my Mormon training hadn't included such things as this. The wind blew all night, and the sand filtered in and into everything. It blew so hard I thought the wind might blow the train right off its tracks. The blowing stopped before morning, however, and by the time we arrived at Basra, the air was clear as crystal. Basra, Sinbad the Sailor's home port, was once on the Persian Gulf at the mouth of the Shatt al-Arab River. The delta built by the river now extends a long way into the Gulf, so boats have to come upriver to get to the port of Basra. The largest oil refinery in the world in 1938 was down the river at Abadan in Iran.

So far, the people we had been traveling with were mostly the Englishmen on their way to Tehran to work in the oilfields. At Basra we four Americans left them and boarded a British India ship, the S.S. *Elephanta,* a small one-class ship of about 3,000 tons with the final destination of Bombay. We boarded on Saturday night and sailed after dark. We passed the huge refinery at Abadan about midnight, and it was lit up with myriads of gas flares. The ship sailed through the beautiful bluish-green water of the Persian Gulf the next day. It was indeed beautiful!

The passengers were mostly English citizens on their way to India. That evening they all showed up for dinner in tuxedos. They really made an event of dining, even though the curried lamb wasn't something I considered a particularly great gastronomical event. I guess it's the thought of bringing civilization to the heathen that prompts this pomp and ceremony.

The next morning at daylight, the cabin boy came to my small cubbyhole stateroom with a pot of hot tea and said, "Bahrain"! I looked out the window and saw the white, palm-fringed beach and knew I was getting awfully close to my destination. The British India ship didn't put in at Bahrain. They sent a lighter out for us, and we and our trunks and bags were brought into the dock. Loading facilities at the port of Al-Manamah on the north end of Bahrain Island consisted of a single long pier jutting out into the water. The pier was made of slabs of limestone pried off the bottom of the Persian Gulf as soft lime mud and left to dry for a few weeks until they became hard as rock.

We were met by Bill Folker, the California Arabia Standard man in charge of loading and unloading passengers and cargo for the Company. He was a big man, clad in khaki shorts and a huge India-type pith helmet and surrounded by a bunch of Bahrain Arabs, all dressed in light, flowing clothes and sandals and wearing skullcaps or headcloths. He spoke to them in English, and we heard him tell them to load the bags in the "jolly boat." He gave them a small piece of paper, which he called a chit, for each bag, and they were paid each day on the basis of the number of chits they had collected.

This was my introduction to Arab laborers, and within a few months I would have a crew of my own doing the manual labor for my gravity meter party. Our people in Arabia usually called them "coolies," but to me this term didn't fit; they seemed on a higher intellectual scale.

CHAPTER 8

LIFE IN THE INTEMPERATE ZONE

BAHRAIN IS A LONG NORTH–SOUTH ISLAND taking its name from the Arab *bahr* (sea) and meaning two or twin seas, the main Gulf on the east and the smaller bay on the west.

Bahrain was the center of pearl diving in the Gulf, and the teakwood dhows with their distinctive sails were seen in all directions. The water is shallow and the divers used no equipment, not even goggles, to collect the pearl-bearing oysters off the bottom. The oysters were not eaten, apparently, for I never saw them on the menu in the Company's restaurants. Most of the pearls were white, but a few were coal black, sold for cufflinks and shirt studs. Al-Manamah was full of pearl peddlers who stopped you and took out a black cloth bag, inside of which was a red cloth bag containing the pearls — *lulus* in Arabic.

In the center of Bahrain Island is a large anticline, and an oil-field was developed there. Although Bahrain was a British protectorate, Standard of California was able to get an oil concession from the Sheikh of Bahrain in the early 1930's. English representatives and Gulf Oil are supposed to have had dealings with the Sheikh prior to Standard's obtaining the oil rights. While the structural significance of the island must have been apparent to the English and American companies operating farther north in Iraq and Iran, the story was that since the producing zones in those fields were of Tertiary age, Bahrain didn't have any oil possibilities because the Tertiary strata were missing, having been eroded away, and only Cretaceous or older strata were present.

In any event, Standard of California got the concession, took Texaco in as a partner because they had marketing facilities in the

Indian Ocean area, and drilled the discovery well that produced from the so-called "Bahrain Zone" in the Cretaceous. A large field was developed and a refinery built on the island. The success at Bahrain prompted the two companies — now operating as Bahrein Petroleum Company — to form a new entity, California Arabian Standard Oil Company (CASOC), and secure a concession on most of Saudi Arabia from King ibn-Saud. A prominent surface dome at Dhahran, Dammam Dome, was mapped on the surface, and a well was drilled to the producing horizon at the Bahrain field. A discovery was made and several development wells drilled which promptly fell off in production. At the insistence of Max Steineke, chief geologist for CASOC, the wells were drilled deeper, and very large production was found in the underlying Jurassic limestone, now called the "Arab Zone." CASOC was now embarked on a geological and geophysical evaluation of the whole coastal province of Saudi Arabia, Al-Hasa, and they needed people like me to do the work.

After our bags and trunks were loaded on the Company launch that went between Al-Manamah and Al-Khubar, the port on the Arabian mainland, I had a chance to think. Here it was, October 24. I had left New York City on September 21, and before me was the Arabian mainland, where I was committed to spend the next three years. I hoped I would be able to learn this new technique of running a gravity meter crew and interpreting the results. I was awfully green in this business and knew it. I just hoped I wouldn't make any mistakes.

As we came into Al-Khubar, I could see the twin hills, called Dhahran, for which the Company town was named. They marked the surface expression of the top of the Dammam Dome. The producing wells, with their gas flares and sulfur odor, were omnipresent — a constant reminder that this was why we were here in this forbidding land: oil!

Americans were welcome guests in this country, and Saudi Arabian customs at Al-Khubar was pretty much a formality. Before the Americans found oil and produced it, the country's only income was from the *hajjis*, pilgrims making their prescribed pilgrimages to Mecca, and most of this income was made in the province of Al-

Hijaz on the west coast. Here in the province of Al-Hasa, except for the few people supporting themselves from date gardens and pearl-diving, the population was Bedouin. They followed the rain and grass with their sheep and goats. Transportation was by camel; donkeys were seen only around the small villages. Camels furnished milk, and meat when they died, and were shaved every spring for their woolly hair, which was sent to India or England to be made into cloth.

Dhahran was a pleasant surprise — clusters of white stuccoed flat-top buildings with palm-leaf roofs for both housing and offices, an attractive mess hall, and a clean kitchen. On Saturday nights a movie was shown in the mess hall. They provided laundry service, and I was given the number 85, for the eighty-fifth American to be stationed in Dhahran.

Dick Kerr met me and took me to supper. He told me Max Steineke, who would be my boss, was in the field and would be back in a day or two.

I had looked forward to meeting Dick. He was a friend of Jim Lund, who had taught me to fly back in Price, Utah. Dick and Jim had known each other in California. When he heard I was going to Arabia, Jim had said, "Be sure to look him up. He's the most innovative, resourceful man I ever met."

Dick was a geologist and a flyer, just missing action in World War I. He took a Ford Trimotor to Alaska from California in the late twenties, before airplanes had radios. He and a group of company geologists were doing some aerial reconnaissance in the Kodiak Island area, looking at the geology, when Dick had engine failure. He successfully landed on the beach of the island, but a storm came up immediately. Overdue at their base, they were presumed lost until a radio station picked up a faint beep in Morse code. It was Dick. He had taken the magneto off one engine, rigged up a hand crank to turn it, put several empty tomato cans together to act as condensers, and rigged up a wire aerial and a spark coil so he could send a message. After they were rescued, Dick came back to the island, repaired the engine, and flew the old Tin Goose to safety.

Dick was in charge of a Geophysical Service, Inc., contract seismograph crew, the first to operate in Saudi Arabia, then working about sixty miles north of Dhahran. He was very interested in the possibilities of the gravity meter as a reconnaissance survey tool to locate geologic structures which could then be detailed with the seismograph. He explained to me that there was a time limit for CASOC's concession agreement with Saudi Arabia, and part of the concession area would eventually have to be relinquished to the Saudi Arabian government. So the entire concession area had to be explored in a hurry. Surface geologic parties were now working previously unmapped areas, and seismograph work was being done on some of the best surface structural features. In the large sand dune areas, where seismograph work was too difficult for checking surface work leads, a core drill crew was drilling core holes to a marine fossil bed that seemed to be widespread — the "Button Bed" named for the characteristic fossil shells found in it. Structure contours drawn on the Button Bed would confirm the surface structure mapping. Gravity meter crews would be able to cover the whole eastern part of the country rapidly if — and this was the big question — the gravity meter data appeared to be significantly accurate in mapping the geologic structures.

I asked Dick about my boss, Max Steineke, whom I had not yet met. Dick told me Steineke was one of the best reconnaissance geologists in the world. Standard of California had sent him to Venezuela and New Zealand before assigning him to Arabia. Max had arrived just as the first wells drilled on Dammam Dome started to decline in production. He took a trip several hundred miles west, looked at the Jurassic rocks where they outcropped there, and when he came back, recommended that a well be deepened to test this part of the sedimentary section on Dammam Dome. This test opened up a new deep pool in the "Arab Zone." Years later, the Arab Zone was to be the main producing horizon in the mammoth fields found south and west of Dammam in the great sand dune areas. However, now the bulk of the exploratory effort was being made north and west of Dammam in the *dikaka* area of small brush-covered sand ridges, mainly because surface geology could be done there.

Dick told me the Company still was not terrifically sold on oil prospects in Saudi Arabia. I asked him why, and he said, "We have drilled four structures so far, and only one has proved productive."

He went on to explain that a beautiful seismic and surface structure just west of Dammam Dome was dry. Another large surface structure near the Kuwait Neutral Zone, El Jauf, had been drilled and was dry. They were presently drilling on the Abu Hadriya structure, 100 miles north of Dammam and, so far, it too was dry. They were drilling at about 7,000 feet and had found nothing yet. Dick said the company felt, and he agreed, that the real potential of the region was in Iran, across the Persian Gulf, where great numbers of large anticlines had never been drilled. He said that if deepening the Dammam Dome wells hadn't proved the Arab Zone production, the Company might have given up the concession on a great part of Saudi Arabia. Fortunately, the Company was able to hang on to this concession and within a few years after World War II, six wildcat wells drilled on the recommendation of Max Steineke, Dick Kerr, and their associates proved up a greater oil reserve than that contained in the whole United States.

In a few days Max Steineke arrived from the field. I liked him immediately. He was a rugged, square-jawed field geologist type, thoroughly at home in his job. He liked what he was doing and was happy with the results.

We discussed the possible role of the gravity meter in exploration in Arabia. I explained how the meter worked, the surveying problems involved in the work, and the personnel needed. He explained that the Company had hired men to run the dumpy levels and plane tables, and they would be on their way to Dhahran soon. The contract Mott-Smith meter and truck had been shipped from Houston and would arrive within a month or so. We agreed that we should start the gravity work on the Dammam Dome, since we knew the most about it. Steineke said he had a hunch it might be a salt-intruded dome, and the gravity meter could prove or disprove that theory. In the meantime, he suggested that I spend some time familiarizing myself with the surface mapping as well as the seismic work.

Dick Kerr invited me to go up to see his operation, where I spent several days. I had never been around a seismograph crew before and was fascinated with their operations. They had two truck-mounted rotary shot-hole drilling rigs, and they drilled their 30- to

150-foot holes with water and mud. Their powder man, Booger Allen, loaded the hole with dynamite after the seismometers, or "jugs," were strung out and hooked up to the recording truck. They recorded sixteen traces on photographic paper as the holes were shot.

Dick showed me the recorder and maps they had made on the Abu Hadriya anticline where the well was presently drilling. Then we drove over the ground so I could see the surface expression of the big anticline. We decided we should run the gravity meter here to see how it checked out with the surface and seismic work.

While we were out checking the surface geology it got dark, and we had to drive back to camp with our lights on. Occasionally we would see small animals in the road, their eyes reflecting in the headlights. Dick told me Booger Allen had come in from the "Jebel" (the camp at Dhahran) with a pretty good load of beer on. He saw a fairly large animal stopped in the road in his headlights, so he threw on his brakes, got out, and made a flying tackle on the critter. He scooped it up in his arms and brought it back to the car, hollering to his partner, "Turn the flashlight on this thing. I want to see what I've caught." The animal was a fox, and it bit him pretty badly. He didn't mind! He had lost fingers off both hands and had that devil-may-care attitude most powder monkeys have, since they live with a constant threat of death if they make a mistake.

A surface party was camped just north of Abu Hadriya, so Steineke sent me there for awhile. Jerry Harris was in charge, and he had an assistant, Tom Barger. They were camped near a dry lake area — called a *sabka* — had laid out a base line and were making astronomical observations on it to obtain their geodetic location. Bill Seale, a middle-aged civil engineer, was camped with them. Seale was in charge of setting up a system of bench marks and geodetic monuments in the form of squares or quadrilaterals. He had a tide gauge on the coast, near the little fishing village of Manifa, and was carrying elevations from mean average sea level. This system of survey points he was setting up was to be the land net to which all our geological and geophysical work would be tied. With no network of townships, ranges, and sections such as we have in the United States, they were starting from scratch in Saudi Arabia. No land surveys had ever been made.

Bill Seale had a Heinrich Wild Swiss-made transit he had brought with him from Mexico. He had been there working in Tampico when the Mexicans moved in and expropriated everything. He said he had picked up this transit and his suitcase and made it out to a Company-owned ship in the harbor. He had lost everything else he owned.

Seale did most of his surveying work at night. He would set up his transit at one corner of the quadrilaterals, which were about ten miles on a side, and put Coleman gasoline lanterns on the other three corners. Then he would measure the horizontal angles very carefully between the three lights. From this he could tie his work into the measured baseline and carry his longitude and latitude from quadrilateral to quadrilateral. This survey went from east to west and ultimately covered the whole province of Al-Hasa. Observations were made at night to avoid the intense distortion of the heat waves during the daylight. As soon as the sun came up, the waves made everything viewed through the telescope appear to dance and gyrate. Also, at night we could shoot the light on the rig at Abu Hadriya. At one location we could actually see the light on the rig at Burgan, Kuwait, where Gulf was drilling what turned out to be the discovery well on the giant Burgan field.

Jerry Harris had been in Arabia for several years and Tom Barger for about a year. Both had picked up a lot of Arabic. They showed me the general theory of verb and noun formation so I could start understanding some of the language. It was rather fun.

While I was camped at Abu Hadriya with Jerry and Tom, I was impressed with how much letter writing Jerry did. Tom told me the letters all went to a nurse at the British Hospital in Bahrain. Her name was Molly Brogan. Tom and I kidded Jerry some about his being sweet on Molly, but I could see Jerry was deadly serious about her.

Later, when I was in the hospital, I got a letter from Jerry every week. At first he didn't inquire about Molly, but when I got to know her better, I kept Jerry posted on her activities.

Molly was a lovely girl — big brown eyes, dark brown hair, and just a slight touch of Irish in her English accent. After the night she stayed with me, keeping me alive through the terrible heart palpitations I had with no doctors available, we became close friends. So I didn't hesitate to question her about the diamond ring she was wearing. She had become engaged to the drilling superintendent on Bahrain, she told me, an older man and a widower.

I knew this was going to break Jerry's heart, so I told her so. Apparently she was unaware that Jerry was in love with her, so I wrote to him, telling him he had better come to see Molly before it was too late. He did, and Molly's diamond was replaced by Jerry's ring. They were married shortly after I left Arabia, and I got many cards and letters from them. They called me "Cupid."

Within three years, however, Molly came down with rheumatic fever in California during the war and died. Her younger sister came from Ireland to take care of her during the long illness. A year later she married Jerry herself, and they had a long and happy married life.

Each camp had a group of soldiers attached to it for protection from the Bedouin, who were pretty much lawless savages. They were armed with World War I Enfields in poor condition. I always wondered just whose side these soldiers would be on in case of an attack. They called themselves *oskaries*, Arabic for soldiers.

Harris and Barger had one man, Khamise, who was most valuable to them, for he was a guide and knew the country very well. They were doing very rapid mapping over long distances and moved the camp every week or so. They had a Ford sedan with large $11:00 \times 16$ tires, and their speedometer and odometer were in kilometers. They were using a scale of $1:1,000,000$ and measured most of their distances to outcrops with Brunton compass and car odometer. Since nearly flat limestone and sandstone outcrops occurred every two or three miles, this method sufficed for rapid reconnaissance. These outcrops were usually three to fifty feet high, and Khamise seemed to know them all. Many had small rock monuments on them called *rijms* in Arabic. Khamise insisted on climbing to the top of each one and looking ahead to the next one. Then we would sight it in with the compass, plot this bearing on the map, and drive to it to measure the distance, then plot the geologic data on the map.

One day we decided to drive to the coast, about thirty miles away, to try to find a place to measure a type section of the Hadrukh formation, which covered most of this part of the country. We drove up to a little tidal inlet and, since the day was hot, we decided to go swimming. Jerry said, "Let's walk over to that little rise and look down into the water first." We did and, while we were watching, a ten-foot shark came slithering out of the dark water and headed out to sea. That was bad enough, but we watched a little longer and saw a huge stingray swimming around in the deeper water. We didn't go swimming!

There was a little village on the inlet with fewer than 100 people, called Safaniya. One of the world's largest offshore oil fields now lies out in the Gulf immediately to the east — its name, Safaniya. Some of the wells are quite near the little inlet where we saw the shark.

One night the soldiers invited Jerry, Tom, and me down to their camp for *gahwa*, Arab coffee. We put on our Arab headdresses — I had bought one in the village of Jubail — and walked over to their camp, which was always placed some distance from our tents, for they banged on tin pans and sang and yelled half the night. I remember how bright the stars were in a dark purple sky as we walked to their camp. The North Star was barely visible above the horizon to the north, and Orion and Sirius were so bright they looked like big lanterns. Betelgeuse, the great red star near Orion, was one of the stars we had astronomical tables for, so we used it in making our observations for longitude and latitude.

We were greeted by the soldiers, and they had their fire built. Now the ritual of coffeemaking begins. First, they roast the coffee beans and grind them up with some cardamom seed. Then they put the coarse-ground particles in the long-necked, Arabian-type coffee pot, called a *nol*. After the water has boiled a while, they bring out small porcelain cups, not much bigger than a thimble. One by one, each guest is handed a cup. Each cup is then filled from the *nol*, starting with the cup near the spout of the pot. The pourer then extends his arms so the small cup precedes the arched trajectory of the stream coming from the long, narrow spout. This small stream is then caught in the cup with a great flourish. This maneuver is a mark of skill and is supposed to be an indication of prowess and hospitality.

The odor of the cardamom drowns the coffee smell. It is almost medicinal in character. But drunk very hot in tiny sips, the *gahwa* is quite delicious. As each cup is emptied, it is refilled with the same flourish. Jerry had warned me that we should drink three cups but no more. If a fourth is offered, one refuses politely by a side-to-side shaking motion of the cup. The server then takes the cup from you. Next comes the tea, or *chi* (rhymes with sky), served in small stein-like glasses with handles on the side, syrupy with sugar and very sweet.

After some talk, the ceremony — which is what it really is — is over, and the incense is brought, little wood pods of myrrh and frankincense placed on hot coals in the serving receptacles, where they put out much smoke. The incense receptacle is a small metal pot with the sides cut out and is swung on a wire handle of some kind. The server swings the incense just below your chin, and etiquette requires you to fluff out your headdress partially around the receptacle and sniff the smoke. This is a head-clearing exercise, since the incense smoke penetrates your nose and sinuses. When all have partaken of the incense smoke, everyone stands and it is time to go. Hands are shaken, and one says *"Fi Iman Illah"* — "Go in the care of Allah." Then back out into the dark purple night and to your own tent and bed. You wonder what these people, who have lived this life for the last 1,000 years or more, are thinking. In the late thirties were we seeing the last of it?

On our day off, which is Friday, the Muslim Sabbath, rather than Sunday, Harris, Barger, and some fellows from the nearby seismograph camp took me to see the ruined village of Sarrar. Khamise, our Arab guide, said it had been destroyed by ibn-Saud during his conquest of Arabia during the early 1920's.

It was difficult to separate fact from fiction on these things, but Khamise's story was that the local Beni Hajar tribe opposed ibn-Saud's conquest, so he leveled their village and banished the tribe from living here forever. The village was mostly a collection of mud huts with one mosque, protected by a small fort on a mesa overlooking the town. The fort was ancient. Khamise said it was built in "the days of ignorance"; that is, before Muhammad, so it was probably at least 1,200 years old. It had several water wells bored down through the bedrock. None appeared to have water in them, for we dropped stones and timed their striking the bottom. One well was at least 150 feet deep, or more; possibly the water table was higher when the well was dug, or the well was deeper and had caved in. The deep furrows where ropes were used to haul goatskin bags of water to the surface testified that water was there at one time.

Very little archeological work had been done in this whole area. Ancient burial grounds were evident in many places, and bits of glass, metal, and other artifacts were strewn about. I hoped that someday detailed studies would be made. During the Pleistocene, when the area was a grassland with live streams, there must have been a human population that would have left much evidence of its culture.

Steineke and Dick Bramkamp, chief paleontologist, stopped by the camp, and I rode back to Dhahran with them. Steineke wanted me to help assemble materials for the two seismograph parties and the surface geological party. Soon there would be another surface party, he told me, and Harris and Barger would each be running parties of their own. This gave me an opportunity to study in detail the structure maps of the Dammam Dome and the Abu Hadriya Dome. I made pantograph copies of these two structures to be used as plane table sheets in locating our gravity stations.

It was the last of November 1938, and I came down with a bad cold and very sore throat. The infirmary at Dhahran suggested I go to the hospital at Bahrain for a few days, which I did. They treated me with sulfa pills, and I felt better. On the way back to Dhahran on the launch on a beautiful sunny day, I lay down in the sun and went to sleep. When I woke up, I had a very sort throat again. I treated the throat as best I could, but when I started running a temperature, they sent me back to the hospital at Bahrain. There my throat got worse, and then one night I developed what I thought was a charley horse in my right knee. The nurse put a mustard poultice on it. Soon I developed a very sore elbow. Then the other knee and then the other elbow went stiff. I was alarmed! So were the doctors!

They took blood samples and tested me for Malta fever. After about a week, they told me I had rheumatic fever. From early

December until Christmastime I got weaker and weaker, until I couldn't turn over in bed without help. Then came the visit from the Greek Orthodox priest and the induced fever treatment I have described.

By the middle of January, I was getting stronger. The doctors suspected extensive heart damage, so they were very slow in letting me get up and around. In early February they finally let me go back to Dhahran.

CHAPTER 9

SURVIVAL IN THE SAND DUNES

In February of 1939 the Mott-Smith gravity meter crew arrived. Alex Peale, a Natchez, Mississippi, native with a degree in electrical engineering, was party chief. Ivan Scherb, a Cal Tech graduate, was assistant, and Stan Head was the party roustabout.

I was only generally familiar with the Mott-Smith meter, which is what Neil Smith's parties in Mississippi had used. It was a large metal box about two feet square and two and a half feet high. Its workings were a quartz pendulum kept at constant temperature by a circulating water bath. The key to its accuracy was a system of thermostats accurate to 1/1000th of a degree Fahrenheit. This temperature control was, of course, very delicate, and the instrument had to be handled with great care as a bump or drop of a few inches could damage it greatly. The meter was mounted in the back of a Marmon Harrington Ford four-wheel drive panel truck. A tripod was lowered through the truck's floor onto the ground, then the meter was set on the tripod, leveled, and read.

The Mott-Smith meter was supposed to be accurate to one tenth of a miligal, or about one-millionth of the total pull of gravity, and was of course affected by the daily tidal effects of the moon and minor earth tremors. Because of the moon or diurnal cycle, a constant change or drift in readings on the meter would occur while it was set up on a station. Consequently, the gravity meter crew had to check back to a base station at least every one to two hours to get a reading to correct for this drift. Speed of operation was necessary for accurate results. Each night the meter had to be taken back to its base camp to have its batteries recharged so constant current would be fed to the delicate thermal system. Flat tires and getting stuck in the sand were minor tragedies, for a whole day's work would be destroyed if the check-back to base station was delayed.

The surveyors had also arrived. Von Hornlein, a former Soil Conservation Service engineer from the Coachella Valley in California, was the only one of them with plane table experience. Hugh Caldwell and Red Nevins from Willows, California, were trainees at running dumpy levels.

We started our shakedown operations on a survey of the Dammam Dome. The surveyors got their Marmon Harrington four-wheel-drive Ford station wagons, with wooden bodies, operating. We put our instruments in adjustment after their long trip overseas. In that era the plane table was one of the surveyor's and geologist's most important instruments. I had hand-carried the plane table alidade, a Gurley, from Houston to Dhahran when I came. A large supply of lath and black and orange flagging cloth for marking our stations arrived as well.

I was to lay out the triangulation stations; the gravity meter would follow me, and the surveyor would follow it. There were some established elevation bench marks around the field, so we had that advantage on the first survey. Putting out a lath with a flag on it to mark a triangulation station proved futile, however. Bedouin camped nearby watched our daily progress and, as fast as I drove a lath and put a piece of black cloth on it, an Arab would come along and carry it back to camp. Later at Ma'gala we solved this problem using very primitive methods.

Around the oil field the roads were not sufficient to put all our gravity stations on their proper mile spacing. This meant driving cross-country trying to leave a trail the meter crew and surveyor could follow. Steineke suggested we get a bulldozer from the production department to build a trail, but we would have had to have four or five to keep up the proper speed. I came up with the idea of dragging a heavy log chain while I made the trail and then driving in a tight circle several times around the gravity station. The deep tire tracks in a circular pattern were easy to see. This enabled the other crews to follow a trail they knew marked a gravity survey and then to find the gravity station by the car tracks. I made a sketch each day of the stations I had laid out and gave it to the gravity crew and surveyors. By the time I made a track, the gravity meter truck followed that track, the plane table man followed it, and finally the level crew came along, we had a pretty well-marked trail.

As we calculated the results of the gravity survey on Dammam Dome, we were elated. A large positive gravity anomaly, virtually the same size and shape as the structure contours, evolved. And in the top of the Dome was an area of less gravity or a negative anomaly. This had to be the salt plug Max Steineke had predicted for the structure. The wells just had not been drilled deep enough to encounter it. It looked like the gravity meter was a valid reconnaissance exploration tool in this part of Saudi Arabia.

Our next trial run was on the Abu Hadriya Dome. We moved up there and stayed in the drilling camp. We still had not received our field equipment — kitchen, tents, etc. We started work on Abu Hadriya. The well was still drilling, so we used the rig as a triangulation point, and the various seismograph roads built by Dick Kerr's party helped us get around the area. The prevailing northerly wind, or *shimal*, had built a vast area of north–south sand ridges, partially brush-covered, called *dikaka*. Travel was easy when we went *with* the grain of the ridges but very rough across the grain. When we used the seismograph roads, which cut across the grain, our progress was greatly speeded up.

Work went faster here than at Dammam. The results, however, were entirely different. There was no strong positive gravity anomaly here; a general nosing of the contours over the crest of the Dome was evident, however. Gravity work in the United States had been pretty well relegated to salt dome areas until now, and geophysicists were just beginning to apply the concept of a regional gravity gradient which would be so large that local gravity anomalies would be masked by it. Alex Peale and I thought this was the case at Abu Hadriya, so we asked Steineke if we could cover an area considerably larger than Abu Hadriya Dome to try to determine the regional gradient. Use of the second derivative of gravity and computer models were a long way in the future. We covered an area more than twice the size of Abu Hadriya Dome. Our coverage was large enough to indicate a regional gravity gradient dipping off to the southeast. Alex and I applied this gradient graphically to our gravity values and recontoured the resulting figures. The new contours revealed a strong positive gravity anomaly along the top of Abu Hadriya Dome. Computers do the same thing now, and it is called modeling, but our crude early work was successful in delineating this low-relief anticlinal structure. It looked like gravity work could be applied to this type of broad low-relief structure with significant results. (Through mid-1982, the last year for which production figures are available, Abu Hadriya had produced more than 520 million barrels of oil.) Max Steineke and Dick Kerr were enthusiastic. Now they had another area they wanted us to try gravity work on, but not until my crew had a weekend off to celebrate Ramadan.

Ramadan is the most important religious observance in the Muslim world. The celebration follows a month-long fast in which no food or drink may be taken during the daylight hours. The Shi'ites, who were in the majority on Bahrain Island, celebrated Ramadan — or Muharram, as they called it, for the first month of the Muslim calendar — with a good deal more gusto than the conservative Sunni Wahabis or Sunnis in Saudi Arabia.

The crew wanted to take their weekend in Bahrain to see the Muharram spectacle. The Company ran a boat nearly every day from Al-Khubar on the mainland to Al-Manamah on Bahrain Island, and it was loaded this time. Many of the production, accounting, and pipeline people were on their way to Bahrain for the same purpose.

My crew filled two taxicabs at Al-Manamah, and we drove out to the Company rest house near the center of the Island. On the way we passed the famous Bahrain laundry, a freshwater pool with a lot of flat rocks sticking out of the water. Some Arab women were there washing clothes, which consisted of soaking the item for a while in the water, then beating it against the flat rocks to get the dirt out. Oldtimers said the pool bottom was covered with buttons. Cotton fabrics held up remarkably well with this treatment, and most of the Island's clothes were washed here.

The next morning we all trooped back to Al-Manamah to the square where the Ramadan exercises would be held. The Company had put up some bleachers for us to get a better view, where we waited and waited for the affair to begin. Finally, after a contingent of soldiers who were there to preserve order left, we discovered that the parade had been canceled. We didn't know why, because there had never been a problem before now.

Stan Head, who was on the Mott-Smith meter crew, had just bought a new camera and was determined to get some pictures. He said, "Let's walk around town and see if they aren't holding it somewhere else."

I agreed, so we set out on foot. In a little while I thought I heard something, so I stopped and listened. There was a barely audible noise, like someone thumping a watermelon, followed by a moaning sound. We headed for the noise.

We rounded a corner in the extremely narrow street and saw throngs of women on the rooftops of the single-story, flat-roofed stucco buildings. The street was too narrow for a car to pass.

It was then that we saw what was making the drum-like noise. It was a company of "chest thumpers," as they were called. There must have been twenty or thirty young men, stripped to the waist, marching in a sort of cadence. Periodically, on signal or by rhythm, they would stop and beat their chests in unison or sometimes one at a time. It was an eerie sound and, as we listened, it was almost nauseating to hear.

We flattened ourselves against the wall and let them go by. By the time Stan had his camera ready, they were past us. He could get only a shot of their backs. As he took the pictures, I heard a hissing noise; it came from a group of women on the roof above. They were expressing their displeasure at his taking photographs. Before I could say anything to Stan, he had stepped out into the street again and was halfway to a sharp bend. He could hear something coming and this time was ready with his camera.

At that moment about fifteen men, stripped to the waist and carrying large swords, rounded the corner. They were covered with blood from cuts high on their foreheads. These were the "head cutters" we had heard about. They were chanting and swinging the swords up to their heads, drawing blood almost every time. Their eyes were glazed, and I smelled trouble. It arrived shortly. They took one look at Stan and his big German camera with the telescopic lens and started to run toward us. They quit chanting and began to scream and swing their swords wildly.

We turned and ran the other way with the maniacs right behind us. The chest thumpers had stopped and turned around to look at us, so I didn't think we should try to go through them. Luckily, a small alley opened into the street from our left. It was full of women, some standing on benches or small bleachers, making their moaning sound. I dodged in behind them, and Stan hit the dirt. I was wearing an Arab headdress (*gutra* and *agal*) and, with my black beard, I looked like an Arab from the chin up. I stood absolutely still and waited. I wanted to be on my feet.

The sword cutters stopped at the alley and looked in. After what seemed like an eternity, they moved on. I was afraid one of the women would give us away, but they didn't. I stood still, and Stan got up. I noticed he had put his big lens away. About that time, another group, the "chain beaters," came along. They carried pieces of tire chain and beat themselves over the back, bringing blood to the surface.

When we could relax a little, I leaned over to Stan and said, "We just about became an international incident." Stan didn't take any more pictures that day. Later we found out that a few years earlier an Englishman had been killed trying to photograph the same spectacle. After thirty days of fasting, I can understand the dazed looks and glassy eyes of the sword cutters. Besides, they were probably in shock from their wounds and well might have cut us up if we hadn't given them the slip. It was a relief to get back to work.

Tom Barger and Ernie Berg, his assistant, were in the process of making a surface structure contour map of a very large anticline about 100 miles west of Abu Hadriya at an area called Ma'gala. The structure was a long north–south anticline which showed up very well in the Eocene limestone outcrops. Steineke had already recommended that the structure be drilled, but he thought it would be helpful to have a gravity survey.

By this time all our field equipment had arrived. Our white tents, lined with blue cloth to control flies, and a large mess tent had been made by local tentmakers. We loaded all the equipment, together with barrels of water and gasoline, on a flatbed truck and headed out from Dhahran with the entourage. It had rained recently, and all the low places were covered with water. In a few weeks grass and flowers would abound where this water had been.

We pitched our camp near Barger's. Our soldiers joined Barger's soldiers, but our cooks and houseboys had their own camp. By this time I had acquired a camp boss, a young fellow from the San Francisco area named Burt Nelson. He was a delightful character who kept our tents and kitchen facilities in great shape.

We were quite an operation. Each surveyor had an Arab rodman and a soldier who accompanied him. Alex Peale had to take a soldier with him in his meter truck. Ivan Scherb, Peale's assistant, couldn't stand the smell of the soldier, as he bathed only in sand, and refused to go into the field part of the time. The headman of my soldiers was called the Emir, and he insisted on riding with me every day. I loaded him in the back seat with his rifle and bandolier of ammunition. He smelled too. I did make him carry his own drinking water in a goatskin bag, which we tied onto the front fender of the station wagon.

Ma'gala was a watering spot on the main caravan trail from Jubail on the east coast to Riyadh, Mecca, and Jidda on the west coast. Nearly every day or two a party of Bedouin or cameleers carrying freight would pass by our camp. With small groves of acacia trees, it was an attractive place.

The water holes, called *dahals*, were actually sinkholes in the Eocene limestone that were so deep they contained water in their bottoms. An agile Bedouin would climb down into the sinkhole, and the others would lower their goatskin bags or *gurbas* to him on a rope. He would fill the *gurba*, tie the bag's neck shut, and it would be pulled up and loaded on a camel or donkey. After the big rainstorm, there were many small ponds of water, and the Bedouin would fill their bags from them — no matter that their donkeys and camels had walked out into the water and relieved themselves there. They just went ahead and filled their water bags anyway! In a few days these ponds would really stink, but the Bedouin didn't seem to mind. These sinkholes were numerous and quite a hazard if one drove at night. One of the Arab drivers drove off into one shortly after we left the area. Luckily he wasn't killed.

Barger and Berg had laid out a carefully measured two-mile baseline and had taken astronomical observations to get their longitude and latitude. They had a chronometer which they checked almost every night by a radio signal from French Indochina (now Vietnam). They kept it in a heavily insulated wooden case, and its accuracy determined the exactness of our astronomical calculations of our location on the ground.

Each night at 8:00 PM we made radio contact with the Company's shortwave radio station in Dhahran. This was a must. Roving bands of Bedouin who were still hostile to ibn-Saud would not think twice about cutting a few Christian throats. Company officials were very concerned about this possibility and insisted on being in constant radio contact with us.

While putting out gravity stations late one afternoon, I drove over a giant-sized sand dune and barged right into the middle of a group of Arabs, all armed and riding camels. I was quite proud of my Emir. He grabbed his rifle and threw in a shell, saying, "MY friends!" I didn't know what he meant, but we were greatly outnumbered, so I said, "*Yawash*" — "Take it easy!" It was obvious he thought they were raiders of some sort. I tried my feeble Arabic on them, and they said they were a hunting party out from Riyadh. They were fairly affluent, judging by their camels and gear, and politely asked if there had been any rain. I told them not recently and then said "*Fi Iman Illah*" — "Go in the care of Allah" — and drove off. I always felt they were a hunting party, but I may have been wrong.

One day a camel caravan came through that included a group of women. They were riding camels, and each had a small canopy built over the saddle, which we had not seen before, to protect her from the sun. One woman had a little rope tied to her camel's neck and was guiding him along the trail by neck-reining him. All of a sudden something scared the camel — I didn't know what — and he ran away with her. A camel-mounted Bedouin chased them and finally headed off the runaway. When he caught the errant camel, he made it kneel down and then took a stick and energetically beat it over its head. The woman was in tears. We didn't approach but watched the affair from a respectable distance. These caravan people were not a bit friendly.

Another day I came onto a small caravan. The camel had straw bags on each side, like panniers on a packsaddle. I stopped, and the cameleer rode up to the car. I could see a young boy, possibly ten years old, in one of the bags. I could tell at a glance he was terribly sick. The cameleer asked for water. We were some distance from the water hole, so I gave him all I had in the goatskin *gurbas* on the fender. It was the first time I had ever seen an Arab act grateful for anything. That night my Emir of soldiers told all the people in camp about my giving the Bedouin water. I often wondered what happened to the boy. He surely must have died soon afterward.

My plane table man, Von Hornlein, had a similar experience. After giving a Bedouin some water, he had his rodman-interpreter ask if the man weren't going to thank him. The Bedouin responded, "I thank Allah for the water." Von Hornlein said, "Ask Allah for water the next time you need some," and then drove off.

One day Red Nevins's rodman saw a little cottontail rabbit and caught it. He brought it into camp that evening and wanted to cook and eat it, but the cook said, "Let's cook it tomorrow." The problem arose as to how to keep the rabbit from running away during the night. Red's soldier said, "I'll show you how to keep him from running away." He picked up the rabbit, promptly broke both hind legs with his hands, and handed it back to the rodman, saying, "He won't run away now." It turned my stomach.

A few days later my Emir saw a huge, fat lizard called a *thub*. The lizard ran into a shallow hole, and the Emir reached in and pulled it out. The *thub* was about a foot and a half long and weighed ten or fifteen pounds, with a square head and jaw and a short, corrugated tail. The Emir wanted to take it back to camp to eat. I had visions of the big lizard getting loose in the station wagon and taking off my hand. But the Emir was resourceful. He took a piece of lath and put it crosswise in the lizard's mouth. Then he took two nails and drove them through the upper jaw, through the lath, and through the lower jaw. He tied a rope around the lizard's head and threw him in the back of the station wagon. The thing thrashed around a little but made no trouble. The Emir had him for supper that night.

It was always interesting to see the actions of the Arabs when they had the good fortune to get a rabbit or a gazelle to supplement their food supply. They would stand for a moment with clasped hands and turn from one side to the other, giving thanks to the two protecting spirits they believed accompanied them everywhere. They have a real, intense belief in the supernatural, and it extends from the two protecting spirits to the dreaded *jinn* which inhabit caves, rocks, ruins, the Persian Gulf waters, etc. Their fear of the *jinn* is very acute.

One day a small group of hunters riding long, lean racing camels stopped for the night at Ma'gala. They were hunting with falcons and carried their birds on their arms, which were protected from the birds' talons by thick leather sleeves. They made camp, and each had a mount for his bird, a small post driven in the ground with a crosspiece about a foot long nailed on top. The falcons were hooded most of the time to keep them docile; the hood was a small, thin leather pouch which fastened around the bird's neck with a leather thong.

None of us had ever seen a falcon perform, so the next morning the hunters showed them off for us. They started with a training session, an exercise in getting the falcon to attack a bird's wing tied to the end of a long string. The falconer would take the hood off his falcon and let the bird watch from its perch. A man would swing the wing on the string around his head until he got it circling at a fifteen- or twenty-foot radius; then he would call to the falcon to attack. The bird would leave the perch, fly over the swinging wing, and then attack with its talons, bringing the wing to the ground. If the falcon was mature or well trained, it would be free to fly to get the wing and would stay with the wing, holding it in a talon, until the trainer took it. If the bird was young and still being trained, it would have a string tied to one leg so it couldn't fly away.

We went out a few miles from camp to a brushy spot, and the hunters showed us how the falcons worked. They took off the hood of a well-trained bird and let him look the brushy patch over carefully. The trainer could tell when the falcon had spotted something. At that time he spoke to the bird and half-tossed him into the air. The falcon circled slowly out over the brushy patch and suddenly swooped very fast toward the ground with his talons outstretched.

We walked over to see what the bird had caught. It was a large grouse-like bird called a bustard, about the size of a male Chinese pheasant. It was dull grey in color and made quite good eating, although the meat was darker than pheasant — more like sage hen, but not with such a strong odor.

The falconers hunted around the area for a day or so and then left just at daylight one morning. The next day one of the soldiers out with a surveying crew spotted an escaped falcon that still had a piece of string around its leg. The string was tangled in the brush, so the soldier was able to catch the young bird. He made a perch for it in camp and fixed up a makeshift hood.

Stan Head, the gravity meter handyman, had watched the falconry with more than average interest. He managed to buy the bird from the soldier and started to train it to work. The bird had to have a name, and one of the Arab rodmen told Stan a common name for falcons was "Ginam." So for the next few weeks, Stan worked with the bird every evening, repeating "Ginam, Ginam" over and over, until we all got tired of hearing the word. And the bird never did learn a darn thing. Stan couldn't get it to chase and catch a bird's wing on a string. He couldn't get it to fly back to his arm, even though he enticed it a hundred times with morsels of meat. All it would do was sit and stare and turn its head from side to side with a vacant, beady look in its eyes. Stan finally got disgusted and gave the bird to a family of Bedouin who passed. We never knew whether they trained it to hunt or ate it!

Tom Barger had done an excellent job getting our astronomical position and had set out a lot of stone monuments, which the Arabs loved to build, sort of like the sheepherders in the United States. The Arabs called these stone piles *rijms*. We used Barger's plane table data and started our gravity survey right over the top of his surface work.

I have mentioned the cloth we used for flagging material to make our triangulation stations. A black two-foot by two-foot flag waving in the wind from the top of a four- or five-foot lath or pole showed up very well from a distance. Unfortunately, the Bedouin women loved the cloth so much that they stole it almost as soon as we put it up. One day I put up a flag on an important triangulation point and then drove a mile or so away to set up my plane table. As I focused the instrument on the flag, I was just in time to see a black-clad Bedouin woman run over to the flag, tear it down, and run back to the camp nearby. Then a boy came and took the lath away.

Von Hornlein was having the same trouble, so we talked to Tom Barger about it. We went down to the soldiers' camp and told them we wanted them to do something about it. They did. The next morning, Von Hornlein loaded the Emir and several of his soldiers in his station wagon, and they drove out to the Bedouin camp.

The Emir and his soldiers went into the camp, and we watched from a distance. The soldiers picked out the biggest and strongest Bedouin they could see and held him while they beat him with their walking sticks. They didn't really hurt him, but he thought they were going to. When we got back to our camp, I asked the Emir how he knew that man was the guilty party. He said he didn't know and didn't care, but there would not be any more stealing of our flags. The man who was beaten would see to it. They didn't steal any more flags. It was certainly a practical way of stopping the thieving, even if not a very judicious one.

When we started to contour up our gravity data, the Ma'gala anticline appeared to be a long north–south gravity high with two separate closures. Tom's work showed only one closure. He and I drove out on the south end of the anticline one day, and there in the bottom of a little draw was his marker bed, a brown siliceous limestone. When he ran elevations on it, he got two separate closures, as we had. This gave me a pretty good feeling about how accurately the gravity work reflected the surface work. But that feeling didn't last long. We discovered that the gravity structure, while being almost a mirror image of the surface structural contours, was offset about four miles to the east. This really baffled us all, and the question was never resolved while I was in Arabia. The Company did drill a well on the Ma'gala surface structure anticline during the next year, and it was dry. I always wondered if the subsurface structural relations might not have been more complicated than I realized and the well drilled in the wrong place. World War II began about that time, and after the war the great emphasis for exploration was south and west of Dhahran.

Our equipment was the best money could buy, but the harsh conditions caused many breakdowns. Among the worst were the small light plants—electric generators run by small gasoline engines. Homelite generators were standard equipment, but about half the time they didn't work. This was particularly important, because we used them to power our nightly radio contact with headquarters at Jebel Dhahran.

Our automobiles were Ford station wagons with Marmon Harrington four-wheel drives, but the fuel pumps would go out constantly. We all carried spare pumps and tools to replace them. One day I went out with Alex Peale, driving his Ford panel wagon that contained the gravity meter. We were doing some spot checking about forty miles south of camp on some old base stations he had previously run. The fuel pump went out. I replaced it with a new one. Within an hour, it too went out. We had another spare. It lasted two hours. There we were, stranded thirty miles from camp. It was either devise something or wait for rescue — maybe the next day.

Alex had a big metal map tube about three inches in diameter and three feet long. He had a small rubber hose he used to put distilled water in the meter's storage batteries. I cut a small hole in the bottom of the map tube, put the hose up through it, and hooked the other end to the carburetor. Then we drained some gas and filled the map tube. Alex sat in the passenger side of the truck and controlled the flow of gas into the carburetor by pinching the rubber hose with his fingers. We made it back to camp in good shape!

One afternoon I was returning to the camp at Ma'gala from laying out gravity stations to the north of the anticline. As I topped a little rise, I noticed a dust cloud several miles to the south. I drove up on a high place and got out my telescopic alidade. Using the hood of the car for a rest, I focused on the dust and was amazed to see at least a dozen automobiles zigzagging across the gravel terrain. They seemed to be going in the same general direction — that is, toward the camp — but none was following the other. They looked remarkably like a bunch of insects darting in and out, each putting up a dust cloud.

I hurried into camp and found Tom Barger. It was the party of Sheikh Abdullah Sulaiman, and his advance car had already arrived. We knew we would have to entertain him, so we hurriedly set up extra tables and chairs in the mess tent and got out glasses and cups to serve cold fruit juice and American coffee.

Sulaiman's black sedan came barreling up and slammed on its brakes. He got out, and we greeted him. Sulaiman was Finance Minister for the Saudi government and a very important man in the country. He was a small man with coal-black hair and the Prophet's pointed beard. His sharp hooked nose set him out as a classic Arab type. He told us, through his interpreter, that he was on his way to Dhahran and the port of Ras at-Tannurah to celebrate the completion of oil-loading facilities there. A three-day celebration was being held, to culminate with an oil tanker being loaded on May 1, 1939. We served him the fruit juice and coffee, and then the sheikh was on his way. He was trying to get to Jubail by dark, but some of his party camped in our area.

I was surprised to see an American, Bill Lenahan, and his wife traveling in the party. They were both dressed in Arab clothes, and she looked tired and sick. Bill confided that she needed to go to the toilet desperately. Since we only had a truck, and people were milling around it all the time, we fixed up a place for her in one of our sleeping tents. Afterward, she looked eternally grateful. It must have been a terrible ordeal to travel over a rough road and not be able to relieve oneself all day. I really admired her for venturing out on that trip.

Lenahan was CASOC's representative in Jidda. He was duty-bound to accompany Sulaiman, the principal figure in the Saudi Arabian government with whom the Company needed to keep a close relationship. I asked Bill why the party's cars didn't all just get on the trail south of the camp and follow it like a road or highway. He replied, "Each driver feels he would lose face if he followed another car, so they avoid it. Instead, they make their own trails." This accounted for the wild, erratic scene I had witnessed earlier.

The next morning, Barger told us he had been warned that King ibn-Saud would be coming to our camp soon. His party got there by early afternoon the next day. I kept all the field parties in, and we all put on our Arab headdresses. We avoided wearing hats because the Arabs believed Muhammad the Prophet had said any-one wearing a hat didn't want Allah to look into his eyes because he was not an honest man.

We cleaned off our table, washed our dirty glasses and cups from the day before, and prepared to serve cold drinks again. Ibn-Saud had a big black Cadillac sedan, and he was accompanied by his eldest son, Crown Prince Saud. Barger and I greeted them, and we used the young rodman working for Von Hornlein as interpreter. Barger was a little reticent in talking to Saud, because when talking to a king one is supposed to use the plural second-person verbs not normally used in conversation.

The young rodman was doing fine, I thought, as he spoke to the king. He was facing Barger and me to see what we said and then turning to repeat it to the king. Gradually he eased his position so his back was partially toward Prince Saud and his father. The prince reached out, took hold of the young man, and spun him around so he was facing the king. The young man had momentarily forgotten that one never turns his back on the king, and he looked terrified when he was corrected.

Prince Saud and his father were both big men — more than six feet tall and heavily built. Ibn-Saud probably weighed 275 pounds and the prince more than 200 pounds. They bore themselves like kings, and you could see how the Saud family had been able to take over Arabia by personal force of arms. As a young man conquering the country, ibn-Saud was supposed to have cut off many a man's head with a broadsword he carried.

Alex Peale had parked the gravity meter truck outside the mess tent, and ibn-Saud asked what it was. Barger gave him an explana-tion, and Saud wanted to see the instrument. Peale had it set up on the tripod, and there wasn't a lot of space between it and the inside of the truck. Big as he was, Saud climbed up into the truck and sat in the operator's seat. Prince Saud was standing next to me, and I didn't know he spoke any English until he said, "The old man is having a hard time getting in the truck." I didn't know whether to laugh or not, so I just said, "Yes, he is!"

You could see the native curiosity these people had for things scientific, particularly those in high government positions; the average Bedouin didn't seem to care. Fifty years and nearly three generations later, this curiosity has resulted in the establishment of a petroleum university now turning out technicians capable of running the country's petroleum industry. Ibn-Saud and company didn't stay long. They too were heading for Ras at-Tannurah. Before they left, however, some of the better-educated Arabs asked Saud for permission to see our water filtering "system." These fellows were not at all impressed with our surveying instruments or the gravity meter but were fascinated with a simple device I had built one day.

The water the Arabs used came from remnants of the rain-filled ponds and the sinkhole wells. It was usually terribly muddy and foul-smelling. I cut the top out of a fifty-gallon metal drum and installed a faucet on its bottom. I put in a layer of charcoal from the campfires and found some clean, well-sorted sand. Then I added a layer of cloth flagging to the drum and alternated layers of sand, charcoal, and more flagging. It was just a big filter. When they poured in the muddy, smelly water and let it sit awhile, clear, clean-looking water came out the spigot. They couldn't believe their eyes. Sahib Walton had created a miracle! Unfortunately, by the time Saud saw the filter, it had been used so much it didn't clean the water as well as it had at first, but he was interested in my little gadget.

That night, after the king's party had left, Von Hornlein came to my tent about midnight and told me we had trouble. His young rodman, the one who had acted as our interpreter with the king, had staggered to Von Hornlein's tent in a state of collapse. He had been stripped to the waist, and his back looked like he had been clawed by a lion from his neck to his buttocks. He was delirious and feverish. We put cold water packs on his back and gave him some aspirin, and he told us what had happened.

The other rodmen and workmen were angry with him because he had been able to talk to the king, and they had held a sort of kangaroo court. They were smoking hashish and beating pans and chanting and decided to teach the boy a lesson for being too smart. They cut a branch from an acacia tree, leaving a knot with a short point or hook on the large end. Then they had beaten him, and with each stroke the hook had cut a swath on his back. It must have been terribly painful.

I feared infection, because any of us who got the slightest scratch immediately had swelling and pus. Frequently so-called "blood poisoning" resulted as a purple welt appeared higher on the limb. We always used hot water with blue vitriol tablets as a disinfectant to soak our infected cuts, but his scratches were too big for that.

Von Hornlein volunteered to drive the boy to Dhahran to be treated in the infirmary. He drove all night, and the boy was patched up without getting infected. In a few days they returned to camp. Although at the time the boy had been highly outraged by his treatment, he came back and took up his work as if nothing had happened. Man's inhumanity to man is always hard to understand. Equally difficult to comprehend is man's reaction to these acts.

A similar case was an incident with the truck drivers at Dhahran. Bill Eltiste, superintendent of transportation, wasn't satisfied with the way the Arab drivers were handling and maintaining their big, expensive Kenworth trucks. He offered a bonus to the driver who, during a certain period of time, kept his truck the cleanest and best repaired. When he gave the prize money to the driver who most deserved it, the other drivers ganged up on him, beat him, and took away the money. The trucks were often willfully damaged so the drivers wouldn't have to work, and the expensive vehicles were treated terribly. It was only after a system of private ownership of the trucks was introduced years later that this problem was solved.

Another staffing problem was the constant turnover among the houseboys. The Company doctor finally told me that the sexual abuse these boys were suffering was so bad that we must get rid of the head cook. Unfortunately, he was the cleanest, most efficient Arab we had ever had in my camp. He was transferred into the main dining room at Dhahran, but we really hated to see him leave.

A few weeks after ibn-Saud's party visited, we had an infestation of horned vipers. I was lying on my cot reading when I heard a commotion outside the tent, right next to my head. Red Nevins had been passing my tent and had killed a viper as it snaked toward my sandals on the floor. The houseboys and workmen found some in their tents as well, so they started sleeping on the flatbed trucks.

The snakes were only about a foot long and absolutely, invisibly, sand-colored. Each viper had a small, half-inch-long horn on its head. They buried themselves in the sand and could only be seen in the evening when the temperature cooled off and they slithered around.

We called in on the radio that night, and the camp doctor told us they were deadly poisonous and there was no antidote. We must have killed a dozen snakes, and then no more showed up. From that time on, however, no one ever picked up anything from the ground or put on shoes or sandals without checking to make sure there were no snakes. The vipers made going to the slit trench at night a hazard, so everyone carried flashlights.

Spring was over and the heat of summer was beginning. Max Steineke had one more structure he wanted us to work before it got too hot to do field work. He had had his structural drill crew working southwest of Dhahran in an area mostly covered with sand dunes. They had found a large low-relief anticline he called Abqaiq. Steineke had an aerial mosaic of the area made from photos taken by Dick Kerr in the early days of the concession.

The Company had bought a Fairchild 71 high-wing monoplane in California and shipped it to Cairo. Dick Kerr uncrated it there and fitted it with extra gas tanks. Then he flew it to Dhahran over the Arabian desert, one of the most desolate regions in the world. With an aerial camera he took some photos of the area around Dhahran. Flying over Abqaiq, he had noticed evidence of an anticline and photographed it as well. The mosaic made from these photos showed the anticline very strikingly. Now we were to run a gravity survey to see how gravity checked the shallow structural drill holes.

Establishing a camp in an area of sand dunes was a little difficult. The northerly winds, or *shimals*, were starting to blow, and our tracks were sometimes drifted full within an hour. When the sand started to move, our radio contact with Dhahran sometimes blacked out from the static electricity generated by the sand grains rubbing against one another. One could occasionally get a real jolt by taking hold of the radio aerial. The sparks would fly.

Each day I had to work only a small area. I would go ahead, laying out the stations, with the meter truck crew following me.

Right behind them were the plane table party and the level party. We didn't get a lot done each day, but what we had done was finished and put on the map. Before we were forced to leave because of the high winds and blowing and shifting sand, we had enough data to indicate the presence of a large anticline. Gravity gradients were low, and I suspected there was a salt layer in the area.

Later drilling proved this to be an *immense* anticline, and Abqaiq became the first giant oil field in Saudi Arabia. Even bigger and more prolific fields were found south and west of Abqaiq, and it was the forerunner of the monstrous oil finds farther south in the Ar-Rub' 'al-Khali desert — the Empty Quarter. By mid-1982, Abqaiq had produced from its eighty-two-plus wells more than six and three-quarter billion barrels of oil, an average of more than 550,000 barrels per day (these figures are the latest available from the *Oil and Gas Journal* in January of 1992).

As the heat of the summer came on, I found I was getting awfully tired during the long hours of field work. I could see Max Steineke was concerned. Dr. Dame told him I had suffered heart damage as a result of the rheumatic fever. I talked to Dr. Dame, who said if I stayed any longer in Arabia, he wouldn't give me more than six months to live. I had thought I was regaining my strength better than that.

CHAPTER 10

HOMEWARD BOUND

MAX STEINEKE SUGGESTED THAT I TAKE UP OFFICE WORK, such as paleontology, but he had no need for me in Arabia since they had two paleontologists already. I didn't know what to do. Then, one night I was over at Bill Isler's place looking at some of his 8 mm. color movies, and we got to talking about my health. He had worked as a driller in the Rocky Mountain area near Rock Springs, Wyoming, and said "Why don't you go back home and start doing field work and forget you have a heart?" I got to thinking this might be the best thing to do, so I wasn't totally unprepared for the word from Steineke a few days later that the Company's medical department in San Francisco had ordered him to send me home.

This meant I was going home in the summer of 1939, sicker than hell, with no job. I had been making $325 a month, and $300 of it had gone into my savings account at Walker Bank in Salt Lake City. I thought, "I've got $3,000 in the bank as a cushion. Maybe I can live on that until I find a job." So I wired Dad to transfer $1,000 into my checking account and prepared to leave. CASOC gave me money to buy a ticket to Salt Lake City by ship and train— about $500. I bought traveler's checks with it.

I boxed up my belongings and had them put on a ship leaving for San Francisco. I packed my clothes in my Gladstone bag and bought a ticket to Baghdad on Imperial Airways. From there I thought I would ride buses and trains through Europe. Imperial flew only twice a week, and sometimes not even then. The Americans called it Yimkin Airlines — using the Arab word for "perhaps." The British didn't think this was funny.

The day I left on the Company launch for Bahrain, the whole geological department came to see me off — Max Steineke, Dick Kerr, Tom Barger, Jerry Harris, and my gravity crew were all there. I certainly hoped I would see them all again. I wanted to prove the doctor wrong about my heart.

The Imperial Airways Short Sunderland flying boat *Coriolanus*, a high-wing airplane with four engines and four bladed props, was a beautiful sight as it circled to land in the Bahrain harbor. I was the only passenger boarding, and a small launch took me out to the flying boat. I took the only vacant seat, immediately behind the pilot's compartment. As we took off to the north, I could see the hills of Dhahran on the Saudi Arabian mainland and wondered if I would ever be back. We climbed to about 5,000 feet, and the temperature was a welcome 85 degrees — a pleasant relief after the 105-degree heat at Bahrain. The Persian Gulf is so shallow that much of its water is only a bluish green and the bottom can be seen. This shallow water would one day be the scene of much oil exploration.

The *Coriolanus* landed in the Shatt al-Arab River at Basra, and we stayed overnight in town. As we unloaded, I had a chance to get a good look at the passengers. Most were British military personnel returning to England from India, leaving the summer heat of Bombay and Karachi for a cool English summer.

We rode a bus to the airport hotel in town, and I sat next to a Chinese doctor. He was from Shanghai and had been educated in the United States. He told me he was tired of being with the stuffy British. He had been flying for three days to get this far on his trip to London. Imperial flew only during daylight hours and on contact flying rules (CFR). Still, it was more enjoyable than taking a ship all the way.

That evening after dinner I saw the Chinese doctor in the lobby, and he said, "Let's take a trip around town." I thought it was a good idea, so we hailed a taxi in front of the hotel. The doctor gave me a good lesson in dealing with drivers. He discussed the whole trip, where the driver would take us, where he would wait and for how long, how much it would cost, and how much tip he would get. Drivers usually tried to stick you with some sort of extra expense, and you had a row with them. We used the same driver all evening, and he seemed perfectly satisfied. The Chinese certainly knew how to deal. We went to several cabarets; I think the doctor liked to look at the dancing girls. They were mostly Persian, Greek, and Lebanese — all sizes and colors.

The next morning we were taken out to the *Coriolanus* and took off for Baghdad. Flying over the Tigris–Euphrates River valley, I was struck by the evidence of ancient agricultural work. There were signs of abandoned canals, ditches, and large fields, all now being covered by blowing sand. Ancient Mesopotamia, which is what Iraq was called when I studied geography, must have been a really rich land. Later I learned that this irrigation system was destroyed by the Tatars in 1258 AD. The present inhabitants certainly don't look like they could build another Babylon with its hanging gardens — one of the Seven Wonders of the Ancient World.

The Tigris River at Baghdad was not wide or straight enough to land the flying boat, so we landed at Lake Habbaniyah, about sixty miles west of town. Within a year this lake would be the site of a bitter battle between Iraqi troops sympathetic to Hitler's Germany and the British Army. I got off the plane and took an airport taxi to town. It was a right-hand-drive Ford station wagon, and I sat in the left front seat — a peculiar feeling riding on the left side and not driving.

I checked into the Claridge Hotel and made arrangements to take the bus from Baghdad to Damascus, which left in two days. Once again I was enthralled by the dining room on the second floor overlooking the river. That evening I took a horse-drawn carriage and toured the residential area of Baghdad. This crossroads city of the ancient caravan routes had a special fascination for me, and I thought, "I may be going home to die, so I am going to live it up for a while."

The next morning I visited the silversmith bazaar and bought some pins and trinkets. These artisans were Christian Arabs and they claimed their process, putting the characteristic black camel and donkey profiles on silver, was handed down from John the Baptist. True or not, it made an interesting selling point to a Christian from the United States.

It was June and the Syrian desert was hot. The bus traveled all night and stopped only at Rutbah Wells for fuel and food. I sat next to an Englishman who had been working in the Kirkuk oil field. A natural rapport existed among oil men the world over in those days. As we approached Damascus, the gray sand and mud of the desert were replaced by the green hills of the Lebanese mountains. The black lava flow on the outskirts of town made me think of towns in Nevada.

I was anxious to see Damascus, the oldest city in the world which has been lived in continuously. Still going first class, I checked into the Omayad Hotel and looked out over the city from my third-floor window. Although I had slept little on the bus, I was bursting to tour the city. A hotel guide took me to the Great Umayyad Mosque, the first big mosque I had ever visited. Hundreds of Muslims were there on their knees praying in unison. The guide took me to the old wall the Romans built around the city and then to the street called Straight, where the Apostle Paul was brought after being struck blind. Syria still had garrisons of French soldiers, and they were much in evidence at many of the cabarets. The French influence on the city was very strong.

No buses ran from Damascus to Beirut, so taxis hauled the bulk of the traffic. The route was through mountains and high mountain valleys with their green Mediterranean-type vegetation reminding me of Southern California. I had hoped to see some of the famous Cedars of Lebanon but was told only one small grove remained, too far from my route to make it worthwhile to visit.

Many of the CASOC people took their summer vacations from Saudi Arabia here in Beirut. It was a sort of Paris of the Near East and had most everything the men were looking for in a vacation spot. I stayed at a clean little hotel a few blocks from the famous waterfront hotels. It was run by a German who spoke English very well. During the early days of World War II this hotel would be destroyed by British forces. The owner had a shortwave radio and was sending military information to the German forces. His hotel had become a center for German espionage.

One of the places I wanted most to see was Cairo. Cook's advised me to take a boat from Beirut to Port Said and go by train

into Cairo. A Greek freighter, the *Andros*, was leaving the next day
for Port Said. I got an Egyptian visa and went aboard a few hours
before it sailed with a variety of freight aboard and several cattle
on the top deck.

That night I had a terrible headache and earache — apparently
an ear infection. I had gone swimming in the Mediterranean and
had scratched my ears with a bobby pin when they itched. I was
running a temperature of 102° F. When we arrived at Port Said,
I got a taxi and went to the British hospital. They put me to bed
and assigned a Russian doctor to my case. He packed my ears with
gauze full of some kind of medication. I lay there in bed very ill for
three days, worrying that this might trigger the return of my rheumatic fever. Fortunately it didn't, and I got to feeling better.

The morning of the third day, a British sailor next to me in the
big ward said, "Yank, look out the window." I did and really got a
thrill. There on the next building flew a huge American flag! I
hadn't realized it was the American Consulate, and today was the
Fourth of July. I felt better already. They discharged me from the
hospital after four days, even though I was still pretty weak.

I took a tour around the harbor facilities and the north end of
the Suez Canal and then caught the train to Cairo. The tracks
followed the canal to Ismailiyah and then turned southwest across
the delta to Cairo. The primitive methods of farming this land, one
of the richest pieces of farmland in the world, were both a disappointment and a revelation. The oxen pulling a crooked stick for a
plow and the donkeys powering a waterwheel to lift water from a
canal to the fields were fascinating to see. The extreme poverty and
filth of the people were not.

A little hotel, the Victoria, a few blocks from the famous
Shepheards had been recommended to me as a clean, cheap place
to stay. The first-class binge I had in Baghdad and Damascus, plus
the hospital bill at Port Said, had depleted my funds faster than I
had thought possible. Nevertheless, I was determined to hit all the
important places between here and England.

My first stop after checking into the hotel was a book shop. I
bought Emil Ludwig's *Egypt* and perused it rapidly. My first trip
was to the Pyramids. Next I visited the Citadel — Muhammad Ali

Mosque, the Sultan Hassan Mosque, and then out to Memphis.

That evening I bought a tarboush and strolled around Cairo in my shirtsleeves. I just mixed with the crowds and was glad I had left my wallet back at the hotel when I was jostled several times by pickpockets. Inadvertently I found myself in the red-light district, consisting of many large, open veranda-type coffeehouses with myriads of people going in and coming out. I had never seen anything like it. There were all shades of skin from ebony to parchment white. There were all sizes from 250-pounders to children. About the only thing they all seemed to have in common was heavy eye makeup. Heavy use of the charcoal-colored "kohl" was typical. To this day, when I see heavy eye makeup, I think of the women of the "Fishmarket," as the district was called.

Athens was next on my itinerary, so I went by train to Alexandria and took a Greek boat to Piraeus. After spending a day around the Acropolis in Athens, I checked at Cook's for a way to get to Rome. No ships were leaving soon, so they advised that I fly there via the Italian airlines. The Savoia-Marchetti tri-motor Alitalia flew from Athens to Rome was a pretty ship. When I took out my camera to take a picture of it as it sat there on the grass runway in north Athens, the flight attendant came screaming at me and wouldn't allow me to take a picture. We took off, flying over Corfu and Albania, and landed at Brindisi, Italy, for lunch.

I was surprised to see Floyd Ohliger, the manager of CASOC in Dhahran. He asked, "Have you heard the news?" There had been a squib in the Alexandria papers about an oil well fire in Saudi Arabia. I told him I had heard there was a fire. "Worse than that," he said. "A well at Dammam blew out, killing the Arab crew and the American driller — Bill Isler." I felt terrible. It was Bill who had encouraged me to leave Saudi Arabia, go back to the Rocky Mountains, and "forget you have a heart."

Ohliger had been in Rome when the news came, and he was flying to Beirut to pick up Imperial Airlines to Bahrain. Bill Isler was married and had been planning to bring his wife to Dhahran in the fall. He was one of the oldtimers in Saudi Arabia, and the Company was making a house available as a special favor for his long service.

One night when I was over at Bill's place watching homemade movies, mine, we had started talking about his Arab drilling rig crew. He said he was having a hell of a time trying to get them to quit smoking on the derrick floor. When they started to drill into the oil and gas pay zone, puffs of gas came up through the blowout preventer, and he was afraid it might ignite and blow up. Bill said the Arabs wouldn't believe there was such a thing as gas. They couldn't see it or smell it, and the Qur'an (Koran) didn't say anything about gas; therefore, it didn't exist!

Ohliger said this was just what had happened. The gas ignited and blew. The drilling mud partially unloaded out of the hole, and here came the oil, catching fire immediately and killing everybody on the derrick floor.

Between Brindisi and Rome, we flew over the Apennines. I was amazed at their size and ruggedness. Ohliger had told me he always stayed at the Flora Hotel in Rome, so I checked in there. The Vatican, St. Peter's, Hadrian's Palace at Tivoli, were all inspiring sights. I felt I was really getting a course in ancient history.

But, as a geologist, what I really wanted to see most were Mt. Vesuvius and Pompeii. I rode the train to Naples and took a tour to the volcano and the buried city. I was not disappointed. The cinder cone even then building in the center of the crater was a real treat to see. I guess igneous geology had always intrigued me, and here I was seeing some first-hand, as it happened. Now I could more easily envision the same condition at the extinct craters in Utah and Idaho I had seen so often. Geology in the making!

There was still one more place in Italy I had always wanted to see. I took the evening train from Naples to Venice via Rome. I thought I would sleep on the train and save a hotel bill. I was traveling second class and wasn't prepared for the melange of people and many children. When I arrived at the Venice station, I took the first hotel porter's offer to carry my bag to his hotel. I checked into a room and slept for a couple of hours. It was a short walk to St. Mark's Square, and I got there in time for lunch and a beer. I still didn't have the stamina I should have, so I rested for part of the afternoon. Toward evening I took a tour of the canals by gondola, which was exciting and included a short visit to some of the art galleries, where I marveled at the Rubens nudes and Titian's portraits of red-haired women.

My travel plans were still rather vague, so I bought a good map of Europe and picked out a tentative itinerary. I wanted to see Switzerland, Germany, possibly Austria, possibly Holland, and England, where I thought I would like to catch a ship for home. With this general route in mind, I bought a ticket to Zurich on an early train so I could see the countryside. (I had also decided on no more overnight train trips.) There were a lot of Americans on the train, mostly college students, but unlike those of later decades, they were clean, neat, and well groomed. These were a credit to their country.

A group of us got off the train in Zurich that night, and we discovered that with a fair going on, the town was jammed. Fortunately, one of the girls from California spoke German and found a clean little rooming house in the old part of town where several of us could get a room for the night — but just one night. I did my best to see the fair and the town the next day. The watchmaker exhibits were beautiful, with large models of Rolex, Movado, and Omega watches.

Probably the most famous place in Switzerland, so far as I was concerned, was St. Moritz, the skiing capital of Europe. Skiing was just beginning to be popular in the United States. Sun Valley had opened a few years earlier in Idaho, and Utah now had lifts at Alta and Brighton. I took the afternoon train to St. Moritz and found a clean third-class hotel a few blocks from the famous international hotel district. Although it was late July, it snowed that night! None of the lifts was operating, but I did get a look at the famous winter resort. The cold felt good, for the heat of summer was taking its toll on my physical well-being.

As a memento of the visit, I bought two Movado watches — one for me and one for Dad. They had to have new crystals and springs occasionally but were used constantly. Fifty-two years later I switched to a new Swiss Army watch my son gave me for Christmas. Such is the superb quality of Swiss craftsmanship.

That afternoon I took the train back to Zurich, got a German visa, and caught another train to Munich, where I stayed for two days. First, I wanted to get a Tyrolean hat and raincoat, which I bought at Hurners, near the famous Hofbrau. Although Munich was bombed extensively during World War II, this store was still in operation when I visited in 1963. Of the group of American students who were on the S.S. *New York* when I was on my way out to Arabia last fall, I had received letters consistently from Olive Holmes, a Barnard student from New York. I figured the group had probably gone for the summer, but I went out to see if I could find them. They had all left a few weeks earlier.

The Reuters news we received in Saudi Arabia had frequently mentioned the arms buildup in Hitler's Germany, but I wasn't prepared for what I was beginning to see. No young men were on the street who weren't in uniform. Armored cars and soldiers were everywhere. There was an almost fatalistic feeling everywhere — not *if* the war comes, but *when* it comes. On the train to Vienna that afternoon, we passed field after field covered with military aircraft, tanks, armored cars. The whole countryside was an arsenal.

Hitler had taken Austria over just a few months earlier, and I thought there might still be hostilities. The only people around the public square in Vienna were elderly. One old gentleman approached me, speaking English, and said that if I bought his lunch he would show me the downtown sights. We walked around the Rathaus, the church of St. Stephen, and Maria Theresa's palace. When we sat down to lunch, I bought us a stewed chicken dinner. I didn't want all my chicken broth, and he asked for it.

My guide told me that, while he was not a member of the Nazi party, economic conditions had been so bad before Hitler's troops came that a lot of people welcomed the change of government. I told him I was on my way to Berlin, and he said I should stop on the way to see Nuremberg, which had a well-preserved old city inside castle walls as well as most of the Hohenzollern Castle. I took his advice and was entranced with the remarkable preservation of this medieval city. The cobblestone rock and massive stone and timber buildings were a highlight of my European trip. I had the feeling I was seeing it before it would be destroyed in the coming war. The United States pounded Nuremberg with bombs incessantly, and I doubt much remained afterward of these original buildings.

My next stop was Berlin, where I found a clean little hotel a block off the main business section, Unter den Linden. It was just a few blocks east of the Brandenburg Gate and the Reichstag buildings, once in Russian East Germany, now united free Germany.

One of the things I wanted to get in Germany was a Leica camera. Germany was promoting tourism then and had issued a special type of money, the travel mark, which was to be used for meals and hotel rooms only. Regular marks were worth about 25 cents, but travel marks cost only half that. I went to a neat-appearing camera shop on Unter den Linden and asked to see the Leica. A tall, dark man about thirty-five who spoke English waited on me. He wanted to know what part of the United States I was from. He told me he had taken the Union Pacific train from Salt Lake City to Chicago, and during the ride had stumbled and fallen getting off the train in Cheyenne, Wyoming. He had broken his leg, necessitating a stay in a hospital there. He said he liked the West and Westerners, and he could arrange for me to draw enough travel marks to buy the Leica. It was their Model III I wanted, which cost $160, but with travel marks it would be $80. He took me to a bank where I cashed traveler's checks in that amount. The banker had to make a notation in my passport of my drawings, however, which bothered me a little because of the omnipresent feel of the police state.

I didn't know whether I should, but I did ask. I wanted to know something about the pogrom against the Jews and the reasons for it. The camera-shop man told me that only a few years earlier his section of the Unter den Linden business district had been nearly deserted. He said that all the shoppers went to the Jewish section of town in the Kurfurstendamm area. Then the Jews were driven out and this area revitalized. The former Jewish district did have nicer shops, as I could see when I visited it, but it seemed a horrible price to pay for equalizing economic opportunities. Anti-Jewish feeling was strong. Everywhere were posters and newspaper cartoons showing long-nosed Jews engaged in various sorts of chicanery. I had grown up in Salt Lake City, where anyone not a Mormon was considered a Gentile, and I was scarcely aware of the presence or absence of a Jewish minority.

The next day, I took the train to Amsterdam. It was a regular coach, and a couple sat across from me who were Germans working for Shell Oil Company in Venezuela, on their way back to Caracas. As we stopped near Utrecht on the Holland border, the Nazi police came through the car, examining passports. They scrutinized mine, and then a discussion arose between two of them.

"Oh, my God!" I thought. They were going to raise hell about those travel marks I had drawn which I knew were more than I was allowed. However, it appeared that they were looking for someone and had thought I was he. They grabbed a man a few seats ahead of me instead and took him off the train. We looked out the window and saw the police slitting the lining of his suitcoat with a knife. In the lining were packages of money—it looked like American money. The man was handcuffed and taken away.

The Shell man said the captive had been trying to smuggle foreign funds out of Germany. He also said, "Look at those dinky little concrete tank traps along the track on the Holland side. They sure won't stop our tanks when we start to roll!" He was certainly right. Within eight months Nazi Tiger tanks would drive across this border like the traps weren't even there.

In Berlin I thought it best to make a reservation on a ship to the United States. I planned to spend a day or two in Holland, three or four days in England, and then sail for home. Since I was running low on money by this time, I wanted to book passage on a small ship that wouldn't cost much.

The man at Cook's in Berlin gave me two choices fitting this condition. One was the Holland American Line S.S. *Statendam* and the other the S.S. *Athena*. The *Statendam* would leave a few days earlier than the *Athena*, so I bought my ticket on it. After the episode at the German-Dutch frontier, I was glad to get out of Germany. The ominous feeling of approaching war was shared by everyone to whom I talked.

I found a small hotel in Amsterdam and went out in search of a place to eat. Crowds of people were singing and dancing in the streets, celebrating the birth of a child to Princess Juliana. I guess I had the look of a Westerner about me, for everyone who spoke to me automatically used English. It was an interesting night. I ate dinner at a modest restaurant–night club and was struck by the great number of young girls, obviously Jewish, who were there plying their trade. The waiter told me that in the last few years Hitler's treatment of the Jews in Germany had forced the immigration of great numbers of Jewish people to Amsterdam. In most cases they had fled without being able to take any of their assets or belongings with them. Many of the older Jews could not find work and had to depend on their attractive young daughters to keep the family in food and lodging.

The next day in Rotterdam I saw the same thing — Jewish refugees everywhere. I took a boat trip around Rotterdam harbor, which at that time had one of the largest volumes of freight in the world. Within a year the Nazis would destroy this harbor and most of the city of Rotterdam, overrun Holland, and sink the SS *Statendam* in the harbor.

I took the boat train to the Hook of Holland, south of Rotterdam, where I boarded the ship for the overnight trip to Harwich, England. The English Channel was fairly smooth that night, and I slept well. Going through English customs the next morning, I was incensed to have the inspectors insist on taking my new Leica camera. They were polite but nevertheless firm. "We will take the camera and deliver it to you on the S.S. *Statendam* when you sail," they said.

Very frustrated, I checked into a small hotel in downtown London. That night they had a practice blackout. All lights were extinguished, and barrage balloons were put up. Large searchlights laced the sky with their beams, and occasional aircraft flew overhead. This was a dress rehearsal for the Battle of Britain, which would soon begin. Surprisingly, the English people I talked to — waitresses, clerks in stores, bartenders, etc. — were usually optimistic about war being averted. They didn't seem to have the gut feeling that war was inevitable.

I took the typical tour to Stratford-on-Avon, Oxford College, the House of Commons, and Westminster Cathedral. Life seemed to be going on at its usual pace. "Maybe they know something I don't," I thought. Still, the legion of men in uniform in Germany, the multitudinous fields of airplanes, tanks, and war matériel I had recently seen haunted me. It must be coming!

The British I had met in the Near East — the haughty men and horse-faced women who, if they deigned to speak to an American, acted as if we were intruders in their backyards by finding oil in Bahrain and Saudi Arabia, the chiselers who insisted on there being two prices for everything they bought, a high price for the Americans and a niggardly lower one for themselves, were not in evidence in London. Of course, I met the "little" people in London, the service people, the salt-of-the-earth types who had to struggle for everything they got. These were polite, decent, nice people. They treated me like a gentleman and expected the same in return. Even the cab drivers were polite!

My father's family was from England. The Reverend William Walton came to Plymouth Colony from England as a Pilgrim in 1630. So I felt a certain kinship with the little people — as well as a tremendous thankfulness that my progenitors had migrated to America. Otherwise, but for the Grace of God, I could be a young Englishman with little or no prospect of ever escaping the entrenched economic caste system.

As the S.S. *Statendam* sailed out of Southampton, I thought, "Well, I've seen most of the Europe I was interested in seeing. Now I am going home to die." Dr. Dame's words kept ringing in my ears. Fortunately, so did Bill Isler's: "Go back home . . . and forget you have a heart"!

My table assignment on the *Statendam* put me with a young American returning from diplomatic service in Japan, a young American girl from New York City who had been visiting relatives in Germany, and a college girl from Minnesota who had made the European tour following her college graduation. We talked about home, and we talked about the coming war. The man from Japan felt it was coming. The girl who had been visiting in Germany said her relatives knew it was coming.

Looking back now on early September of 1939, it seems absolutely ridiculous that something couldn't have been done to stop it. We were so helpless, like people watching a lumberjack cutting at the base of a tree. With each stroke the tree shudders, and we know if the cutting isn't stopped the tree will topple, but we watch, mesmerized by the whole process. The world must have been mesmerized too.

British customs had taken my Leica, all right, but when I boarded the ship it was nowhere to be found. I raised hell with the customs people, and they had the gall to say they would find it and deliver it to me, because "We never make a mistake." As it turned out, they were right. It had been given to the ship's purser, and he had mislaid it — purposely or not, I will never know. Anyway, three days after we sailed I found a note from the purser to come and get my camera! I was really overjoyed.

We docked in New York City in the evening. The customs people took us in alphabetical order. It was three hours before they got to me. Finally, I made it through and out the gate, and there was Dad waiting for me. I had written him that I was coming on the *Statendam*, but I didn't expect him to meet me. He had ridden the bus all the way from Salt Lake City and had gone to the Governor Clinton Hotel and reserved a double room.

I was awfully glad to see him. We had hunted, fished, played football and tennis together while I was growing up and, now that Mother was gone, we had grown even closer. He had been terribly worried about me when I was in the hospital so long, and I could see the relief on his face at seeing me still in one piece, although there was also shock at my appearance. I was thin and tired, and he showed his concern. The ear infection that had put me in the hospital at Port Said had flared up again, and I was half sick from it. He had hired a taxi to take him out to the dock and back, and we loaded up my two bags and went to the hotel. I was very tired and went to bed immediately. I refrained from telling Dad I thought I had come home to die.

The next morning I felt better. I found a doctor to treat my ear, and we went on a rubberneck tour of the city. It was an adventure for Dad. He had never been east of Omaha, where he had once taken a load of lambs to market. We went out to the World's Fair for a couple of days and saw the sights.

Next day I checked with a car brokerage outfit that many of the returning CASOC employees used, and they found a grey Mercury convertible with a black top. It cost me a big chunk of my bank account — $960. I thought, "What the hell! I'm going home to die. I might just as well go in style." We left the next morning for

Washington, D.C., and when I turned on the car radio, we heard that the *Athena* had been sunk! It really stunned me to realize how close I had come to being on that ship. Leaving Washington and driving out through the beautiful farmland of Virginia, I did a lot of thinking about myself. Maybe I wasn't supposed to die now. I had missed being on the *Athena*! Maybe that was a good omen.

We drove west across the Appalachians, across the corn belt states, and into Kansas and eastern Colorado. We stayed at the little town of Cheyenne Wells. Next morning we drove on to another small town, Hugo, for breakfast. As we walked out of the cafe, I heard someone call my name, and there was Con Shafer, with whom I had worked in Utah in the Soil Conservation Service. He was home on vacation visiting his folks. We went and had coffee with them and shot the bull for a while. Con told me that since I had left the Soil Conservation Service they were expanding operations, and I could probably get back on with them if I wanted. This sounded good because I was sure Standard of California didn't have any domestic jobs available.

As we drove into Denver and then up to the mountains to Estes Park, I thought, "I'm home now. I'm going to try to remember Bill Isler's advice." It wasn't easy — particularly after old Doc Sundewall put me to bed for a week and had me take digitalis to strengthen my heart. I was weak and had many fits of depression, but I finally fought my way back to good health again. I was home.

EPILOGUE

WHEN I WROTE TO STANDARD OF CALIFORNIA to let them know I was home and sick, C. C. Gester, the chief geologist, answered, saying my employment was terminated.

The Soil Conservation Service didn't have a job for me either, so I decided to enter the University of Utah to work on a master's degree in geology (with a minor in metallurgy), which I got the next spring, in June 1940. The next two years I spent at Massachusetts Institute of Technology, working on a PhD in geology. I did my dissertation work in the "Geology of the Cretaceous in the Uinta Basin, Utah," and received the degree in June 1942.

The Texas Company hired me to go to Denver and work in the Rocky Mountains. I was with them for two years and left to become division geologist for J. Paul Getty's company, Pacific Western Oil. That is where this yarn about Saudi Arabia began and now ends.

Since August 1990, when Iraq invaded Kuwait, I have tried to keep abreast of the war and subsequent operations.

The area north of Abu Hadriya along the Neutral Zone boundary, where Tom Barger, Jerry Harris, and I were doing our surface geological work, was the staging area for the Allies' land battle with Iraq. Our tanks were moved in from Dhahran and Jubail to the south and deployed westward along this sandy desert by night. Then they crossed into Iraq and attacked Iraqi forces from the rear, crushing them.

The little village of Jubail, which had a town watering trough outside its walls where we filled our tanks and barrels with potable water, is now a huge industrial complex with chemical plants, manufacturing companies, etc. From a population of fewer than 500 people, it has grown into a city of more than 50,000.

The oil field we found in the Neutral Zone near Jebel Fuwaris was named Wafra, and through mid-1985, according to *Oil and Gas Journal*, it produced 1,254,000,000 barrels of oil (an average of 85,000 barrels per day). Before the invasion by Iraq in 1990, the field was producing 130,000 barrels of oil per day, according to the *Wall Street Journal* for February 7, 1992. As Saddam Hussein was driven out of Kuwait, he set fire to the oil fields. Wafra was the first to ignite; however, since its wells do not flow, they were relatively easy to extinguish. At Burgan to the north, where gas and oil pressures were high and the wells flowed, the fires were terribly difficult to put out and the oil flows difficult to control afterward.

Part III
WILDCATTING

The beginning of a lifelong love affair: College student Paul Walton making a topographical and geological survey of the brand-new Dinosaur National Monument in the Uinta Basin, Utah, 1934.

Three States Natural Gas Company's H. E. Walton #A-3 well (named for Betty Walton, the author's wife), at 150 million cubic feet of gas per day, the largest well in the Clear Creek gas field, near Huntington, Utah, 1952.

The discovery well, Mary Durkin Kearns #1, of Three States Natural Gas Company's Flat Canyon gas field, near Huntington, Utah, 1953.

Paul Walton alone and with a passing Bedouin in the Sahara Desert, near a promising iron deposit in the province of Fezzan, Libya, 1961.

The rich iron deposits at Wadi Shatti that led to successful negotiations, hopeful investment, and ultimate frustration; province of Fezzan, Libya, 1962.

CHAPTER 11

THE UTAH OIL AND GAS STORY

WHEN I DECIDED TO LEAVE PACIFIC WESTERN and the Getty group, I made a trip to Salt Lake City to see the Morgans — Nick Senior and Nick Junior. I had met them on one of my trips to Utah some years earlier, and we had kept in touch. The Morgans sold Pacific Western leases covering the big Teasdale anticline in Wayne County, Utah, and the Gordon Creek structure in Carbon County, Utah. Pacific Western had drilled both structures and made a carbon dioxide gas discovery at Gordon Creek, but Teasdale was dry. I had made a plane table structure map of both anticlines and staked the locations for the test wells.

At this time, 1948, the Morgans had a large lease block covering the Big Flat structure in Grand County in which they were partners with Glen Ruby, an internationally known geologist with the firm of Hoover, Curtice, and Ruby. This firm had consulting jobs for the Navy on the Alaska North Slope and for the Chilean and Argentinian governments in the Tierra del Fuego area, near Cape Horn. Tidewater Oil bought the Big Flat "play" from the Morgans and Ruby and had made an apparent oil discovery in the Mississippian limestone in their first well. A few months earlier the Ashley Valley field in Uintah County had been discovered by Equity Oil, and now an apparent discovery at Big Flat made Utah look like a real oil state. The Morgans were anxious to continue their lease business but needed geological guidance. They had approached me to go to work for them before I went to Arabia.

I went to their offices in the Wasatch Oil Building, later the Phillips Petroleum Building, and told them I was ready to make the move to Salt Lake City. We formed a three-way partnership called

[179]

Morgan and Walton Oils, and they guaranteed me $800 per month salary for a year.

Dad seemed happy I was moving back to Salt Lake City and said he would build an extra bedroom on the house for our two children if we wanted to move in with him. He was living alone and wanted to get better acquainted with his grandchildren, who were two and four years old. It took a few weeks to sell our house in Casper, and we made our move to Salt Lake City on June 20, 1949.

Reporting to the Morgan offices for work, I found they had good rapport with Bob Bernick, then business editor for the *Salt Lake Tribune*, and he wrote a big story for the financial page on my Saudi Arabian Neutral Zone trip for J. Paul Getty. It got quite wide coverage, and I was a minor celebrity for a while.

I was interested in acquiring leases in several areas, so I went to work drawing up geologic maps so the Morgans could file federal and state oil and gas leases on them. Advance rentals were only 10 cents an acre; and I expected the Morgans to have the necessary capital to pay for these filings. I was amazed to learn that they brought other people into the deals to pay the rentals and thereby gave them a half interest. This reduced my interest in any play we took to one sixth, which didn't set very well with me.

My principal interest in Utah was the Uinta Basin, where I had done my doctoral dissertation, and we filed on leases in an area near the axis of the Basin, about fifteen miles west of the Colorado line; I called it North Bonanza from the nearby gilsonite mining town of Bonanza. Another promising area just south of the town of Duchesne in Pleasant Valley featured surface structures with Green River formation oil possibilities. That year Carter Oil (Standard of New Jersey) drilled a discovery well on the Roosevelt anticline on the north side of the Uinta Basin which produced oil from the Green River formation. Many oil companies, I thought, should start to consider the Uinta Basin as a major oil-producing area.

I thought it would be easy to sell or farm out our Uinta Basin acreage blocks or plays, so I took them to Casper and tried to interest some of the oil companies. No luck. I went to Denver and met the same stone wall. I was really discouraged. I felt that if I couldn't sell some of these plays, my connection with the Morgans would terminate, and I would have to move back to Casper or Denver and get another job.

On one of my trips to Casper, I had a chat with Ray Chorney, who had been my assistant at Pacific Western and was now district geologist for Wilshire Oil. He advised me to take a good look at the Mush Creek and Fiddler Creek fields in Weston County, Wyoming, on the east side of the Powder River Basin, saying the economics were good for a small independent company.

Emmett Schieck of Morton Oil Company, which was doing a lot of drilling in the Mush Creek area, had just written a paper for the annual Wyoming Geological Association "Field Trip Guidebook" on the Mush Creek Field. His paper showed the oil production was from the Newcastle (Muddy) sandstone which appeared to be a stream channel or offshore bar deposit of some kind. The wells were shallow and inexpensive for Wyoming, and the production was fair (20 to 50 barrels of oil per day). It seemed an ideal place for a small independent to try to get production. That was what I was after for the partnership, so I contacted Emmett, whose company was putting together a lot of drilling deals by selling interests.

I got the data on the drilling deals and took them to Salt Lake City. The Morgans thought they had some people who would be interested in participating, so we took a half interest in two wildcats drilled by Yellowstone Drilling Company for Morton Oil. One was in the Mush Creek trend and the other in the Fiddler Creek trend. The wells were more than sixty miles from a town, so we stayed out at the location in a trailer and did our own cooking. I shot an antelope, which was great fare for a few days. Ray Chorney came out to see how we were doing, and we had lots of other visitors, but both wells were dry. I went back to Salt Lake City pretty blue.

However, while the wells were drilling, I had done some field work, looking at the outcrop of the Muddy sand along the west side of the Black Hills; these outcrops showed where the two productive sand development trends came to the surface. It occurred to me that there ought to be similar trends of the Muddy on the east side of the Black Hills which might also be productive. I discussed the possibility with the Morgans, and they thought it was a good idea too.

We had just bought a Willys four-wheel drive jeep station wagon, the first of its kind. It was painted a hideous maroon and yellow, but it was a good field car. I loaded my family into it, and we headed for the east side of the Black Hills, staying in Rapid City, South Dakota. I followed the Muddy outcrop from Rapid City to Sturgis and was excited to find two areas of thick sand. Also, I found an electric log of the water well the Air Force had drilled at their B-36 base east of Rapid City, which showed 20 feet of good Muddy sand in that hole.

I was enthusiastic about the play, so I called Marv Wallway in Casper and got him to come and check the records to see who owned the land in the two trends. It was all patented farmland. We contacted all the landowners and held a meeting at the little town of Boxelder to explain that we would like to lease their land. No one had ever leased for oil in the area before, and they were willing. We leased about 40,000 acres in the two plays and had a solid block except for the state land. The Morgans brought Thomas F. Kearns into this play, and he put up the money for the leases.

Emmett Schieck heard about our leasing activities and expressed an interest. I told him we would put the state land up for bid and buy it, and then we would like to get some wells drilled. That winter Nick Senior and I flew to Pierre, South Dakota, and were the only bidders for the state leases, paying the minimum figure of 10 cents an acre. Now we were ready for some drilling.

The next spring Merle Morton, president of Morton Drilling, came over to Salt Lake City, and we worked out a farmout. Morton was to drill three wells on the south trend and two wells on the north trend for a half interest in the leases. Morton and Schieck worked out a deal with Amerada to take an interest in the drilling and by midsummer had moved a rig in on the south trend. We found beautiful porous Muddy sand in two of the three wells, but absolutely no shows of oil. Then they moved to the north trend and neither well found any good sand. What a disappointment! Since then, several dozen more wells have been drilled in this area and no production found. The idea was a good one, but the oil just wasn't there.

Tom Kearns, who had financed this lease play, was a son of the discoverer of the famous Silver King Mine at Park City, Utah. Tom had grown up in the mining business, had fought in World War I as a fighter pilot, and then had been an almost hopeless alcoholic for twenty years. By the time the Morgans interested him in the oil business, Kearns was a confirmed member of Alcoholics Anonymous and a pillar of the Salt Lake community. His family owned the *Salt Lake Tribune*, the morning newspaper, which was run by publisher John Fitzpatrick, a former aide of Tom's father, Senator Kearns. Tom Kearns and John Fitzpatrick drove to Rapid City while we were drilling the first well on the north trend. They were there several days, and I got to know them quite well. Both were intrigued by the oil and gas business and seemed to want to stay in it until they found some production. This helped to cheer me up after the five dry holes.

In the meantime we had been approached by Clair Senior, a prominent Salt Lake attorney, to purchase my much-shopped-around North Bonanza block. The deal was on an option basis for a major company, and they would pay $3.00 per acre for the 5,000-acre block, plus a 3 percent overriding royalty. Of course the Morgans had other partners in this deal, so my net was about equal to half a year's salary and one half of 1 percent overriding royalty. It wasn't much of a deal, but at least it was the first one after a year of no lease sales whatsoever. The company buying this block was Standard Oil Company of California, and they ultimately drilled a well to the east of this block, finding a field they called Red Wash. They eventually moved over onto our block and found production on about three square miles of it. Production was small, the oil was heavy and waxy, and it sold for about $1.50 per barrel, so my one half of 1 percent overriding royalty made me just a few hundred dollars a month. It was better than a kick in the fanny, but, being a perpetual optimist, I figured this was just the beginning.

We had taken a few other large blocks in the Uinta Basin based on my surface and aerial photographic work, which we sold that year, 1950. One, going to Carter Oil (Standard of New Jersey), went for $10 an acre. Another went to Union Sulphur on a generous cash bonus, and still another went to Conoco. A small gas field was eventually found on the Union Sulphur block, called Moon Ridge. The royalty from it was so small it hardly paid the office rent.

When I first moved to Salt Lake City, I had made a down payment on a two-acre lot in the Walker Lane–Cottonwood area near the stream course of Big Cottonwood Creek, which flows westward out of the Wasatch Mountains. Unlike most of Salt Lake Valley, it had natural cottonwoods and birches due to the high water table, and I had always wanted to have a home in that area.

While things were still pretty shaky financially, I decided to start building a house on the lot so we would have more room for the two children as they grew up. Walt Henoch, a friend of mine from engineering school days at the University of Utah, was working for a local architect, Bill Monroe, and together we drew up plans. We followed my wife Betty's basic idea for a U-shaped house facing the mountains, with a patio. We were able to engage two carpenter contractors who would build it as cheaply as possible between their other jobs. It took nearly two years to finish. Betty and I did most of the painting, and we built it for $10 a square foot — a record even for those days.

Before beginning construction, I applied to Mountain Fuel Supply Company, the local gas distributing firm, for a gas line connection. I was told there was no gas available for new houses in the Salt Lake Valley. This was quite a surprise! I investigated further and found that Mountain Fuel's reserves, which were in southwestern Wyoming and northwestern Colorado, were very limited in extent. There just wasn't any gas available. I was forced to put in oil-burning furnace equipment — with a monthly fuel bill three times more expensive than gas during the winter. Clearly, what Utah needed was a new gas supply. This set me to thinking.

Looking around at the Rocky Mountains, I saw that the great bulk of the gas reservoirs were in Cretaceous rocks at depths from 2,000 to 7,500 feet. Most gas was produced from these Cretaceous rocks when they were located on anticlines or structural terraces. Was there an area in Utah where Cretaceous rocks could be found at these depths and where there might also be anticlines to trap the gas?

The Cretaceous was eroded away from most of southern Utah; it was too deep in the Uinta Basin, where there were no obvious structures. One area of Cretaceous rocks was the high, mountainous region of central Utah called the Wasatch Plateau. Here upper Cretaceous rocks were on the surface, and there might be anticlines not yet discovered in the heavily forested mountainous area. Some wells had been drilled on the eastern edge of the Plateau, but only one, at Gordon Creek, had any gas or oil shows. Still, the region intrigued me, and I felt there were possibilities there for major gas reserves. I discussed the idea with the Morgans, and they brought in Tom Kearns and John Fitzpatrick. They said, go ahead, and we will finance the lease acquisition.

The Soil Conservation Service had aerial photos of most of the area, and I sent in an order to cover everything from Soldier Summit on the north to Salina Canyon on the south and from the Book Cliffs on the east to Sanpete Valley on the west — an area sixty miles long and twenty miles wide. I spent a good part of the winter of 1949–50 working these photos. There was some prior mapping in the area by E. M. Spieker for the U.S. Geological Survey, principally for coal beds, but it covered only the eastern portion of the area. This work helped me in recognizing the various stratigraphic units on the photos. I couldn't get out into the field to check my work until April, after the snow started to melt. However, I had seen enough on the photos to be sure there was a large fault-closed structure near the coal mining town of Clear Creek, another fault closure in the Flat Canyon area south of Clear Creek, a very large structural closure on the west side of the Joes Valley graben valley, and two smaller fault closures north of the town of Scofield.

Nick Morgan checked the records and found the federal and state lands all open for filing. At Clear Creek some patented coal lands were leased to an independent oil company from Tulsa, Mid Continent Petroleum. Tom Kearns put up the money, and we filed oil and gas leases on nearly 100,000 acres for a little more than $25,000.

Now I waited for spring to get in on the surface and make a plane table structural map of the five different structural closures I had found on the photos. When the weather broke, I bought a new Dietzgen alidade and plane table and, since I couldn't afford a rodman, I made a stadia rod that I could place in an automobile wheel and stand up at a fixed point to take readings. I had already bought two Paulin altimeters, which I used for determining elevations where it was impossible to run plane table surveys.

I started on the Clear Creek area, staying at the Utah Fuel Company's bunkhouse and eating in their commissary. The coal miners were friendly and helpful. I discovered from my photographic work that the coal beds and coal workings that Spieker had shown on his U.S. Geological Survey map would be the only stratigraphic unit I could recognize over the whole structure. He had done a good job correlating the various coal beds, and his correlation checked with the structural attitudes I had found on the aerial photos. Using elevations from the topographic map of the area, which was quite accurate, I was soon able to delineate the structure at Clear Creek pretty well. I was amazed at its size; it covered at least 25,000 acres and was closed on the east side by a big graben fault valley.

Preparing the structural contour map gave me an exhilarating feeling. In my experience, this excitement in geologic discovery has almost always been an indication that the area will be oil- or gas-producing. Some old-time cable tool drillers used to say they could feel whether an area would produce oil or not — something akin to water dowsing, I guess.

Proceeding north from Clear Creek, I was able to map the Northeast and Northwest Scofield structures using the Castlegate sandstone as the key horizon. These worked out to be pie-shaped fault blocks with about 5,000 acres or more within each of the closing contours. Then I went down to Huntington and stayed there while I did what mapping I could on the Flat Canyon structure. Again the Castlegate sandstone occurred over much of the structure and, using elevations from the topographic map, photo data, and plane table elevations, I was able to rough out the broad outline of the anticlinal fold. It was closed on the west by the large Joes Valley graben which, at this point, had more than 3,000 feet of vertical displacement. This was a good-sized structural closure of more than 15,000 acres, and I felt it should have good gas possibilities. Now, all I had left to map was the large Joes Valley structure, but I would have to hurry to get it done because of other developments.

During one of my infrequent visits to the office that spring, Paul English, an independent operator, came in. He was working with a firm called Byrd-Frost of Dallas and said they were backing a proposed gas pipeline from Boundary Butte on the Arizona line to Salt Lake City, solely within the state of Utah and therefore not subject to the dictates of the Federal Power Commission. State of Utah approval was all that would be needed for the authority to build it. The pipeline firm, Utah Natural Gas Company, was headed by John McGuire, a lawyer from Massachusetts, and it had an impressive board of directors. They were planning to file an application immediately. Byrd-Frost would be interested in finding gas to help fill the line. Reserves backing the line were to come from the Boundary Butte field, the Monticello area, and the Last Chance field in central Utah.

My first reaction to English's proposal was that they had insufficient reserves to back such a line. However, his statement that Byrd-Frost would want to drill some wildcat wells looking for gas sounded good. The Wasatch Plateau structures I had worked out needed to be drilled, and maybe this pipeline project would aid in their development.

Mountain Fuel Supply Company was the sole producer and gas distributor in the region, and they were paying only 5 cents per thousand cubic feet for gas in Wyoming and Colorado — a price that certainly gave no incentive to anyone to explore for gas. A producing well would barely pay itself out, which was the reason Mountain Fuel had few gas reserves and why I was unable to get a gas connection for my new house. On the other hand, gas in the San Juan Basin in New Mexico was bringing 10 to 15 cents per thousand cubic feet and was being piped to California. English said these prices should apply to Utah, but Mountain Fuel would fight it. After all, they had a monopoly.

We told English we would cooperate with him and would dedicate any gas we found on our drilling prospects to the Utah Natural Gas pipeline if they would do some exploratory drilling. So, on May 30, 1950, Utah Natural Gas Company filed its application to build a pipeline from the Four Corners area to Salt Lake City. Both the *Salt Lake Tribune* and the *Deseret News* ran big headlines on the story, and my name was prominent in the writeups. The cost of the line was estimated at $25 million, and it would be financed by Lehman Brothers. Utah Natural hired the firm of Van Cott, Cornwall and Bagley to handle the application. Sid Cornwall and Cliff Ashton were to present evidence supporting the application at a hearing scheduled in September. They told me they wanted me to be a witness to describe the gas possibilities of the Wasatch Plateau. I agreed.

This meant I had to finish my mapping of the Joes Valley structure, which was to be a big job. The structure lies in the tops of the mountains, at elevations from 9,500 to 11,500 feet, with no roads and only a few Jeep trails. I used a combination of aerial photos, Paulin altimeter, and plane table alidade to locate and run elevations on key horizons. By late summer I had a rough map. It showed two separate areas of structural closure, one on the north and the other on the south. At least 80,000 acres were included in the closing contour, which necessitated our acquiring more leases around the original 40,000-acre block.

Again I was able to use the Castlegate sandstone as the mapping datum for the structure contours, although I used strata 2,000 feet above it in the North Horn and Flagstaff limestone formation as well. This structural closure was immense; it was cut off on the east side by the Joes Valley graben fault, which has 3,000 feet of vertical displacement in some places. I felt this was a wonderful gas prospect.

It was apparent that the shallowest drilling depth and the easiest area in which to make a well location was the Clear Creek structure. Our only problem was the Mid Continent in-holding of the Utah Fuel coal lands, which included the bottom of Long Canyon where we wanted to drill and had no lease. Nick Junior and I went to Tulsa to see their landman, Hugh Key, and he was agreeable to a farmout — a free well for a half interest. Paul English had told us we should also get a call on their share of the gas. I wrote up a letter of agreement setting out the deal, and it contained a call on their share of the gas at 10 cents per thousand cubic feet, twice the going price in Utah. Key said they were happy with the deal since they were getting something done on their leases, which were to terminate in two or three years. (This letter of agreement would come back to haunt me.) Key told me they had done some gravity work in the area and had found a positive anomaly, taking their leases on it. We now had the lease block in good shape for drilling on Clear Creek.

That fall I took Jack Frost of Byrd-Frost, Paul English, and Paul's son Bill down to Clear Creek and drove them around the structure. We walked up Long Canyon to my proposed well location, and Frost was impressed with the geologic structure. He told me he would like to drill it. I was gratified, for Jack Frost was a successful operator, a geologist with great experience, and a very likable, modest gentleman.

Shortly after this trip, the hearings started on Utah Natural Gas Company's application before the Utah Public Service Commission. Utah Natural Gas had their experts and consultants, including John McGuire, the president, who testified about proven reserves backing the line and their ability to finance and build it. Then they pulled in other interests: Glen Ruby, the internationally known geologist, told of the oil and gas possibilities of the Paradox Basin in southeast Utah; Dorsey Hager, who wrote the first book on petroleum geology in the United States and was a renowned geologist, gave testimony on the gas prospects of the state of Utah; K. W. Willson, another successful geologist, took the stand, then Cliff Ashton and I testified concerning the gas possibilities of the Wasatch Plateau.

In my testimony I made an estimate of the amount of gas that might be contained in each structure if it proved productive. I said Clear Creek should make a little over 200 billion cubic feet of gas. I noticed W. T. Nightingale, the president of Mountain Fuel Supply — who was there opposing construction of the line — guffawing over my figure. Years later, after Clear Creek was producing more than one third of the gas Mountain Fuel distributed, I found out that Nightingale had written to Glenn E. Sorensen, president of the Kemmerer Coal Company (which owned a small uncommitted acreage on the west side of the structure), that the area had absolutely no possibility for gas production. I guess I have the last laugh, since Clear Creek ultimately made just a little less than my 200 billion cubic feet estimate.

Some business attitudes are really peculiar. Here was Mountain Fuel Supply Company, short of gas, unable to serve new customers, opposing a gas line which would bring new supplies to them and enable them to expand their service area, and they fought it tooth-and-nail. They just didn't want to let anything threaten their monopoly, I guess. This attitude has prevailed for many years among many utilities and gas companies, I'm afraid, and the great gas shortage of the winter of 1976–77 was one of the results. The greed and stupidity of many businesses is sickening to observe. If there were a better system, I would be for it. Unfortunately, like Western-style democracy, it is not the best system — just the least bad!

The most flamboyant witness at the hearings was Colonel D. H. Byrd of Byrd-Frost. Trained as a geologist, he had built with Jack Frost a multi-million-dollar company from their wildcat oil and gas discoveries. Byrd was a colonel in the Texas Air reserves, and a big bronze plaque was placed in his honor at the old Love Field terminal building in Dallas. His initials, D. H., prompted his nickname, "Dry Hole" Byrd. It was said he drilled more than sixty dry holes before finding a producer. Colonel Byrd told the commission that Byrd-Frost would spent $5 million exploring for gas in the state. This put the pipeline effort in a very good light. Mountain Fuel certainly wasn't spending anything like that in exploration.

The pipeline hearings were adjourned until December, when the opponents were to cross-examine Utah Natural Gas's witnesses and supply their own testimony. A few days before the hearings were to continue, the papers carried a lead story on a new company, Utah Pipe Line — a wholly owned subsidiary of Delhi Oil Company, a Clint Murchison company from Texas which had filed with the Federal Power Commission to build a line from Aztec, New Mexico, to Salt Lake City. This proposed interstate line would bring New Mexico gas to Utah.

Utah Pipe Line asked to intervene in the re-convened hearings for Utah Natural Gas. The Public Service Commission ruled the company could intervene only on a "limited basis," and only in opposition to Utah Natural Gas's proposed line, but "not for purposes of presenting its own case." This ruling came after a spirited exchange between Sid Cornwall, lawyer for Utah Natural Gas, and Glenn Turner, representing Utah Pipe Line.

This time Utah Natural Gas had some help from gas users like Utah Home Builders, Draper's Lions Club, and various towns along the route. But companies such as Mountain Fuel, Union Pacific, Utah Coal Operators, and D&RG Railroad were there *en masse* to oppose the line.

The weakest link for Utah Natural Gas was the reserves they said they could put in the line. I thought they were much smaller than the estimate, and I hoped their promise to explore in the state would influence the Commission to grant the pipeline, which was vital to my whole Wasatch Plateau play. It was eighty miles to a pipeline connection, and, if this line was not built, I could see that it might be years before anyone would drill there. Certainly Mountain Fuel would not.

In ten days of hearings over a seven-week period, Utah Pipe Line went straight to the issue of reserves behind Utah Natural's line. Their expert witness attempted to tear to shreds K. W. Willson's earlier geological testimony. On rebuttal, Cliff Ashton told the Utah Pipe Line expert that Mr. Willson had been responsible for several oil and gas discoveries.

"How many oil and gas fields have *you* found, Mr. Dougherty?" Dougherty, Utah Pipe Line's expert witness, flushed and said, "None." Ashton turned to the Commission members and said, "I would place my faith in a man who has been successful in finding a gas field." By the looks on their faces, this had obviously made a favorable impression on the Commission members.

As the hearing came to a close, Ashton asked the Commission to give a conditional certificate of necessity for the building of the line. Cornwall said, "Byrd-Frost is willing to spend its own money to find what the gas reserves are in Utah, but it must have the protection of a certificate from the Public Service Commission." Strenuous arguments were made against this proposal, with Utah Natural Gas painted as a villain, a promoter, etc., by Mountain Fuel and Delhi and the Utah Coal Operators.

The Commission's decision seemed a little long in coming. Editorials in both the *Salt Lake Tribune* and the *Deseret News* called for the granting of the certificate. Then the decision was announced: Within one year, or by April 1, 1952, Utah Natural Gas must show it had proper financing, adequate reserves to pay for the line, and signed contracts with pipeline construction companies. Utah Natural Gas really had its work cut out for it to do all this in one year. Newspapers announced an imminent Utah drilling boom. Byrd-Frost announced locations at Boundary Butte, Monticello, Last Chance, and Clear Creek. It looked like my geology would be given the acid test on the Wasatch Plateau.

In the meantime, Utah Pipe Line appealed the Public Service Commission decision to the Utah Supreme Court. Cliff Ashton argued the case for Utah Natural and Calvin Rampton, attorney for the Public Service Commission, argued their right to give a conditional certificate. C. W. Wilkin was the attorney for Utah Pipe Line. The Supreme Court eventually upheld the Commission's right to grant the certificate.

By midsummer I went with Hicks Allen, engineer for Byrd-Frost and the drilling superintendent, to stake the location for the wildcat well on the Clear Creek structure. We were committed to drill a well on the Mid Continent leases, and I staked the location in Long Canyon on the exact top of the structure, according to my field work. Subsequent drilling showed this was indeed the highest point on the whole Clear Creek structure.

Drilling commenced in September 1951, and by the middle of October the first objective horizon, the Ferron sandstone, had been encountered. The drillers took several cores that were hard and impermeable and had no odor of gas or oil. My heart sank! I returned to Salt Lake, expecting to come back when they got into the Dakota sandstone, about 1,000 feet deeper. The next day I got a call from Allen. He said, "This is extremely confidential, but I need a pitot tube."

My heart went up into my throat. I knew he had found gas. A pitot tube is used to measure the volume of a flow of gas as it is discharged out of a pipe into the atmosphere. After calling Nick Morgan to tell him it looked like they might have something at Clear Creek, I threw my sleeping bag into the Jeep and headed out. When I got to the well location, they had the gas flaring. It was making a flare about 60 feet high out of 4-inch tubing. My, what a beautiful sight!

Hicks Allen and Jim Edson, geologist on the well, told me what had happened after I left. The tight, impermeable sandstone in the upper part of the Ferron sandstone, which I had seen in the first cores taken, apparently persisted for about 300 feet. Then, while they were drilling instead of coring, the well started to lose circulation; that is, the mud system which cools the bit and brings the rock cuttings to the surface started to filter back into the rock formation. This occurred at a depth of 4,704 feet. Allen mixed more mud and drilled on to 4,734 feet, when the entire contents of the mud pit disappeared into the well. Allen mixed up some new mud and put in lost circulation material, cotton seed hulls, and regained partial circulation. There were no shows of gas bubbles or odor in the mud. At this point, Allen ordered a Halliburton drillstem testing crew to the well to test the apparently porous lost circulation zone. I will be eternally grateful for his decision. Most drilling superintendents would be worried about losing the hole and would never test under these circumstances. Hicks Allen was looking for gas, and he found it! When the drillstem testing equipment was run in the hole and opened, mud, water, and lost circulation material started flowing out. No gas showed for nearly an hour — only gobs of mud and cotton seed hulls. Then came the gas, just a little at first and finally, after seven hours, the well was making a lot of gas. Allen let the well blow for eighteen hours, at which time the gas was blowing at the rate of 7½ million cubic feet per day. In the meantime he had casing brought to the well, and after running an electric log, he ran and cemented the casing in the hole. He gravel-packed the hole opposite the Ferron sand and ran tubing for further testing.

It was clear that we had an important discovery. Charlie Hauptman, the U.S. Geological Survey engineer, came down to assist in the completion. Mountain Fuel's district geologist came out to the well and gave me a long dissertation on how this probably was just a small gas field and we should sell out now, while it looked good. "This is one we will play to win," I told him.

Within a few weeks the Utah Pipe Line appeal to the Utah Supreme Court came up. They questioned the reserves at Boundary Butte and Last Chance, but the attorneys for Utah Natural Gas highlighted the important discovery at Clear Creek.

Calvin Rampton questioned the "sincerity" of the Utah Pipe Line intervention. "They qualified to do business in Utah only two days before the hearing began," he said. A few days later Utah Pipe Line asked the Supreme Court to dismiss its action against Utah Natural Gas and the Public Service Commission. Its gas reserves, which had been committed to the Utah pipeline, had been sold instead to El Paso Natural Gas Company for transmission to California. Mr. Rampton was later elected Governor of the State of Utah for three four-year terms.

The winter of 1951–52 was a busy one. Byrd-Frost merged their Utah interests into a new company — Three States Natural Gas Company, headed by John McGuire. Three States took over operations at Clear Creek and kept a rig busy all winter. They drilled several more wells both north and south of the Utah Fuel #1 discovery well. All were productive.

W. T. Nightingale of Mountain Fuel met with our group and wanted to get into the act. He wanted to try to get a deal on our land in Clear Creek or, failing that, work out a deal to take over the Flat Canyon structure. I asked him if he was ready to drill on Flat Canyon. "Well, no," he said. "We want to do some magnetic work and some seismic work to see if the fault on the west side of the structure exists." I said, "The Flagstaff limestone is opposite the Castlegate sandstone, indicating a vertical displacement of at least 3,000 feet. Isn't that enough evidence of a large fault?" He hemmed and hawed and said what he really wanted to do was "break John McGuire's back." Later that day he called me over to his office and said he understood I wanted to get gas for my house and he would authorize a connection, which he did.

Jack Frost and McGuire had already told me they wanted to drill Flat Canyon by August 1952 and drill two wells on the separate Joes Valley structural highs. I held a meeting with Tom Kearns, the Morgans, and Fitzpatrick and said I thought we ought to get John McGuire up to Salt Lake City and finalize a deal with him. McGuire came up, and we worked out an exploration agreement on all our holdings on the Wasatch Plateau. Three States would drill the initial wells free to us and finance our share of the subsequent wells for a 50 percent undivided interest. When the deal was consummated, Bob Bernick featured it in a front-page spread, with photos, in the *Salt Lake Tribune*.

Then my telephone started to ring. People assumed I had become a millionaire overnight. Anyone with something to sell or an angle of any kind would call at any hour of the day or night. I hadn't yet realized a dollar out of the Wasatch Plateau!

That summer Three States moved on to our leases and started to drill, first the H. E. Walton #1, then the P. T. Walton #1–X. The latter well came in for 136 million cubic feet of gas per day — probably one of the biggest gas wells ever drilled in the Rocky Mountains. It was followed by the H. E. Walton #A–3, which was even bigger. It looked like we had a major gas field.

In the summer of 1952 Three States moved a rotary rig onto the Flat Canyon structure and commenced drilling. They encountered lost circulation almost immediately in the Mesaverde formation. Of course this was common at Clear Creek, and the practice was to drill with water through the Mesaverde and Mancos shale to the top of the Ferron sand, then run casing at that point. Then they drilled through the Ferron with oil-base mud or with gas from an adjoining well. This gas drilling was to protect the Ferron sand from mud and water invasion that would plug its producing zones.

The Flat Canyon well, known as the Mary Durkin Kearns #1, had been drilled only a few thousand feet deep with the rotary when Three States decided to move in a large cable tool rig. This solved the lost circulation problem, but progress was slow. They finally encountered the Ferron sandstone, and it was really hard and tight. Only a small flow of gas resulted, about 250,000 cubic feet per day. Three States elected to continue to the Dakota sand — fewer than 1,000 more feet of drilling — but it took nearly a month to drill that small amount of hole. Three States must have had nearly half a million dollars in the well by that time. However, at just a few feet below 7,000, they encountered the Dakota, and the well started to make some gas. By the time they were at 7,739 feet, they had about 1,700,000 cubic feet per day — not much for that depth.

During this time, Three States had developed a technique at Clear Creek of "shooting" the Ferron section, when it was tight and nonproductive, with nitroglycerin. The most spectacular result obtained there was at the Colleen Kearns Steiner #A–1 well, the most southerly one drilled on the structure. Natural flow from the Ferron was about 2 or 3 million cubic feet of gas per day. After shooting it with 200 quarts of nitroglycerin, the well flowed more than 100 million cubic feet of gas per day. It was decided to shoot the Flat Canyon well in the Dakota sand level. This proved only slightly helpful, for it merely doubled the production.

With the production obtained at Clear Creek, Utah Natural Gas now appeared to have the green flag to construct a pipeline from Clear Creek to Salt Lake City. In the meantime, John McGuire had sold a controlling interest in the company to El Paso Natural Gas. Paul Kayser, El Paso's president and founder, came to Salt Lake to appear before the Public Service Commission. He said he could build the line and have it completed by late 1953. Part would be 16 inches and part 18 inches, and the line would have an initial capacity of 50 million cubic feet of gas per day, which could be increased to 100 million per day with additional pumping stations. Utah Natural would purchase gas from Three States and sell it to Mountain Fuel for distribution in the Salt Lake City and Provo areas. The Public Service Commission gave its approval, and construction started early in 1953. R. H. Fulton of Lubbock, Texas, was the builder for the pipeline and also laid the twenty-mile field gathering system at Clear Creek.

Gas pressure in the line at Clear Creek was held at 496 pounds per square inch. At its lower terminal, some 5,000 feet lower in elevation, the pressure was 513 pounds per square inch. At this time Clear Creek was the highest gas field in the world, parts of it more than 10,000 feet above sea level. Utah Natural also built a dehydration plant near the top of the highest point in the field to extract the small amount of water contained in the gas.

Now our wells were hooked up and ready for production. They went on stream in the fall of 1953. It appeared that our wells would soon pay out, and we might start to receive some income. But a fly appeared in the ointment.

About the time the wells went on stream, the sheriff came to our office to serve a summons. Mid Continent Petroleum was suing to declare the call on their gas in our original farmout null and void. This agreement called for the drilling of a free completed well, which had been done, and a call on their gas at 10 cents per thousand cubic feet, which was twice the going price at that time. However, by the time El Paso took over Utah Natural Gas Company, the price of gas had risen to 12 to 15 cents in the San Juan Basin, so El Paso signed us up for 15 cents per 1,000 cubic feet, with escalation to 18 cents over a twenty-five-year period. We had assigned our call on Mid Continent's gas to Three States, which then sold the gas to Utah Natural. Again I was thunderstruck at the business tactics of oil companies, this time Mid Continent. Why hadn't they come to discuss the matter with us before filing suit?

We were using Dick and Louis Callister as attorneys at the time, and they suggested we call in Harley Gustin, a prominent Salt Lake City trial lawyer. Gustin got in touch with Mid Continent's lawyers, and they sent one to Salt Lake City. We met with him, and I have never seen a more arrogant, egotistical person. I thought Tom Kearns was going to whip him before the meeting was over. He offered nothing, said we had no rights, and proceeded to tell us how many lawsuits he had won. To a man, we agreed to have our day in court with such people. It came in Wilmington, Delaware. Nick Morgan, Gustin, and I were there. Mid Continent's attorneys blew and blustered and then sat down. Gustin got up and said, "Mid Continent says the sentence in the agreement which says Morgan-Walton has a call on Mid Continent's gas doesn't mean what it says."

He went on to show how we had drilled a well on their land, making a valuable discovery for them in which they would make millions of dollars, and they hadn't even the courtesy to try to work something out. Gustin made a good impression, and the judge took the case under advisement.

We had a meeting when we got back to Salt Lake City, and John Fitzpatrick offered to go to Tulsa on business and "accidentally" run into the Mid Continent attorney and have a talk. By that time we had exchanged legal briefs, and ours was obviously better than theirs. Fitzpatrick made the trip, met the attorney, and worked out a deal for them to buy our call on their gas. They offered to pay $1,050,000, and we accepted. My share was about $150,000 after expenses.

Four years later the Internal Revenue Service declared this ordinary income, subject to excess profits tax and five years' interest.

They threatened to attach our production at Clear Creek, and we were advised by our tax advisers and attorneys to settle. We did. I had to pay $155,000 tax on the $150,000 income, and that was with no penalty or fine — just interest and excess profit treatment of the money. What a blow! This was just the beginning.

Three States drilled two more productive wells on the top of Flat Canyon. Now they thought it was possible that the Flat Canyon field and Clear Creek were all part of one big field. They were in the same fault block, with only a small structural saddle between them, and I have to admit I was favorable to the concept. John McGuire had to show large reserves to keep his credit good with Lehman Brothers, who were financing his drilling operations. He and Jim Edson, the geologist, decided to drill a well to test this theory part way between Flat Canyon and Clear Creek. It was known as Flat Canyon Unit No. 4, the structure having been unitized — that is, the leases had been placed in a federal oil and gas unit in order to have regular, ecologically sound drilling practices and production and to maintain the leases. Water was found in both the Ferron and Dakota, and the well was plugged. It was a real disappointment.

Meanwhile, Three States had "spudded" a well on the north closure at Joes Valley. It had continuous lost circulation problems and was finally abandoned at a little over 3,000 feet. Three States had nearly $600,000 in it by then. This was another blow.

By mid-1954 Three States had started to run back pressure tests on the Clear Creek gas wells. They showed an alarmingly steep pressure drop as gas was produced. Our reserve estimate for the nearly 20,000 acres that appeared to be productive had been on the order of a trillion cubic feet of gas. It looked like we would have to reduce this potential reserve drastically. That winter, after the Colleen Kearns Steiner #A–1 well on the extreme south end of the field had been completed, it was impossible to lay flow lines due to frozen ground, so the well went unconnected for six months. When we connected it in the spring, we found the well had declined in pressure without being produced! It became obvious that the Clear Creek Ferron sand was a fractured, limited-volume reservoir, so we had to revise our figures downward again. We were down to a quarter of a trillion by now, still enough to make money, but nothing of major importance as we had first thought.

Mountain Fuel was still short of gas, so Clear Creek was produced at rates up to 50 million cubic feet of gas per day during the winter months. I felt this was too much for the reservoir to stand; however, Three States needed the money to pay its debts, and the wells suffered accordingly. While the field was still producing from two or three wells until 1980, many of the wells were watered out before their time, and much of the gas originally in the reservoir will never be produced because of water coning and other problems. Proper conservation, I feel, would surely have lengthened the life of the field a great deal. Ultimately it produced only 132 billion cubic feet of gas — far less than the one trillion we thought it should contain.

During 1954 Utah Natural connected the three wells at Flat Canyon to their gathering system, but they didn't perform very well. It seemed ludicrous that while about 60 percent of the area within the closing contour at Clear Creek was productive, fewer than 1,000 of the 24,000 acres in the Flat Canyon structural closure were productive.

In 1955 Three States commenced drilling another well on the north closure of the Joes Valley structure. By October 17 they had encountered the top of the Ferron sand at 7,100 feet. They ran casing and started to drill in with air, and gas immediately came to the surface. Within a day they had a flow of 15 million cubic feet per day, only 164 feet into the 525-foot-thick Ferron sand.

I drove down to the well with my son, who was ten years old at the time. With more than two feet of snow on the ground, we barely made it into the well location. The gas flare lit up the whole country, and I thought we really had something this time. The Joes Valley structure had more than 80,000 acres within its closing contour — twice the size of Clear Creek. It had more than 3,000 feet of structural closure, also twice that of Clear Creek. This looked like the makings of a major discovery. That night, while slowly drilling into the Ferron sand, we hit water less than a third of the way through the Ferron. This meant we had another little bubble of gas on a great big beautiful geologic trap. Why? Oh, Why?

They shut the well down for the winter, and the toolpusher for the drilling company nearly lost his life a few days later when he got his car stuck in a snowdrift and tried to walk out. He lost most of his fingers and toes. Later, the Three States production superintendent on this same well did lose his life: he went into the cellar of the well when there was a gas leak and was asphyxiated. What a bedeviled well!

Next spring Three States completed this Joes Valley well and then drilled an offset to it to the Dakota sand, about 1,000 feet deeper, where they made a small well which was non-commercial at that depth. While they did connect the three wells they had drilled on North Joes Valley to their gathering system, the wells never paid out. I will never know why this structure was such a bust. It had all the makings of a major gas field. I used to tell my wife, "If J. Paul Getty owned it, it would have been the greatest field in the world." Of course that isn't so, but I can never understand why these large, broad structures had only a little bubble of gas on their tops and that is all.

Three States subsequently drilled a well on the south closure of Joes Valley. It was hard and tight in both the Ferron and Dakota sand levels with no shows. It is ironic that the Frontier sands, the equivalent of the Ferron and Dakota sands, have been productive of gas and oil all over nearby Wyoming but had such poor reserves in Central Utah. Many years later Tenneco Oil drilled another well on south Joes Valley, and it was dry too.

Despite the disappointments of the larger project, Clear Creek made a nice income for Tom Kearns, the Morgans, and me for many years. Kearns made more than a million and a half dollars on his interest alone. My share, of course, was much less, but it came when I needed it most. It bought a ranch in Jackson Hole, Wyoming, and financial security for many years.

For ten years after production began at Clear Creek, I worked on the possibility of getting some company to drill a deep well to test the Pennsylvanian and Mississippian formations. During that time, Mid Continent's interest was bought by Sunray Oil Company. Then Three States sold *its* interest to Delhi-Taylor, the Murchison company. Then Delhi-Taylor sold *its* interest to Conoco and Tenneco. As each new interest owner arrived on the scene, I talked "deep test." Sunray was interested for a while. Delhi-Taylor never was. Finally, I got Conoco and Tenneco to consider it. Conoco was interested; the Tenneco people dragged their feet. Finally, Tenneco said they would go, but they insisted on being operator. I would have preferred Conoco. Tom Kearns's son-in-law, Dick Steiner of American Linen Supply Company, wanted to pay our share for a sliding-scale interest dependent on the well cost.

Despite warnings from me and from Conoco's geologists, Tenneco insisted on locating the deep test on the highest ridge on the structure, near the old Utah Fuel #1 discovery well. Conoco and I wanted the well in the bottom of a protected canyon, where there would be 1,500 feet less drilling and weather protection. Not Tenneco. Their arrogance prevailed. By the time they had drilled through the Ferron and set protective casing in the gas sand, they had more than $600,000 in the well. At that point our wells had cost $125,000.

That was just the beginning. The well was scheduled to about 16,800 feet to test the Mississippian Madison limestone, and we estimated $800,000 at the beginning. By the time they got to 12,000 feet they had more than a million dollars in it. Most of the cost was a result of lost circulation trouble brought about by their high topographic elevation. They had drilled to the Permian Kaibab limestone and Coconino, or White Rim, sandstone, when their protective intermediate casing started to go to pieces, and they continually got stuck coming out of the hole. Then, in the lower Permian, they accidentally cemented their drill pipe in the hole while setting a lost circulation plug. This ended the ill-fated venture. One and three-quarters million dollars in the hole, and the objective never reached! And so there it sits today, a big, beautiful structure which has never had a meaningful deep test! I had to adopt the Arab Muslim philosophy, "If Allah wanted me to be a rich man, I would be rich."

CHAPTER 12

THE URANIUM BUG

ONE DAY IN THE FALL OF 1953 I got a call from Dewey Anderson, a land broker friend of mine. He said he had something he wanted to talk to me about, so we met. Years ago I had worked in Southern Utah with Dewey's older brother, a student at the University of Utah who had volunteered after Pearl Harbor and become an Air Force pilot. He was shot down and killed in an air battle over Britain. Dewey had been a bombardier in a B-24 but had come through the war in good shape. He and his father were actively acquiring oil and gas leases in the big Central Utah lease play that followed our gas discovery at Clear Creek in 1951.

Dewey said he had the uranium bug and told me he had an option to buy a group of claims, the "Swede claims," just a mile north of Charlie Steen's big Mi Vida mine near Moab, Utah. Steen's discovery, reported to have over fifty million dollars' worth of uranium ore in it, had really put Utah on the map as a uranium producer. Mi Vida was located on the west flank of the Lisbon anticline, and Steen had found it by drilling shallow core holes.

The Swede claims were located in just about the same position as Steen's mine, on the west flank of the Lisbon anticline, and had never been core drilled. The Swedes wanted $40,000 and a small royalty for their claims, and it did look like an attractive deal. Dewey wanted me to finance the purchase and carry him for an interest. Clear Creek was starting to bring in some money, so I was financially able to handle it. I told Dewey I would go down and take a look at the claims and let him know.

I was doing a lot of field work in Wyoming's Green River Basin using a Jeep, but this trip was a long way, so I took the family

DeSoto station wagon. My son, Paul, Jr., frequently accompanied me on trips to Wyoming, but this time his little sister Ann thought it was her turn to take a field trip with me. We drove to Green River, Utah, on a Friday and stayed all night. The next morning we drove down through Moab and La Sal to the north end of the Lisbon anticline. There was a little snow and mud, but we managed not to get stuck.

Nothing on the surface suggested that the geology of the Swede claims should be any different from that of the Mi Vida area. There was a little more overburden, however, and the drilling would be a little deeper. Ann and I drove around the whole area and got a pretty good feel for the surface geology. State Section 16 lay immediately west of the claims on which Dewey had filed a uranium lease. I looked over the ground there and thought I detected a subtle flattening of the dip of the Wingate sandstone over it. I decided this could mean subsurface structure, which might indicate an oil and gas trap at depth. We tried to file an oil and gas lease on it, but Pure Oil Company beat us to it. Ultimately, they drilled four or five gas distillate wells on this section. Lisbon anticline was a remarkable geologic structure, with uranium, gas, and oil on its flank and magnesium and potash salts on its crest.

When I got back to Salt Lake City, I called Dewey Anderson. He told me he had been talking to a core drill contractor from Casper, Wyoming, who would like to drill these claims for an interest. His name was "Friday" O'Connell. Things started to happen pretty rapidly. Whitney Brothers, who had underwritten several penny uranium stock companies, approached Dewey and me to do an underwriting. We ended up buying the Swede claims, signing a contract with O'Connell to do some drilling on them, and then putting the whole deal in a company called Federal Uranium for some money and stock. The Whitneys had no trouble selling the stock, and the company was in business.

At about this time, Floyd Odlum, a famous financier and president of the 100-million-dollar Atlas Corporation, was assembling uranium leases on the south end of the Lisbon anticline. He had the wherewithal to put together a big uranium company, and we in Federal thought we ought to approach him about merging our holdings with his. We met with his Utah representative, C. L. Davidson, who set up a meeting with Mr. Odlum in New York City. Reed Brinton, Federal's president, Howe Moffat, a director and attorney, Bob McGee, an accountant, and I made the trip.

Mr. Odlum had us come to his apartment in the River House, on Seventy-Second Street near upper Fifth Avenue. He carried on much of his business from his home, either here or at his ranch near Indio, California. He was a soft-spoken, kindly man, a lawyer by training, who had started his business career as an attorney for Utah Power and Light Company in Utah. The only flamboyant thing about Floyd Odlum was his wife, Jacqueline Cochran, the famous aviatrix. She had won the Bendix race once in a Republic airplane, and the seat and part of the cockpit had become conversation pieces in the apartment foyer. Later, Jacqueline was the first woman to fly the Atlantic solo and to break the sound barrier in a jet. Quite a gal!

Odlum's philosophy was that oil and gas were dwindling in importance as energy sources, and uranium would be the next great source of power. He had vast business interests in Northwest Airlines and a movie company, and he was an adviser and confidant to Howard Hughes. I didn't share his opinion on oil and gas versus uranium, but it appeared that he could do a great deal for Federal Uranium if we could interest him in it.

He *was* interested in Federal, and it seemed to fit into his overall plan of proceeding step by step, taking control of several small companies and eventually merging them into a large entity. It looked like we might be able to work something out, so we planned another meeting for Odlum's next trip to Salt Lake City.

At the Salt Lake meeting, we proceeded with the general evaluation processes necessary for putting properties into a big package. Of course everyone in the country who had a uranium claim wanted to be included. Much of the screening had to be done by Odlum's geologist, Ray Wimber, and me. Ray Wimber had been a student teacher in mineralogy at the University of Utah when I took the course in my sophomore year, so we already knew each other. He was a careful, competent mining geologist, and I learned a great deal from him. My experience was almost completely in oil and gas, so this was a new discipline.

Mr. Odlum had global business connections, and I soon discovered that he intended to acquire uranium properties all over the world. He had been contacted by people with uranium holdings in Portugal, Spain, Ethiopia, and Yemen, and he approached Wimber and me to make a geologic investigation of them as soon as possible. He suggested that we take our wives along, so that we would appear to be on a grand tour.

Wimber and I got our affairs in order and, with our wives, Eva and Betty, left for Washington, D.C., on August 26, 1954, to start getting the necessary visas and gathering maps of Yemen. Odlum was dealing with a European who had reportedly been granted a mineral concession on the whole country of Yemen.

We had already had some of the necessary shots for typhoid, typhus, etc., in Salt Lake City, but we needed yellow fever shots. Our first stop in Washington was the U.S. Public Health Service, to complete our inoculations and get our official health records. Next, we went to the Army Map Service and found they had only very sketchy maps of Yemen. We got copies of these, but couldn't get much of anything on Ethiopia.

Since it was the weekend, we all took a tour of Mt. Vernon, Arlington National Cemetery, Lincoln Memorial, and the Smithsonian Institution. Sunday we flew to New York City and stayed at the Ambassador Hotel, one of Mr. Odlum's investments. Mr. Odlum invited us to his River House apartment for cocktails. Madeline Jenkins, his private nurse, was hostess. She was a lovely lady whose hot packs and massage each day kept his arthritis under control.

Next morning, we had a conference with Mr. Odlum at his 33 Pine Street office near Wall Street and then went to the Egyptian and Turkish consulates to start the process of getting visas. That evening we went to Sardi's for dinner and later saw the stage production of *The Solid Gold Cadillac*.

Worried that we wouldn't have our visas on time, Mr. Odlum called former U.S. Ambassador Patterson, who put his limousine and driver and a Mr. O'Brien at our disposal, and we went from embassy to embassy gathering all the visas in record time. I was really impressed with Mr. Odlum's connections!

That evening we had dinner at Toots Shor's, went to Radio City Music Hall, and had an after-theater supper at Lindy's. I said to Wimber, "We may not be finding any uranium, but we sure are having a good time!" And our wives were eating it up!

The next day, Mr. Odlum's chauffeur drove us to Idlewild (now Kennedy) Airport, where we boarded a Pan Am DC-6 for Lisbon. Lisbon was our first destination because officials of Dresser Industries had contacted Mr. Odlum about some uranium properties available in Portugal. After stopping at the Azores to refuel, we landed in Lisbon at about 8:30 AM. We were met by a Mr. Karamza, a middle-aged Hungarian engineer who had a disconcertingly dishonest look in his eye. All four of us immediately distrusted him. He hired three taxicabs, all small British Morris compacts, and we loaded ourselves and our luggage and headed for our hotel. Karamza checked us into the Grande Borgas Hotel, a smelly fleabag joint we instantly despised. He took us to dinner at the Negrese restaurant, which also smelled, and we went back to the hotel for the night.

The next morning Karamza sent Mrs. Rieber, who turned out to be his mistress, to take us out to Estoril and check us into the Hotel Paris. It was considerably better than the Grande Borgas, but still poor. After we were settled in our rooms, we went down to the big rotunda on the south side, which overlooked the coast highway and the ocean. It was a beautiful Sunday morning, and we were really enjoying the rest. All of a sudden, we heard a big bang on the highway and saw that a small green sedan had run into a heavy-set elderly woman and knocked her sprawling on the roadway. We hailed the waiter and told him to call an ambulance. While he was trying to get to the telephone, the two men in the car got out, picked the woman up, loaded her into the car, and drove off.

An elderly English couple were sitting at an adjoining table, and I said, "My God, what do we do now?" The English lady replied, "Nothing. This happens all the time in this country." I guess I hadn't realized what conditions were really like under their dictator, Salazar, who was in power from 1933 to 1968. It took a while for everyone to get over the shock.

We still had not met any of the principals of Dresser Industries, or anyone who could tell us about them. The next day, after we had walked around the beach at Estoril all morning, Mrs. Rieber picked us up and took us to the house of Senhor Juan Baptista da Silva, a beautiful summer home in Cintra, a suburb of Estoril. We were surprised to hear that houses in Cintra didn't have addresses; they had names instead, spelled out in tile on the front gates.

Juan Baptista was a fat, fortyish Portuguese wheeler-dealer with interests in business in Portugal and the Azores, from where he had just returned. He had with him a British mining engineer, Rod Lewis, and a Portuguese engineer named Martins. At last we had met the principals.

After an amazing dinner, which we had to eat with our fingers from a lavish table spread with roast suckling pig, lobster, barnacles, and several kinds of fish, as well as cakes and cheeses, we got down to business. Juan Baptista would have Mr. Lewis and Mr. Martins take us to the properties, which would require several days. We were to leave in the morning, if that was agreeable. The next morning Wimber and I were picked up by Lewis and Martins in a big black Chrysler limousine, and we headed north, following the Tagus River valley. The country looked much like central California, even to the big oak trees, except these were cork oaks and their bright red color, after the bark had been peeled away, was eye catching.

Our first stop was Castelo Branco, near the Spanish border. Much of central Portugal is underlain by a granite batholith, and the uranium minerals in the various properties we looked at were fillings of thin fractures in the granite. The yellow carnotite and associated greenish-yellow minerals looked pretty, but their percentage of the total rock volume was very small. No large minable tonnage was apparent in any of the prospects. We continued north to the town of Guarda, which had the best occurrence of uranium. It was a filled fracture in the granite about six or eight inches thick, dipping about 60 degrees to the horizontal and exposed in a shallow pit for about five or six feet along its plunge. It was pretty, but it would have to widen out or be very long or deep to be commercial.

Martins had found most of these prospects while searching in the area for rare earth minerals that occurred in similar thin fracture fillings in the granite. He had a small mineralogical lab in Guarda, where he had brought pieces of the rare earth ores and refined them by gravity means during World War II. The metals of principal interest were scandium, lanthanum, cerium, and thorium, and Martins indicated that he had sold concentrates of these metals to both the British and the Germans.

Wimber had his Geiger counter with him, and for some distance we tried to trace the showings, but they didn't have much extent. We asked Lewis how these mining properties had been acquired. In the United States most uranium mines are on federally owned land and are staked as claims by someone. Here, however, most land was privately owned. Many pieces of land had been divided for so long that individual olive trees were separately owned by heirs of the original owners. Many of the heirs now lived in Brazil, so much correspondence and even separate purchases of rights to certain olive trees were required. It had been a tremendous job for someone to assemble the leases on these prospects.

Lewis and Martins took us north to the head of the Douro River in a terraced, timbered area where they had more thin veinlets of uranium ore. The volume of ore was so small it was hard to feel very much interested. The country, however, was fascinatingly primitive. There were still many groves of hardwood trees, and we visited a sawmill where all the power was human muscle. We watched two men with a long buck saw that had a handle on each end cut inch-thick boards out of a twenty-foot log. It would take them all day to cut just one board. The country was so lush, I couldn't understand the level of poverty. Black cloth was the principal clothing material, and it was common to see three or four generations of patches on patches on men's clothes.

The large vineyards appeared prosperous, and Rod Lewis told me that in the mid-1920s a disease of some sort, probably a virus, had killed almost all of the grapevines in Portugal. The new vines had come from roots and stubs imported from California!

We passed several small villages where agricultural fairs were being held. It was fascinating to see the girls in brightly colored dresses walking along the dusty dirt roads in their bare feet, carrying their only pair of shoes. When they got to town, they put their shoes on for the dances and social events. It made me think of my days in Mississippi, when we used to see the young black girls doing the same thing. I said to Rod Lewis, "The Negroes around Natchez used to call Saturday 'tight shoe' day. What do they call it here?"

"They don't have a specific name for it here," he said. Lewis would have known, because his mother was Portuguese and his father English, and he had been raised here.

That evening we drove into Porto for the night. I had always heard the city called Oporto, but Lewis explained that the "O" was the article for the Porto. My next impression, of course, was that this was the home of Port wine, a highly revered beverage. Lewis told us that most Portuguese didn't like Port wine, so it was all exported. Lewis and Martins took us to a combination bar and eating place, where we heard some good music and had a tasty meal. About that time, a couple of girls got their eye, and Wimber and I went back to the hotel.

We left just after daylight the next morning. It was less than fifty miles to Lisbon, but travel was slow on the narrow, winding roads. Since we had seen all the mining properties, Lewis took us to a few of the tourist sites. I was impressed with the many fortresses on prominent hills along the way. Lewis explained that these were Portuguese forts built during the conquest by the Moors, who had held Spain and Portugal for so long after the great Arab conquest of North Africa and the Iberian Peninsula. We visited the university at Coimbra. The so-called *fado*, the folk song of Coimbra, happened to be very popular even in the United States at the time, and it was interesting to see where it had originated.

We got to the hotel at Estoril fairly early and found we all had been invited to a supper club overlooking the sea. The Baptista da Silvas were our hosts. John the Baptist, as we now called him in our private conversations, really put on a spread—complete with crêpes suzette. Da Silva's attorney, Caster Neves, was there, and he entertained us with his amazing stories. Particularly appealing to us was his recounting of all the free lunches he had been invited to on his last trip to New York City and how much his taxi bills had been. He said, "I'm eating free, but I'm going broke paying taxi fares to get me there!" Our recent trip to New York City had been much the same for us; riding from River House on Seventy-Second Street to the Waldorf, to the Pierre, really rolled up the cab fares.

Karamza got drunk and tried to bully Wimber and me into telling what our report to Odlum on the properties would be, but da Silva shut him up. I had the feeling Karamza's whole livelihood depended on his selling da Silva on uranium, and he was desperate to make a deal. If he hadn't been such a despicably slimy character, I could have felt sorry for him. We told da Silva we would be in touch with Mr. Odlum, and they would hear from him. We had no authority to deal on the properties in any way. It was a perfect out, since Wimber and I didn't want to have to take a lot of flak because the properties were not interesting.

We left the next day on an Aero Portuguese Airlines DC-3 for Madrid. They flew low, and Wimber and I could see where we had looked at properties at Castelo Branco. We checked in at the Palace Hotel, and it was surely a pleasant change after the Hotel Paris in Estoril. Mr. Odlum had an interest in the Irving Krick weather modification company here, which had a contract with the Spanish government. A Mr. Glasier was their local representative, and Odlum wanted us to check in with him and talk to him about exploring Spain for uranium. We phoned Mr. Glasier's office and were told he would be gone until Sunday.

This left us some time for sightseeing, so we all went to the Prado Art Museum and the Retira Gardens and walked around downtown Madrid. Then we took a rubberneck tour of the city. I learned of a bullfight on Sunday, so we went. I was surprised at the gore, but happy that they no longer let the bulls gore the horses, now protected by large mattress-like pads. Actually, the play with the capes was very exciting to watch, and I marveled at the dexterity and nimbleness of the toreadors and matadors. However, it was spoiled for me when the picadores started the kill by sticking the bull with their lances. I am more in sympathy with the Portuguese bullfights, in which they accentuate the play with the capes and do not kill the bulls. After the bullfight, we were able to meet with Mr. Glasier, and he took us to dinner. We went at 10:00 PM, which I considered late, but Blanca, his Spanish wife, informed us that we were actually gauche in being so early, because the elite never show up at supper clubs until midnight.

Mr. Glasier was a banker who had stayed in Madrid during most of the Spanish Civil War, from 1936 to 1939. He had had to hole up in his basement during some of the shelling, but he said both sides realized the importance of keeping a bank open and had left him pretty much alone. He said that once a Russian-trained officer had insisted on seeing what was in the vault, and Glasier took him there alone. Glasier had taken his revolver from his desk drawer and carried it with him during the inspection. The officer looked around and then left and never came back. The Glasiers had moved to New York City for a time after the Civil War, but Blanca could never get used to the early rising, the lack of servants, and no siesta time, so they came back.

The next day Glasier picked the two of us up in his car and drove us around the northwest outskirts of the town, showing us the trenches and shell damage to the buildings that still hadn't been repaired. We discussed the possibility of uranium exploration in the country, and he said it would take some arranging to get permission. He promised to talk to the authorities about the matter and get in touch with Mr. Odlum later. Neither Wimber nor I ever heard any more from him, so we figured there was too much red tape involved. Spain is one of the areas where the earliest mining, particularly for mercury, was undertaken, and it should have had some possibilities for uranium.

Later that afternoon we all left for the airport, and our plane, a Venezuela Airlines Constellation, was four hours late. After we were finally checked in and our bags loaded, a uniformed customs man came over to me and wanted to see how much money and traveler's checks I was carrying. I showed him what I had in my wallet, and he said, "You had more when you came into the country." I said, "Yes, I did, but one book of traveler's checks is locked in my bag, which is on the plane." He insisted on seeing the money, so a baggage man and I had to climb up into the plane's baggage compartment, retrieve my bag, and take out the checks. When I brought them back to the counter, the officer said, "Count them."

"Count them yourself," I said. "You're the one who wanted to see them!" So he did, and then he let us all board the plane. He had been keeping everybody off the plane until now. We were now five hours late, and we didn't get to Rome until 10:00 PM.

We had wired ahead through Pan Am Airlines for reservations at the Hotel Majestic on the Via Veneto. The rooms were dirty, with no hot water, and the toilets were down at the end of the hall. And, to make it worse, Wimber had a terrible headache and was sick. Next morning Betty was sick too, and Wimber was sicker. We got a doctor to see them both, and he gave them some sulfa pills which made them feel better. Wimber stayed in bed all day. I hired a horse-drawn hansom cab and took Betty and Eva to the Colosseum, Baths of Caracalla, the Victor Emmanuel Monument, the Catacombs, and along the Appian Way. We had quite an afternoon. When we got back to the hotel, Wimber was up, saying he couldn't stand any more foreign food, so we went to what was advertised as an American restaurant. We had steak and pie, but it still tasted Italian.

We had come to Rome to meet Theodore Montague, a Frenchman who was supposed to have a concession for mineral exploration on the whole country of Yemen. He had sent a copy of this document to Mr. Odlum, and I had read it. It was a simple but comprehensive agreement, and I thought it would be adequate to cover any mining activities.

The next morning we located Mr. Montague at the Hassler Hotel and met him for lunch. He was short and dark, in his fifties, apparently a man of means who had worked all over the world. He had been a mining engineer and geologist originally, but now was more a financier, dealing in mining properties. Montague spoke of being in deals with Herbert Hoover, the Hochshields, and the Rothschilds. He spoke in French, Italian, Spanish, Portuguese, and English and was a typical polished European gentleman. He rang almost true, but I was still a little suspicious of him. Wimber and I wanted to find out more about his reason for taking the concession.

"Have you seen any indication of uranium in Yemen?" Wimber asked.

"There is a whole mountain of carnotite there," he said.

"Have you seen it yourself?"

"Yes."

"How did you know it was carnotite?" we asked.

He bridled at that question. "Anybody knows carnotite when he sees it. It's canary yellow!"

"Have you tested it with a Geiger counter?"

"No, it wasn't necessary. I know carnotite when I see it!"

Carnotite, the canary-yellow ore of uranium and radium, was common in southeastern Utah and southwestern Colorado. Wimber and I had seen lots of it — never in volume the size of a mountain. Carnotite usually occurred as a thin veinlet or as a replacement for petrified wood cells. Yellow ochre and clay sometimes looked remarkably like it but were not radioactive, as carnotite was.

"Can we proceed to Yemen to see the deposit?" This, after all, was the main reason for our trip.

"No. There has been a revolution. The crown prince just killed the king, and the country is unsafe for travel." This was disturbing news, but I have to admit not overly disappointing to me. I had dreaded going back to another primitive Arab country. I know Betty and Eva were relieved. Ray and I had planned to leave them in Cairo and go down alone.

Mr. Montague showed us some pictures, black-and-white prints he had taken around Yemen. One, a picture of the crown prince, was startling. The prince clearly had Down syndrome. He probably had impaired intellectual capacity and obviously had criminal tendencies, for he had personally killed his father, the king. Montague said he would keep in touch with Mr. Odlum and let him know when it was safe to visit the uranium deposit. A few days later, *Time* and *Newsweek* carried articles on the Yemen revolution. (About a year later, Wimber made the trip to Yemen. The yellow stuff was hydrothermally altered volcanic ash, a light yellow color, but not carnotite and, therefore, worthless. Our opinion of Montague as a geologist and mining engineer fell pretty low.)

Wimber wired Mr. Odlum of our inability to go to Yemen, so he instructed us to proceed to Ethiopia, where there were some people he wanted us to see. We would have to fly from Cairo to Addis Ababa, so we had a choice in the route we took from Rome.

I suggested we go by way of Athens and Istanbul, which we did. With difficulty, I was able to get four seats on KLM to Athens, but no promise of a hotel room. The DC-6 got us to Athens before dark, and we had a lovely view of the Acropolis before landing. KLM had a hotel for us — in Delphi. It was a flophouse. You could smell the single toilet for each floor as soon as you got off the elevator. The beds were small, with straw ticks for mattresses. Betty and Eva were desolate, so we took a cab down to Constitution Square and had a beer on the terrace of the King George Hotel.

The next morning we hired a woman guide in front of the King George, and she drove us to the Acropolis, where we toured the Parthenon. I was relieved to see nothing had happened to damage the antiquities during World War II. The Germans had occupied Athens and had been driven out. There had been great worry about possible demolition, in both Athens and Rome, but none occurred. The beautiful lines of the Parthenon should be perpetual inspiration to all people, no matter what their political or religious beliefs. We drove around Athens and saw the business and residential areas before departing for the airport.

KLM had reservations for us on the TAE Turkish Airlines. The plane was a DC-3, the passengers mostly peasants who had been visiting their families in Greece. Their baggage was amazing. Baskets and woven sacks of reeds contained loaves of bread and vegetables. One woman even had two live chickens, which she stowed on the shelf above the seats. Luckily the flight over the Dardanelles and the Sea of Marmara was smooth, and nothing fell down on us from above. We got rooms at the Pera Palace, an old and only partially used hotel that had probably been considered a grand hotel a hundred years ago. The lobby, filled with inlaid tables and native furniture, was poorly kept and dirty.

Ever since I had hurriedly passed through Istanbul in 1938, I had hankered to return to see the city — particularly the mosques. Downtown was a disappointment, with its narrow, dirty, smelly streets. However, the Blue Mosque and the Mosque of St. Sofia were outstanding. The domed buildings, with their stained glass and slender, graceful minarets, are an exciting feature of the skyline of

Istanbul. But these are not the only mosques. We stood on the old city wall at the Adrianople Gate and counted twenty-seven.

The famous Golden Horn bazaars proved to be extremely interesting to the Wimbers. Ray taught mineralogy at the University of Utah and knew his gems pretty well, so we spent several hours looking at the offerings of the many jewelry and precious stone shops. Ray bought a set of alexandrite ring and earrings for Eva. Of course there was much drinking of heavy Turkish coffee and tea at the various shops we visited.

We took a launch ride across the Bosphorus to Haider Pasa. It was a rerun of my trip to Saudi Arabia sixteen years earlier, when I had admired the magnificent view of the Istanbul skyline from the Asian side. I was still entranced by the sight.

Our KLM flight to Cairo was delayed, and we didn't arrive until 1:00 AM. Fortunately, the airline had Shaffi, a dragoman, waiting to take us to our hotel, the Semiramis. I arranged for Shaffi to meet us the next morning, and he drove us out to the Pyramids. We had lunch at the Mena House and then toured the Pyramids. We even had our pictures taken riding camels in front of the Sphinx. It was pleasant to be back in Cairo, where I had spent a lot of time during 1949, working on Getty's Neutral Zone concession.

BOAC seemed our best bet to get to Ethiopia: they had two planes a week. The other lines only went once a week. We had the possibility, but no promise, of reservations for three days ahead. I spent at least an hour every day in their office, working on getting tickets, but the delay gave us time to see Cairo.

Shaffi took us to belly dancing clubs at night and to the tombs at Saqqara and Memphis, the Egyptian museum, the bazaars of Khan Khalili, and the Muhammad Ali mosque during the day. I had been to all these places before, but it was interesting to see them again. The 5,000-year-old paintings at Saqqara were a particular thrill to see. The bull sarcophagi seemed an amazing but wasteful exercise in construction and artistry. I am always appalled at the effrontery to man's intelligence of building these beautiful, highly polished stone burial boxes of black andesite to serve as the final resting places for the remains of sacred bulls!

We finally got our tickets for Addis Ababa, but such a schedule! We left the Semiramis Hotel at 1:30 AM by cab for the BOAC office, from where we were taken to the airport. Then the plane, an Argonaut, similar to a DC-4, took off an hour late, at 5:00 AM. Not only that, they served stewed kidneys for breakfast on the plane. We landed at Aden after an interesting six-and-a-half-hour flight over upper Egypt, where we could see the Nile flooding. Along the west side of Yemen, we had a distant view of San'a, the capital, where we were scheduled to go.

It was hot in Aden, and we had to wait some time to board our DC-3 for Addis Ababa. I couldn't believe my eyes when we got on. The plane had at least twice as many seats as it should have had, and it was jammed full of freight. The runway was at least 7,000 feet long, and the plane used it all! It was so loaded, the pilot couldn't climb more than 100 feet above the water of the Arabian Sea until we were halfway to Somaliland (now Somalia), where we landed. Fortunately, many of the passengers and much of the freight were unloaded. Addis Ababa is at 7,000 feet, and we never could have made it otherwise. It still took two and a half hours to climb up over the green lava hills before we dropped into the Addis Ababa airport.

It was the rainy season, and everything was wet. A pall of eucalyptus wood smoke hung over the city. We checked in at a little hotel, the Ras, and Wimber got in touch with Swede Galeen, who ran Ethiopian Airlines. He was our contact in Addis and was a former associate and employee of Floyd Odlum. By this time I had a terrific case of food poisoning from the breakfast of stewed kidneys. I was sick all night, and the next morning Wimber found a Swiss doctor who came and gave me some sulfa and a penicillin shot. I soon felt somewhat better — and I had to! Galeen had made an appointment with Emperor Hailie Selassie I for 4:00 PM.

Wimber briefed me further on the reason for the meeting and for our coming to Ethiopia. Swede Galeen was Odlum's listening-post in Ethiopia and had recently discovered that an itinerant German geologist had been in the country looking for uranium. Apparently the man had found a yellow mineral which he thought was carnotite, and his Geiger counter had indicated that it was highly radioactive. He had approached the emperor for a mining concession, and Galeen had contacted Odlum for him to try to get a concession as well. The geologist had left some samples of the yellow mineral with the emperor, and the meeting was set up for us to look at the mineral and test it with Wimber's Geiger counter.

On shaky legs I accompanied Wimber and Galeen to the palace. We were met by a distinguished-looking black man in a military uniform, who instructed us how to enter the room, greet His Majesty, and leave the room. He would also act as interpreter. Swede Galeen accompanied us; he was used to meeting the emperor, and that helped. After some small talk and niceties with His Majesty, we were shown the yellow rocks. Wimber put his Geiger counter on them and got nary a click. I said, "Do you suppose the counter has been damaged in transit?" I had been carrying it in my heavy Halliburton suitcase, wrapped in clothing.

Wimber asked, "Has anyone got a radium dial on his wristwatch?" Swede did, and the counter really clattered with the sonde close to the watch face. "Well, there's nothing wrong with the counter," Wimber said. I had to agree. "But why the geologist's report that the yellow rock had a high radiation count?"

Galeen later determined that the German's counter must have been damaged before he tested the yellow rock, and it had given a false reading. What a wild-goose chase! It appeared that our Ethiopian investigation was coming to naught. We both thought the country should have uranium resources, but we had neither the time nor the wherewithal now to check on anything further.

"Would you like to have this Geiger counter?" Wimber asked, turning to Hailie Selassie. The emperor looked over the slender black vinyl-covered instrument with its slightly tarnished brass probe and somewhat worn appearance. He turned to the interpreter and said something which came out: "The Emperor would like you to come back sometime soon and bring him a new one"! Apparently a little honest wear was more than he could stand.

I had really hoped he would take the counter. Every customs officer who went through my baggage suspected that the instrument was some kind of infernal machine or a bomb. I had been held up at almost every port of entry because I was carrying it. But I was doomed to take it to the United States, although I got it pretty well wrapped up in clothes, so it wasn't found every time.

It appeared that our meeting with the Lion of Judah was coming to a close, so we thanked him and excused ourselves. Wimber and I did our best to follow Swede Galeen's backing-out procedure. He bent slightly at the waist and then backed out of the room so his back never faced the emperor.

Galeen took us to his apartment in the Jigjiga Building that evening to show us pictures of his big-game safari in Kenya and Ethiopia, and we discussed the possibility of sending a field party to look over the whole country for uranium. Geophoto Corporation had had a party here looking for oil prospects for Sinclair Oil some years ago, but conditions were really unhealthful, and it was hard to get geologists to stay very long. We said we would take it up with Odlum when we got home.

The celebration called Finding of the True Cross was going on at the time. Ethiopians are generally Christian, and the kings of their royal Meneluk line are, so the story goes, descendants of the Queen of Sheba and Solomon. Many young people and villagers from the countryside were parading through the streets with long lances of bamboo. They were exuberant but not boisterous, and they waved gaily to us as they marched by — an interesting bit of local color.

The next day some people from the U.S. Embassy who were in Ethiopia on the USAID program came by to see us. A Mr. Andrews drove us out to Lake Bishoftu, which occupies an extinct crater. A resort-type restaurant on the shore of the lake afforded a lovely view of the blue water and green hills. Sitting on the terrace was a problem, however, because of the flies. They were omnipresent. Andrews' job in USAID was to bring in new industry. He was attempting to get a coffee-growing economy going, and his figures showed it would cost $5,000 per acre and take seven years to put a coffee plantation into production. We told him we would pass the data along to Odlum; I knew he would not be interested, however.

That evening three of the TWA personnel who helped operate the Ethiopian Airline had us to dinner. They were all big-game hunters, and their apartment was lined with animal heads from

Kenya. They were insistent that we not venture outside the buildings at night, even in the outskirts of Addis Ababa, because of the great number of hyenas that raided the garbage cans and chicken coops of the city dwellers. Hyenas had been known to kill a person who was encountered unexpectedly.

We left the next morning for Cairo on the Ethiopian Airline Convair. We landed at Asmera for lunch and again at Port Sudan for fuel, arriving in Cairo at dark. The Wimbers left us there. They had always wanted an ocean voyage, and now was their chance. They were going to London to sail home on the *Queen Mary*.

Betty and I got visas to stay a few days in Cairo. We were both sick. Betty was quite sick that night, so I asked the desk clerk to call a doctor. When he came, he took her temperature, which was high, and prescribed a penicillin shot. He gave me a prescription, which I got filled at an apothecary shop across from the hotel. In those days, penicillin came in powder form with a bottle of sterilized water; you injected the water into the bottle containing the powder. When I returned, the "doctor" didn't even have a hypodermic needle. (I don't really believe he was a doctor.) Fortunately, I had one and mixed the medicine and gave Betty a shot. She felt better the next morning, so I guess that was the important thing.

I spent most of the next two days in airline offices, trying to confirm passage back to the States via India, Burma, Thailand, Singaport, French Indochina (Saigon), Hong Kong, Japan, and Hawaii. I also wrote a short report to Mr. Odlum on our trip so far.

Thursday, September 30, we left for Bombay on a TWA Constellation at 9:45 AM. We flew over the Sinai Peninsula, across the northern Arabian desert, over Dhahran and Bahrain Island. I was able to point out to Betty some of the areas where I had worked in Saudi Arabia. We flew nonstop to Bombay, landing at about midnight. Even at midnight, India's civil servants took two hours getting through the paperwork and customs at the airport. We checked into the Taj Mahal Hotel near 3:00 AM.

We got up a little late the next morning but, after checking with Air India, we took a sightseeing bus to the Gate of India, the Queen's Necklace, Malabar Hill, and the Hanging Gardens. We saw the college, the burial buildings of the Parsees (where vultures devour the corpses), and the shopping district and slums. The view of the city from Malabar Hill was outstanding! The physical port of Bombay is fascinating; the human side is not. The street people, who have no homes and live, procreate, and die on the sidewalks, are a depressing sight. The smell of urine around every building and the constant crush of humanity everywhere were sickening.

The Taj Mahal Hotel was an architectural masterpiece. Its outside form is like a Hindu temple, and the large, high-ceilinged rooms were practical for the hot weather. Servants of rich people, who had to sleep outside the doors of their masters' hotel rooms, seemed pitiful until you realized that they did have food, shelter, and clothing — more than many others in the country.

We flew to Delhi on an Air India Vickers Viking and stayed at the Ambassador Hotel. We took a cab around the beautiful new red government buildings in New Delhi, which are lined up in a mall, much like the Capitol, Washington Monument, and Lincoln Memorial in Washington, D.C. Our driver pointed out some of the people cutting the lawn with hand scythes as lepers. Apparently there were no leper colonies in India, and the afflicted roamed free to take care of themselves. We also saw the site of Mahatma Gandhi's funeral pyre.

The Red Fort in Old Delhi was another architectural wonder. The area surrounding it was mostly marketplace, teeming with Indians of all walks of life, from Brahmins to holy beggars, whose painted faces and bodies marked them as objects of public almsgiving. We walked around Connaught Square and found the Imperial Hotel, then one of the fanciest hostelries I had ever seen. We had a lime squash on its terrace and were treated like royalty. I could really see why so many Englishmen "went out to India" and were never the same again. The opulence of the life of the wealthy in India of the late eighteenth and early nineteenth centuries must have been fantastic.

I made arrangements to be driven to Agra, so we left New Delhi at 6:00 the next morning. Our driver was a bearded, turbaned Sikh and our guide a Hindu in his mid-thirties. We drove south on the Grand Trunk road, passing sacred cows, water buffalo, jackals, goats, even flocks of vultures on the way, and reached Agra at 9:30, in time to see the Red Fort both inside and out. The Red Fort of Agra is a much greater and more interesting edifice even than its counterpart in Delhi. At Agra the fort is on the Jumna River, commanding a magnificent view of the Taj Mahal, about a mile downstream. In particular, the view of the Taj Mahal from the rock-latticed windows in the cell where the father of Shah Jahan lived as a prisoner while the Taj was being built is especially beautiful. But the irony of the emperor son imprisoning his deposed father spoiled the gorgeous view for me.

We had tea at the Imperial Hotel in Agra and then drove to the Taj Mahal. From inside the large red stone gate, the view of this most beautiful building in the world is breathtaking. Its white marble dome and slender minarets are so delicate and beautiful from a distance that one is hardly aware of the intricate inlaid designs of semi-precious gems in the walls that materialize as one moves closer. This beautiful mosque, built as a tomb for Shah Jahan's favorite wife, carries on the Mogul architectural tradition — even though the architect was French! While it was built in the seventeenth century, it looks only slightly weathered, the marble taking on a slightly off-white patina. The tomb of Akbar the Great, another red sandstone monument, was interesting mostly because of the bands of monkeys inhabiting it. They are fed by the sightseers, most of whom are Indians.

Before leaving Agra, we had an early dinner at the Lauries Hotel. Here I saw a most unusual thing. An old man had pet birds which appeared to be a species of sparrow. He had taught them to catch a playing card when he threw it into the air. They never missed catching and returning it to him. Then he would spread the deck face up on the floor, and one of the birds would pick out the six of diamonds and bring it to him every time, even after the cards had been shuffled and re-spread. I had never seen birds do tricks like this before. Of course, there were the usual snake charmers with their weaving cobras, but I don't like snakes very much and didn't spend much time watching them.

On the way back to Delhi, about twenty-five miles out of Agra, a wild monsoon rain and windstorm struck the area. Earlier it had rained a lot, and the trees lining the road were standing in water.

When the winds hit, trees toppled and fell across the road. Many had dead monkeys in them. We had to pick our way through the fallen trees, sometimes pulling them out of the way so our little Chevrolet sedan could pass. Finally, we came to a stretch where the road was completely blocked. By this time it had become pitch dark. Facing a night and part of the next day in the car, with no bathroom facilities for Betty, the guide suggested backtracking to a small town where Betty and I could catch the train. We got to the station all right, and found the train would be coming through about 10:00 PM. So they left us there. The station was small and cramped for sitting space on the bare wood benches, and the sight of bright red spittle on the floor — from passengers who were chewing and spitting betelnut bark — became quite nauseating.

Betty got faint, and we went to the soft drink counter to buy her a bottle of Coke. The old man popped the lid off and then rubbed his dirty hand over the top of the bottle, "to wipe the dirt off," he said. I thought Betty would "pop her cookies." His hand was filthy. We took her handkerchief and wiped it again, and the liquid did help her nausea. Finally, the train came, and we sat on more wooden benches, arriving in Delhi at midnight. We took a cab to the hotel.

I found the long day to have been one of the most interesting in my whole life.

The next morning, our guide and driver showed up and told us they had found another way home and had been in Delhi by 9:00 PM! Oh well, they thought they were doing the right thing in having us catch the train, I guess.

The guide took us on a more complete tour of the government buildings and then to the extremely ornate Lakmi Narayan Mosque. Jawaharlal Nehru was in office at this time, and India was still unpartitioned; Pakistan had not yet broken away. The British influence was far from gone. One of the most outstanding examples in New Delhi is the George V Monument and the Gate to India, built to commemorate George V's visit to India. The civil service system the English instituted was still carried on, and among the better educated, English was pretty much the common tongue of the whole country. It is clear that England, like the earlier Mogul conquerors, had left a lasting and deep impression on the country.

That night we boarded a Pan Am DC-6 for Bangkok, arriving the next morning after passing through a monsoon which tossed the plane around like a Piper Cub. We were fortunate to find a room at the Oriental Hotel — the classic hostelry of the city. The Oriental is located on the Chao Phraya River, with a terrace from which we could watch the busy river traffic. Boats of all descriptions go up and down the river, which is about a quarter mile wide at this point.

We took a taxi to see the Temple of the Emerald Buddha and the adjoining buildings in the castle grounds. The outside of these buildings is a mosaic material consisting of bits and pieces of crockery, porcelain, and glass, all stuck in a cement. While rather tacky-looking close up, at a distance it makes a distinctive texture. One of the most interesting parts of the city was the floating market with its early-morning activity. We took a launch at 6:30 and toured the various waterways where the farmers sell produce from their little boats. While I expected to see fruits and vegetables as the main items, there were also quantities of bread, coffee, cloth, and other kitchen staples for sale. The people in the boats and those in the houses along the waterways appeared to be very clean. They could be seen bathing, brushing their teeth, and washing their hair in the light-brown water of the river. Not exactly sanitary, but it rearranged the dirt each day, anyway. That afternoon we visited the Temple of the Reclining Buddha — a hundred-foot-long, gold-covered full-length statue. The marble courtyards of the temples were particularly beautiful and well maintained.

The next morning we took an early flight to Singapore on a Garuda Airline Convair. We flew south across the Malay peninsula and passed over several open pit and placer mines. These were the famous tin mines the Japanese took so early in World War II. I wondered, looking at them, if there might be some primary uranium mineralization in this area and took notes to discuss it with Wimber when I got back home.

I had always heard that Singapore was a rough–tough seaport town, consisting of rows of tin-roofed shanties and brothels. Nothing had prepared me for the beautiful, clean city and the charming Raffles Hotel. The racetrack and adjoining polo fields were completely foreign to my image of Singapore. Naturally, the next few days there were delightful. We visited the papaya and tapioca groves and saw rubber trees and all sorts of exotic citrus trees. We secured a driver and guide who took us to Johor Baharu. I wanted to see the bridge where the Japanese had come in the back door and taken the city without a fight.

I was getting anxious to get home and take care of business, so we skipped Saigon and went directly to Hong Kong on a BOAC Argonaut. We stayed at the Peninsula Hotel in Kowloon. Hong Kong has grown so much since 1954 that it is hard to think of it as the jewel of the Pacific, but it really was then. We enjoyed the sights and bought a teakwood chest. We went to dinner with an American from San Francisco who knew a geologist who had worked in Casper, Wyoming. He was a manufacturer's representative and came here often. He took us to a Chinese restaurant frequented mostly by Chinese. The food was similar to Chinese food in the States, but the service was different. All during the meal, a fifteen-year-old girl stood at the end of our table and, after each course was served and eaten, she would present each of us with a hot, perfume-scented towel to wipe our hands and faces before we embarked on the next course. It was unique, but the next morning we were both sick to our stomachs.

We took a later afternoon Pan Am flight to Tokyo and arrived the next morning. The moon was full, and Fujiyama showed its snow-topped crest beautifully. We wanted to stay at Frank Lloyd Wright's Imperial Hotel, which had been the only major building to survive the 1922 earthquake, but it was full. We found space at the Kokosi Konko, a new little second-class tourist hotel. However, we did visit the Imperial, where a Geisha prepared a broiled beef and vegetable lunch for us — somewhat different from the sukiyaki then available in Salt Lake City. We toured the royal palace gardens and the downtown shopping district — Ginza Street.

In late 1954 Tokyo was just beginning to be rebuilt. Many remains of the burned-out blocks were still evident. Time after time as I drove around Tokyo and saw the flimsy houses and the limited extent of their industry and business, I wondered, "How did they ever expect to beat the United States when they attacked us at Pearl Harbor?" Theirs had to be some special kind of madness to think they could prevail over a country with the size and resources of the United States. It was October 13, and we knew there would be snow in the Wasatch Mountains in Utah. It was cold here, but no snow yet.

We flew by Pan Am Boeing Stratocruiser to Honolulu by way of Wake Island—seven hours to Wake and another seven to Hawaii. We had been gone nearly two months, and America looked awfully good. I rented a car and we drove all around Oahu. We ate fresh pineapple and went swimming at Waikiki. We called Salt Lake City and told the kids when we would be home.

The trip had been a wild-goose chase as far as finding any uranium reserves. But we had checked out two good leads — one in Portugal and the other in Ethiopia. Wimber would later check out the one in Yemen. It was becoming evident that our best uranium possibilities were probably in the United States — most likely in Utah — so we would work toward that end.

I called Mr. Odlum as soon as I got home. He suggested I come down to his ranch at Indio, California, and meet with him, Ray Wimber, and Allen Ellgren, a Salt Lake City attorney. I flew to Palm Springs, where Odlum's driver picked me up and drove me to the ranch. It was about 900 acres and included a nine-hole golf course; citrus trees and date gardens comprised the rest of the area. The main house sat on a small hill, and all our meetings were held there and on the terrace overlooking the swimming pool. The guest houses, of which there were a number, were nearly always filled with Odlum business associates and Jacqueline Cochran's friends; General "Tooey" Spatz of the Air Force and Ambassador Bill Pauley were guests during my visit. Mr. Odlum had a skeet range, and one afternoon I shot with them. I was surprised to make the second-highest score, particularly since I had never shot skeet before.

Although Miss Cochran was usually either just coming or going somewhere in her twin Beach airplane, she happened to be there at the time, and when I told her I was from the Rocky Mountain area, she said what a shame it was that all the water was now polluted. This was considerably before ecology and pollution became a cause célèbre, so I was surprised at the remark. I told her there were still many untouched areas in the Jackson Hole region of Wyoming and the Uinta Mountains of Utah where pure springs still could be found. She obviously didn't believe me. Then she said how fortunate it was that, since we were running out of oil and gas, uranium was going to take over powering the needs of the country. As an oil and gas geologist, this rankled me, so I said I expected to see my grandchildren still heating their homes with gas. She didn't appreciate this remark at all and acted as if I were a traitor to the uranium cause. While a brave and gutsy flier, she was obviously only partially aware of the activities of Mr. Odlum, for I knew he was negotiating at that particular time for an oil and gas concession in Argentina and was talking with others about drilling for gas in the San Juan Basin in New Mexico.

General Spatz had been in charge of the commission to find a site for an Air Force Academy and had just announced that Colorado Springs would be the location. One evening he gave us a short résumé of the problems involved in the process of choosing the location.

Ambassador Pauley, having recently served as Ambassador to India, was an expert on Far Eastern affairs. One evening over cocktails he lamented the manner in which Mao had taken over China without the United States lifting a finger to prevent it. He was really bitter about our being sold out by our representatives who called Mao "an agrarian reformer" rather than recognizing him as the Marxist he really was.

Our business discussions led Mr. Odlum to consider the possibility of combining all his holdings with Federal Uranium and bringing other properties into the same package. Later, we held meetings in Albuquerque, Beverly Hills, and Salt Lake City to further the merging of the various properties. Our meeting at the Beverly Hills Hotel was interesting because Mr. Odlum had to leave suddenly in the middle of the discussion. He went outside and got into an old Plymouth coupe driven by a dark-haired man with a black moustache. They drove off together and didn't come back for an hour or so. I was mystified until Madeline Jenkins, Mr. Odlum's nurse and special assistant, said, "That was Howard Hughes. He wants to talk to Mr. Odlum about TWA."

Odlum wanted me to be president of Federal Uranium during this transition period and to supervise the core drilling he was doing on some claims on the south end of the Lisbon anticline — not far from Steen's Mi Vida mine — and on some claims in the Jacob's Chair area west of Blanding, Utah, near the White Canyon uranium district. This would free up Ray Wimber, who was exploring some properties in Australia. I agreed to this and made several field trips. Ken McGriffin was the geologist on the Lisbon properties, and Lou Davidson looked after the Jacob's Chair claims. We opened an office for Federal Uranium on the eleventh floor of the Walker Bank Building, and I hired Betty Allen, a former Texaco land secretary, to run it. My office was on the fifth floor.

About this time, Federal began to need money to operate, and Mr. Odlum brought in more directors, who were asked to buy blocks of Federal stock; the old directors were expected to come up with like amounts of money. Most of them did, but I felt I was spending a lot of time without compensation, and I didn't want to have to invest money as well as time. Besides, the oil and gas business was starting to pick up, so I wrote to Mr. Odlum, saying I wanted to resign. He accepted with a nice letter. Meanwhile, more properties were being put into Federal, companies were being merged, and a large uranium company appeared to be aborning. The stock was selling for about fourteen dollars a share, and my stock was worth more than half a million dollars. Then it happened!

Those of us who were in early had agreed not to sell any stock until the concern was into production and well established. Not so those who came in later. Large amounts of stock were dumped on the market, and the price went down and down. Even the University of Utah, to whom Odlum had given a block of stock, dumped theirs. The price went down to less than a dollar, and lawsuits and countersuits sprouted. Most were finally resolved, and today Federal Resources is a viable operating company with a stable stock price and a sizable income from minerals other than uranium. However, not a single officer of the company or any of its stockholders know that claims I bought and put into Federal were the basis for its beginning. Oh, well! I held on for years as a stockholder and finally sold at around a dollar a share. Finally, after more than twenty years, uranium ore was found on my original "Swede claims," and I was paid a small royalty for a year or two.

Ray Wimber's trip to Yemen had proved the Montague story of a mountain of carnotite a myth. While on a trip for Odlum to South America, Ray and his wife Eva went down in a plane in the high Andes. Their bodies were never discovered.

When I got back into the oil and gas business, I found that Betty Allen was tired of Federal Uranium too, and she went to work for me as a land secretary. She is still with me after thirty-eight years.

After Mr. Odlum died in 1975, his beautiful Indio ranch was subdivided into home sites, and I now own a condominium there. I have never tried my hand at uranium since.

This story of the beginnings of a small natural resource company may be useful in showing that the exploration for and exploitation of needed natural resources don't just happen. It takes endless and infinite effort and luck for such enterprises to succeed.

In contrast to my work for J. Paul Getty in the Neutral Zone, which secured for him the largest single asset in his company, this uranium expedition — which started with apparently equal possibilities and opportunities — contributed nothing to the assets of Federal Uranium. This is the luck factor! Or some other factor? Who knows?

CHAPTER 13

LIBYAN ORDEAL

BETWEEN 1956 AND 1960, LIBYA was very much in the international oil development news. All the major American oil companies had concessions in the country, and several oil fields had been found. As it was a large, undeveloped country, the first concessions, granted principally in the Sirte Basin, were very large. Later concessions were granted in nearly all parts of the country, including areas along the western border with Tunisia and Algeria as well as the eastern border with Egypt.

Large discoveries of natural gas had been made in Algeria some years earlier, so adjoining areas in Libya were looked on as favorable for oil and gas prospects. However, the most fruitful region during the early years of exploration was the Sirte Basin, where companies carried out photogeologic and geophysical surveys of all types, and followed them with exploratory drilling. Concession agreements provided that the companies had to relinquish from a third to a half of their original concession area after the first five years. A great amount of potential oil land would thus become available for leasing by other, smaller companies.

My landman, Jerry Guinand, was approached by a Denver-based landman, Don Christopher, a former Conoco hand, to join him in putting together a syndicate to try to acquire some of these areas in Libya. Christopher was being touted on the idea by a Denver-based geologist, Ray Thompson, a former classmate and friend of a geologist in the U.S. Geological Survey who was currently working on a USAID program of geological mapping in Libya. They knew of my experience in Saudi Arabia with the Getty interests and wanted me to join them. I was naturally intrigued with the idea but against our joining, because I knew the tremendous costs and the time and effort involved in dealing with Arab governments.

I did consent to talk with Christopher and Thompson and flew to Denver to see them. They painted a rosy picture, claiming to have Occidental Petroleum lined up to back us in the venture. They also had a geologic report on a huge deposit of hundreds of millions of tons of iron ore in the middle of Libya that was not under concession and that we might be able to obtain with the U.S.G.S. geologist's help. It was their plan to form a Swiss company, financed by American money, and have the advantage of Swiss international money dealings and the flavor of a neutral non-aggressive country for company background. With considerable misgivings, I agreed to join the group and consented to go to Libya with them to have a preliminary look at the situation.

It was December of 1960. On the way to Libya, we stopped in Switzerland to meet Thompson's brother-in-law who, we were told, was a president of the Swiss railroad. Although he was a charming fellow, I later learned that he was actually the president of his local labor union. We also met a friend of his, a banker from a small town in eastern Switzerland. They gave us some advice on forming a Swiss company and some names of law firms that could handle the legal details.

Then we headed to Tripoli via the twice-a-week flight of Alitalia from Rome. The plane arrived after dark, and the airport bus unloaded us at our destination, the old Uaddan Hotel. It was Tripoli's best, but dirty and unkempt. It did have an Italian kitchen and dining room which was quite good.

Thompson had written Gus Goudarzi, his U.S. Geological Survey friend, that we were coming, but Goudarzi was out in the field. However, Mrs. Goudarzi was in town and invited us to accompany her to a cocktail party given the next evening by American Ambassador Jones. The party was attended mostly by Embassy personnel and USAID organization types — generally nice people, but obviously underworked, overfed, and over-consumers of alcohol. There were a few oil company personnel there, and I recognized a geologist with Standard of New Jersey who had formerly worked in the

Uinta Basin in Utah. Of course he wanted to know what I was doing there, and I said, "Just looking around."

When Goudarzi returned, we discussed with him the possibility of concessions coming available. He didn't seem to want to talk about it, and I had the feeling Thompson was imposing too much on their friendship. Gus was an Iranian who had been taken to the United States at an early age and had grown up in Butte, Montana. He had graduated from the Montana School of Mines as a mining engineer. He looked like the Libyans and got along well with them; he was an excellent contact, I thought. Gus took us to the Embassy to talk to the man in charge of economic affairs, who gave us a rundown on Libyan contacts to see about oil concessions.

One who sounded like he might be most helpful was a former Palestinian lawyer, Anis al-Qasem. Al-Qasem had been head of the Petroleum Department and had drawn most of the petroleum law prior to the granting of the first concession. He had worked closely with King Idris and his cabinet advisers during the granting of many of the concessions. Now he had his own law office.

We met with Qasem in his office. He appeared to be fifty or so, slightly balding, with dark hair and eyes. Actually, he was only thirty-five. He was a graduate of Lincoln Inn, London University, and spoke English very well. He said he could help us to get a concession but wanted a retainer now, more money while he was working on the concession, and then more money when he delivered the concession. He also wanted an overriding royalty. He said Wendell Phillips had received an overriding royalty from an American oil company as a result of Qasem's introducing him to King Idris and presenting the king with a handsome sword. This royalty ultimately made Phillips a multi-millionaire.

Christopher told Qasem about his supposed Occidental connection, and Qasem said we would have to establish a headquarters and office in their name before he could start negotiations. He knew of a villa we could rent — he owned it — which would suffice as a base of operations. His office would be our business address. We looked at the villa the next day and rented it in the name of Occidental Petroleum. Then we had to find some furniture to get it ready for occupancy. Fortunately, we were able to buy some used beds, a sofa, and a radio-phonograph from an American airman attached to the Air Force at Wheeler Field, who was being transferred home.

Goudarzi introduced us to his assistant, Chase Tibbitts, a field geologist who was looking after a number of water wells being drilled down near Sebha — about 500 miles south of the coast and the capital of the Province of Fezzan. The iron deposit was seventy miles from Sebha on the Wadi Shati, and Tibbitts had some work to do in that area. If we could go to Sebha with him in a day or two, he would take us around the iron deposit.

This was an opportunity, so Thompson and I flew with Tibbitts to Sebha. We stayed at the Hotel Morsi, owned by a character out of the Arabian Nights named Haj Morsi. He was one of those people who, like a cat, always lands on his feet no matter how he is thrown about. Morsi had come down to this former French outpost, complete with a fort on the hill, as an Italian merchant and trader before World War II. He was actually Jewish, but the Italians owned Libya then, so he became an Italian and bought the hotel. Then, when the area was liberated by the French armies, he posed as French for awhile, until they left the country to the Arabs. Then Morsi became a Muslim, complete with two wives, one an Italian, and even made a trip to Mecca — and was thus able to go by the name of Haj, which indicated to all that he was one of the faithful who had made the pilgrimage to the Holy City. Morsi was a salesman, and he did his best to find out what we were doing so he could sell us something. He dabbled in everything from used cars to influence.

Tibbitts came by the next morning at daylight, and we headed for the Wadi Shati, where the iron deposit was located. About twenty miles out of Sebha begins a sand sea of solid sand dunes, called the Rebiana. A trail across it was marked with metal poles, but many were blown down.

Tibbitts' Chevy pickup was a four-wheel drive, yet we hit some very soft spots where we nearly got stuck. He carried two small metal ladders, called sand ladders, which we could put under the wheels if they got stuck in the soft sand. They are quite effective. Some of the Americans in Sebha said they had had to use those ladders continuously for miles, sometimes, after a strong blow of wind had softened the sand.

The drive was interesting. The Rebiana sand sea occupies a depression and stretches several hundred miles to the west. Most of the dunes are the crescent-shaped barchans made by the prevailing southwest winds. Some thin, straight sand ridges cut across these crescent dunes at an angle, however. They were sometimes miles in length and as narrow as a car track on their crests. They looked for all the world like a sand dike that had been intruded into the thick barchan sequence.

We spent the next two days going to all the locations where core holes had been drilled into the iron ore. Goudarzi had been in charge of the work, and we had his report as a reference. The iron ore was a blanket sedimentary deposit stretching for more than thirty miles. The iron bed had a little dune sand on top of it, but it showed up as a long series of benches or mesas. There were hundreds of millions of tons in sight!

The iron deposit was Pennsylvanian or Mississippian in age and lay as an outcrop on the south side of the Jebel Soda uplift. Dips were less than 1 degree to the south. Only about 50 to 100 feet below the ore lay a porous Devonian-age sandstone. It was the aquifer of the region, and the springs in the Wadi Shati came from water in this reservoir. There was plenty of water here for mining operations and for domestic use in a mining camp. The ore was red oolitic hematite and looked beautiful. It could be stripped by surface mining without any trouble. The only problem was that it was 450 miles from the Mediterranean and the seaports.

I took many samples and had a whole gunnysack full of specimens. I wanted to get enough ore to be able to send some to the Colorado School of Mines for analysis and recommendations for any treatment necessary.

It was January and cold at night but crisp in the daytime. The air was clear, and no wind blew to move any of the dune sand. We drove back over the Rebiana sand sea without difficulty and stayed at Morsi's hotel until the next plane left for Tripoli. I figured we had enough information now about the iron deposit to be able to decide if we wanted to try to get a concession on it; that is, if the ore analysis in Goudarzi's U.S. Geological Survey report checked out.

When we arrived back in Tripoli, we found that Christopher had been in touch with Occidental Petroleum, and they were dragging their feet on trying for an oil concession. He suggested that we try to interest El Paso Natural Gas, which was currently operating on an oil and gas concession in Algeria. El Paso had a Paris office, and Roy Allen, their exploration manager in Algeria, would be there the next week. We decided it would be a good idea to talk to Allen, and I suggested I might stop off in London to talk to J. Paul Getty about entering Libya as well.

We got our plane tickets on UTA, the French line, and went to the airport to leave for Paris. The customs people were suspicious of the big bag of ore samples I was carrying and declared that our exit visas were not in order. Fortunately, before the plane left, they relented, and we arrived in Paris and checked into the Crillon Hotel. Roy Allen wasn't back from Algeria yet, so we spent some time with Jerry Fiedler of the U.S. Embassy nearby, who had been a friend of Christopher's in Denver.

We met Roy Allen the next day and told him about the oil concessions to be granted in Libya in the near future from the land which must soon be dropped by the major companies operating there. He said he knew there were great oil possibilities in Libya, but we would have to talk to the El Paso people in their main office. He thought our connection with Anis al-Qasem could get us a concession, and we should take the matter up with Roland Hamblin, their company landman in El Paso, Texas. We said we would.

I flew on to London, called the Tidewater office and told them I had worked for Mr. Getty in Arabia and would like to see him. They gave me a number to call and said to talk to Miss Lund, his private secretary. I called the number, talked to Miss Lund, told her who I was and that I would like to see Mr. Getty. She said to hold on a minute and, when she came back on the line, she said to come out to Sutton Place and have tea with Mr. Getty the next day. She explained in detail how to get there.

The next afternoon I took the train from Waterloo Station to Woking and found a taxi to drive me to Sutton Place. The butler was very polite and took me into the sitting room. Sutton Place is a two-story stone and brick castle set in the middle of a large estate of rolling green hills with scattered deciduous trees. A small bunch of sheep grazed outside the grounds. Being a cattleman, I didn't think much of this arrangement. Mr. Getty joined me in a few minutes and was very cordial. He said, "You don't look a bit different from the last time I saw you." This was January 1961, and he had last seen me in November of 1948. I told him he looked just the same, too. And he really did.

"I have always wondered how you got to Washington from New York City when you left me at the Pierre," he said. He was referring to my trip to Washington to get maps and visas and to meet with the Saudi Arabian ambassador prior to my trip to Saudi Arabia to negotiate for the concession on the Kuwait Neutral Zone. I didn't think he would remember this incident, the foul-up of airline reservations and my having to go by train.

He not only remembered that obscure incident, but we reminisced about other events in the negotiations for the concession on the Neutral Zone. I told him I understood he had found some nice oil production there. "We drilled five dry holes," he said, "and then we went down by that surface structure you thought you saw from the airplane and found a giant field. DeGolyer–McNaughton says we have nine billion barrels of oil in it." This firm certified to the amount of oil in oil fields all over the world and were considered the best in this type of engineering calculation.

"What are you doing now, Paul?" he asked.

I told him I had been down in Libya attempting to get an oil concession. I said, "You should come to Libya. Your name would be magic down there." His face really lit up. He knew I hadn't meant it as flattery. I knew that if he wanted to, he could get a concession there and find more oil, and he recognized my appreciation of that fact.

He wanted to know about the types of reservoirs found in Libya. Were they like the Neutral Zone or more like those in Texas and Louisiana? I told him more like Texas, which appeared to disappoint him. I told him about my connection with Anis al-Qasem and the huge areas coming up for awarding of concessions. He seemed interested. I told him further of the deal that had been broached to us by a representative of the "Black Prince," a brother of King Idris, in which an oil concession would be delivered for a payment to the prince of a million dollars. "That would be dangerous to go on a deal like that," Mr. Getty said. "The concession could be set aside!" I had to agree.

"When you get back to the States, talk to George [Getty, his son] about this," he said. He indicated his companies didn't have the funds then to embark on another concession. I knew he wasn't selling all the oil he would like from the Neutral Zone, and, with his tremendous capital investment connected with that oil development, he was probably short of ready cash to embark on another concession.

Mr. Getty asked if I would like to have a tour of Sutton Place, whereupon he took me up to the Great Hall on the second floor and around through the lower hall, where many of his paintings were hung. The large tapestries in the Great Hall were a magnificent sight. Then he had the butler call me a taxi, and I returned to London.

The next day I went sightseeing around London. I hadn't been there since before World War II, and I was anxious to see Piccadilly, St. Paul's, and Westminster Abbey again. I was surprised to see there were still some bombed-out areas left as remembrances of the Battle of Britain.

My flight to the States left the next day, and I went as far as Denver. I arrived home in Salt Lake City on January 27. I had been gone nearly two months and had missed Christmas with my family.

The ore samples arrived in Salt Lake City, and I sent some representative specimens to the Colorado School of Mines for analysis. In the meantime, my partner, Tom Kearns, had looked up L. F. Rains, an old friend of his who had built the first steel mill in Utah. Rains had pioneered in the coal and coke business in Utah before building the steel mill at Ironton, just south of Provo. Later he had been president and director of several steel companies, as well as machinery companies, so we felt he could advise us on the iron ore situation.

When the results came back from Colorado, we showed them to him. He laughed and said, "The iron and steel industry in the

United States was built on iron ore that isn't that rich." This made us feel pretty good about going ahead and trying to get a concession on the iron ore. I did, however, discuss the situation with Ken McGriffin, a consulting mining geologist who had worked for me in Federal Uranium and later with another company, U.S. Lithium Corporation. McGriffin did some research and came up with a short report that said the steel companies were trying to move away from the sedimentary hematite iron ores in favor of the higher grade igneous origin ores. He pointed to new finds in South America and Australia which were the latter type and were being put into production at that time. This made me unsure about going ahead with the iron concession.

Christopher and I made a trip to El Paso Natural Gas Company's office to talk about their backing us in acquiring an oil concession. We talked to Roland Hamblin and worked out a deal to front for them in Libya. El Paso would pick up the expenses and carry us for an overriding royalty. Their attorneys had started to draw up the papers for the arrangement when we got a call from Hamblin at our motel. The weekly *Oil and Gas Journal,* which had arrived after we left his office, had an article saying all new concessions in Libya would be up for public tender or auction. Hamblin said this would eliminate the advantage al-Qasem would have in negotiating for a concession with his friends in the Libyan Petroleum Commission who granted them.

We wired Qasem to see if this were true, and he replied that it was. I had planned to talk to George Getty, president of Tidewater, about an arrangement with him on the same terms, but this new tender arrangement shot us out of the water with all the companies we might contact. We discovered later that Libya did not actually adhere to their public tender policy at all. What they did was to work out a deal with an oil company, then open the bidding for one day and award the concession before anyone else had a chance to bid. But with the publicity given the public tender in the trade journals, we found it impossible to interest any company in backing us.

I met with our Denver partners, and they were anxious to pursue the iron concession. They didn't have their share of the money required just then, but they said they had talked to a Japanese company that was ready to take the concession off our hands when we got it. But the company acquiring it had to be from a neutral country, like Switzerland, to give the deal a non-American flavor. I discovered later that this was untrue.

We had been in touch with Qasem. He agreed to the Swiss idea and wanted to meet us in Switzerland to form the company and prepare to apply for the concession. Christopher and I flew to Paris in April, where I bought a Volkswagen bug for $1,200, and we drove to Geneva. Qasem was already there. We drove around the city the next day, Sunday, and then started to work drawing up the Articles of Incorporation for our company. The name we chose was African Resources Company — AFRESCO.

After spending several days getting the documents ready, we engaged a Swiss law firm recommended by Thompson's relatives, and it was a bad choice. Their services were poor, they had only one lawyer who spoke English, and their charges were outrageous — $6,000 to form the company, and I was paying! Christopher and Thompson didn't have their money lined up yet. Swiss law required that the company's board be controlled by Swiss, so Thompson's relatives were put on it. Christopher tried to convince me that everything would be all right. I wasn't so sure.

While we were in Geneva, we went to the United Nations library in the old League of Nations building. Qasem wanted to see what they had in the way of mining concession agreements for the various countries of the world. We found quite a few, and the ones we liked best were those from Venezuela. We decided to write up a concession agreement immediately and be ready to present it to the Libyan government when we got to Tripoli. Qasem wrote and I typed. We cut and pasted and reworked it. As a landman, Christopher helped a lot. We had it pretty well drawn up by the time we left Geneva. We drove on down to Rome, stopping at Milan and Siena. The road was slow, but the scenery was gorgeous over the Alps and down through Italy.

We arrived in Tripoli on April 23, 1961. We started in again on the concession agreement, and Qasem commenced translating it into Arabic. We had been only about three weeks getting the company formed and the concession agreement written, and now we were ready to submit it to the Libyan government. This was pretty fast progress. We submitted the agreement to the Minister of National Economics on May 9. Then began a series of long waits. The ministers changed positions. Their assistants changed places. They brought in a German mining engineer to study the agreement. Christopher had to leave. I wanted to leave but stayed. It looked like I would be there all summer, so I cabled my wife Betty to come to Tripoli, from where we would go to Rome, pick up the Volkswagen bug, and drive around Europe for a couple of weeks, then put the car on a ship and take it home. She arrived in Tripoli on June 5. Four days later Qasem informed me that I had to go to Sebha to meet with a man named Arabi who could get the concession granted. Arabi was in the government of the Province of Fezzan, where the iron ore was located, and had a lot of influence with the Wali or minister of the province.

I took copies of our proposed agreement with me and flew to Sebha. I had planned to go down one day and back the next but ended spending nearly a week. I met with Arabi several times. He told me, through his interpreter, that the concession agreement looked all right. He said the next step was to take it up with Seyfal Nasr, an adviser to King Idris.

Chase Tibbitts was in Sebha and wanted me to stay at the so-called rest house where the USAID employees were billeted. It was terribly hot, over 120°F., during the heat of the day, and all activity came to a halt. They turned on the fans, and everybody stayed inside and gasped for breath. I came down with a high temperature, a desert bug of some kind. A French doctor in town came and gave me some antibiotics, however, and I soon felt better.

When I got back to Tripoli, Qasem tried to get in touch with Seyfal Nasr, but he had left the country for the summer, and nothing could be done until he returned in the fall. Betty and I flew to Rome, picked up the VW, drove up through Italy, Switzerland, Germany, Holland, Belgium, and France. We loaded the little car on the *Queen Elizabeth* on June 30, arrived in New York City on July 5, unloaded the VW, and drove through the Holland Tunnel to New Jersey for the night. We arrived back in Salt Lake City on July 12.

We still had a long way to go to get our concession on the iron. The summer of 1961 rolled by with no word from Qasem on its status. By early 1962, I was beginning to wonder if any action would ever be taken on our application. In March I sent Jerry Guinand, our landman, over to Tripoli to find out what had become of the application. After two weeks there, he wired for me to come over, and I arrived in early April. Qasem was trying to get the people in the Fezzan provincial government to grant the concession. Arabi and Seyfal Nasr met with the federal people at Baida, the new capital city of Libya. But nothing happened. I was disgusted and told Qasem I was leaving on the first of May unless something happened. It didn't, so I went back to Salt Lake City.

The only bright spot of this trip was a day spent with Chase Tibbitts and his two Italian friends, Mario Bertiolli and Mario Mancini. They took us quail hunting about seventy-five miles east of Tripoli, near Misurata. We hunted Mediterranean quail, which winter in North Africa, fly to Europe for the summer, and then migrate back to Africa. There were small flocks of them in the bean and berry patches on some farms owned by Italians who were friends of the two Marios.

The quail were small, about half the size of American quail. They would flush out of the bean patch and fly about four or five feet above the ground at a blinding speed. I shot at several before I got my reaction time speeded up to aim the shotgun and pull the trigger. It was an interesting day. We each shot more than fifteen birds, so we stopped at one of the farmhouses and gave them part of our bag. They brought out some of their homemade wine and poured us all a big glassful. At one of the farms, the hired man was a teenage boy who entertained us by playing his accordion. We had left Tripoli before dawn and had stopped at an Italian bakery for some loaves of fresh-baked bread. The Marios had brought along some home-cured ham and wine. We arrived back in Tripoli way after dark, tired but appreciative of the wonderful day we all had enjoyed.

I had been in Salt Lake City about two weeks when Qasem cabled me to return to Tripoli; we were to have a big meeting about the concession with the Minister of Industry. So I headed for

Tripoli again, arriving on May 19. Qasem had been talking with Arabi again and said it looked like the concession was about to be approved. On May 22, the day for the big meeting, Qasem informed me that the Minister of Industry had decided to call it off. Instead, they were going to meet without us and would probably ask Gus Goudarzi for his advice on granting the concession. I wondered why I had flown 10,000 miles just to be told this.

I met with Randy Bomar, USAID representative in Sebha, who told me that Muhammad Bey, Minister of Fezzan, disliked Qasem, and that was a problem. I had not yet met Muhammad Bey, but his reputation was frightening. He was said to have recently killed two men with his pistol, which he always carried, and, at King Idris's insistence, he was not prosecuted, merely placed under house arrest, so to speak. He wasn't supposed to leave the province of Fezzan for a year. Gus Goudarzi later confirmed the Wali's enmity toward Qasem. The trouble was that Qasem had an interest in AFRESCO, the company we had formed to acquire the iron concession, and we were obviously committed to him. I decided we would have to sink or swim with Qasem. We had no one else to carry the ball on negotiations.

During the remainder of the month and into June, Qasem and I carried on further negotiations with Khadir, the Minister of Industry's representative. We negotiated on royalties, rentals, and amount of work to be done, and finally reached an agreement. Qasem said the concession would be granted immediately. When it wasn't forthcoming, he inquired as to its status. The Minister of Industry told him that Khadir had been repudiated. The minister said, "Your terms with Khadir are just an offer. Now, let's start negotiating the concession!"

I told Qasem I wanted to meet again with the minister and tell him these terms were *it*. If they didn't accept, we were finished. Qasem set up the meeting, and I told the minister just that. Arabi was there and tried to be helpful. The provincial government of Fezzan had been very helpful. We came away from the meeting feeling we had struck out. The minister called us to another meeting the next day. I told him of the new iron discoveries in Mauritania and in Spanish Sahara and how much richer they were than

Libya's. I explained how Libya's iron would have to be unburdened by high royalties for it even to meet expenses, etc. But I did suggest that, if it were profitable, Libya should have a sliding-scale interest in the profits. This seemed to sit well with him and his adviser, a Dr. Afiefi. Then they called us to another meeting the next day to try to chisel on the terms we had agreed to two days earlier. It was disgusting. They acted like street peddlers.

Qasem met with Khadir again the next day, with no results. We had now been meeting with them almost every day for a week. Khadir and Qasem began re-drafting the parts of the concession agreements we had agreed on until now. Khadir informed Qasem that the Minister of Industry had moved to Baida, 600 miles east of Tripoli, and we would have to go there to negotiate further. By this time Don Christopher had arrived from Denver, so he and Qasem and I flew to Benghazi. We had to wait there two days before we could find a car to rent to drive to the ancient Greek city of Cyrene, where we would stay, since Baida had no hotel or public accommodations.

The old two-story yellow stucco hotel, set in a small grove of pines, was to be our headquarters for the next month. It was of pre–World War I vintage, with big, high-ceilinged rooms and one toilet and bath for each floor. The hotel sat atop a 3,000-foot escarpment and was within walking distance of two sets of ruins. The oldest were mostly hollowed out gray limestone caverns, which had been used by the Greeks as burial places — hence the name, the Necropolis. Then, built above these extensive caverns were a series of Roman temples, complete with pools and stone walkways. Situated some 3,000 feet above the Mediterranean, Cyrene (in Arabic, Shahat) has a pleasant climate during the hot North African summer. The United States maintained an Embassy here, and we were invited to the cocktail party Ambassador Jones gave on the Fourth of July. The ambassador wanted to know how we were coming on the concession, and I said we were making progress but very, very slowly. He wanted to know what we would do with the iron deposit, and I said we would have to get some partners to help us, then we would try to start some operations. He seemed satisfied with this plan.

Qasem presented us with the redrawn concession agreement, and it was terrible. I wouldn't agree to a single article. We would even be prevented from exporting any ore! Dr. Afiefi, the Minister of Industry's adviser, had taken over for Khadir, and I told him they were acting in poor faith to try to shove such an agreement down our throats. Dr. Afiefi called another meeting with the minister, and we started at the beginning, again. After three days, we still had no consensus past Article II. We argued and argued to no avail. The minister said he needed to study the situation further. "Would you prepare a memorandum of objection to our agreement?"

"Yes, we would," and I spent the next two days typing one up. The minister had us meet with him again, and we argued again. I felt we were never going to get an agreement we could live with, and it was July 12. We were still miles apart on most issues.

We met with Arabi, who said he thought the agreement was all right. We should retype it, hand it to the minister, and go back to Tripoli. Then he would see Seyfal Nasr and get him to approve it. This looked like a way to circumvent the Minister of Industry, and I felt that was the only way we could ever get the thing ready for signing by the provincial government of Fezzan. Arabi said Seyfal Nasr and Muhammad Bey could force the federal government to sign if they signed. So we delivered a newly typed — by me — copy of the agreement and left Cyrene for Benghazi, stopping before we left to pay our respects to Ambassador Jones. We arrived back in Tripoli, where I drafted a new map for the concession agreement, which Qasem sent to Arabi. Christopher and I saw Arabi, who said it would be at least two weeks to a month before the ministers could meet again and suggested we go home and wait. It was awfully hot in Tripoli, so we agreed. I arrived back in Salt Lake City on July 22, still with no concession.

On August 10 I received a cable from Qasem saying to come to Tripoli. I left Salt Lake City two days later. I met with Qasem on the thirteenth, and he said he'd heard from Arabi that our draft was being accepted and we would have to go to Sebha for the signing. Bill Henebry of the U.S. Embassy sent word he wanted to see me; so I stopped in, and he took me to Ambassador Jones, who wanted to know how the concession agreement was coming. I said it appeared that we might be getting it, and they both expressed satisfaction and offered any help I might need. I thanked them.

Qasem, Christopher, and I flew to Sebha on August 17. Chase Tibbitts met us and took Christopher and me to the rest house to stay. Qasem went to the hotel.

It was Chase's birthday, and his two Italian helpers had cooked a lavish Italian dinner for him. Pasquale Vento—Pasquale Wind— lived up to his name, keeping us in stitches all evening. Before dinner started, he proposed a toast: "Here's to Chase! I liked him better yesterday because he wasn't so damn old!" It was a very enjoyable evening, even though there was no air conditioning and the temperature outside after sundown was over 95°F. The big ceiling fans kept us from melting, and we stayed until almost two AM.

We met the next morning with Arabi. He said Seyfal Nasr was ready to sign the concession agreement for the Province of Fezzan and asked us to get it typed up on a stencil so that several mimeograph copies could be made.

Randy Bomar of USAID got us a typist — a man, and very inaccurate. It took all afternoon and half the night to get the document typed. I had to help him with every page.

The next day we took the agreement out to Seyfal Nasr's villa, and he signed all six copies. Every time he signed his name he said, *Bismallah* — in the name of Allah.

I signed as president of AFRESCO and Qasem signed as secretary. Qasem had said we should bring some liquor for the signing, and I had two fifths of Grants Scotch with me. After our pictures were taken during the signing, Seyfal Nasr and Arabi proceeded to drink most of the two bottles. They made me think of some Mormons who, like the Muslims, don't believe in drinking, but once in a while, when they do drink, they really tie one on.

That evening Nasr hosted us at dinner in his villa. He had pretty well sobered up. Of course it was strictly a men-only affair. Tibbitts and Bomar joined Christopher, Qasem, and myself. This was no desert Bedouin meal. We had roasted partridges, fresh vegetable salads, wine, and pastries. We didn't get back to the rest house until 5:30 AM.

The next day Muhammad Bey, Minister of the Fezzan, and Mr. Orfelli, his secretary, came by to offer congratulations. The minister kept looking at his wristwatch in an obvious fashion. It

was the watch Christopher had given Arabi the day before as a gift
for signing. I guessed it meant Muhammad Bey wanted us to know
he knew everything that went on and would always have a piece of
the action.

That afternoon we flew back to Tripoli pretty happy with ourselves. We had the concession and pretty much on our own terms.
Its modest royalties, rentals, and work requirements should make it
attractive to iron companies around the world as well as in the
United States.

Now the work of setting up an operating company in Libya
began. It required a new account in the National Bank of Libya for
the rentals due. We had to get a resident agent in Sebha to take
communications to AFRESCO. Then we had to go to Switzerland,
hold a directors' meeting, and approve taking and paying for the
concession.

Qasem had told me that when we got the concession we would
have to set up an office in Tripoli with a manager. I had broached
the subject with Chase Tibbitts, and he seemed interested in the job.
He was due for a vacation to the States in December, and he came
to Salt Lake City to talk more about it. I worked out a job contract,
including salary plus expenses and educational expenses for his children, and he decided to go to work for AFRESCO. He left the U.S.
Geological Survey early in 1963 and moved into our villa in Tripoli.

In the meantime we worked up a brochure with maps and reports on the iron concession. Now we were ready to start the job of
interesting some companies in joining AFRESCO to carry on the
necessary exploration work, help pay the rentals, and carry the ball
in putting the property into production.

A local stockbroker asked me to submit the deal to a large construction and mining company with whom he had close associations.
We went to their San Francisco office, and they said they were interested and would probably join us. But they delayed and delayed,
so I thought it prudent to talk to other companies. I went to New
York City and talked to a friend at one of the large international
mining companies. His company wasn't interested because their
other holdings in Africa, particularly black Africa, were the object
of political unrest, and they feared expropriation.

They said, "Your biggest problem is next door in Egypt —
Gamal Abdel Nasser. He wants to unite all the Arab nations into
a United Arab Republic, and Libya is next on his list. If Nasser
takes over, your iron concession will be expropriated." Everywhere
I went in New York City, I heard the same opinion. I talked to
several banking and investment houses, and this was uniformly their
attitude. It was discouraging. This same attitude prevailed throughout the mining community as well. Christopher and Thompson's
Japanese company said they were no longer interested.

Chase Tibbitts wrote, asking me to come to Libya to talk over
some of his problems there. I went by way of Madrid to see Holly,
my oldest daughter from an earlier marriage, who was at the University of Madrid for her junior year. Chase was having some problems with the Libyan government bureaucrats and needed someone
with whom he could talk. He also thought we should contact the
Italian government steel company, Italsider.

We flew to Rome to their main office. They referred us to their
Milan office, so we went there. Milan referred us to their Genoa
office, and we went there. This was the operations office, where
we were received very courteously. We had a long talk with their
exploration and mining staff. In essence, they told us we had taken
the iron concession at a very unfortunate time. A very large iron
deposit was just going into production in Mauritania, and with
55 percent iron ore, it was richer than our 50 percent ore in Libya.
Also, rich new deposits had been found in Nigeria and Liberia, and
the iron ore supply was soon going to be much greater than the demand. However, they said that if we could get some American
partners in the venture, they might be willing to take a quarter interest. "The deposit is practically in our backyard, so we have to be
interested in it," they said. We were somewhat encouraged.

There was another possibility, they said. A new process had
been developed that used natural gas to make what is called sponge
iron, and Mexico had just put a plant into production. Sponge iron
is used as a substitute for scrap iron in the smelting process, and at
that time Europe imported more than 60 percent of its scrap from
the United States. If a sponge iron plant were built in Libya using
Libyan natural gas, much of which was going to waste by flaring,

the owners should be able to sell its product to European steel mills.

Chase and I talked over this possibility. We decided that I would pursue the matter at home, with American oil companies operating in Libya. Production would be a profitable way for them to use their flare gas. One company had even plugged and abandoned a gas well about seventy-five miles north of the iron deposit, and they might want to develop their gas to use in a sponge iron mill.

I had one more company I wanted to see before heading home: Axel Johnson, the largest Swedish shipping company. They had contacted me for a contract to ship the ore once we were in production. I flew to Stockholm to see them. The man I had been corresponding with, Walter Hogland, was in the office when I arrived unannounced. We had a long talk followed by dinner that night. He seemed sure we could develop a market in Europe for the ore. I left even a little more encouraged.

Back in the U.S., I went to the Pittsburgh office of the oil company with the shut-in gas well. They said they were getting ready to *relinquish* their concession; besides, they had been bitten by the "beware of Nasser" bug. They were even contemplating pulling out of Libya altogether, but they agreed to think about my venture. (Eventually they did pull out of Libya completely.) During the next six months, I talked to all the oil companies operating in Libya. None wanted to increase investment there; they all had the "Nasser bug." It was little satisfaction that all agreed the iron ore was a tremendous resource and would be developed someday.

I received a disturbing letter from Chase. Seyfal Nasr, who had signed our concession agreement, had fallen out of favor with King Idris and had been banished to Egypt. Arabi had left government service in Sebha. New government bureaucrats were demanding that we do some expensive exploration work and were saying our rentals were too low and should be raised.

Worse than that, Christopher and Thompson were in arrears on their share of the expenses, and I was fearful that Kearns and I would have to pay all the rentals ourselves and carry on the work of the concession with only a 40 percent interest in it.

I wrote Chase that I didn't think we were going to be able to continue in light of these developments and to prepare to back out.

He informed the Libyan government that we couldn't continue unless we got an extension on the rentals. They refused an extension, so he sold all our belongings in Libya and came back to the United States. He was pretty blue and so was I. I continued to pay his salary until he found another job. He went to Chad to supervise the drilling of water wells under a USAID program, a similar job to the one he had had in Libya.

Fourteen years later, a Japanese company had the iron concession and was preparing to develop it; however, the glut of iron ore on the world market has made the Libyan deposits non-commercial for the present. The Nasser threat never materialized. Nasser died and Sadat took his place in Egypt. King Idris was dethroned and Qadaffi rules the country. Qadaffi offered to merge Libya into Egypt; Egypt refused.

So ended my attempt to develop a large iron ore deposit in Libya. As in the oil and gas exploration business, I just drilled a "dry hole."

Occidental Petroleum entered Libya and obtained a concession without consulting Christopher and Thompson. They drilled and found several large oil fields. Christopher and Thompson sued, but before the case came to trial, Christopher was killed in an automobile accident. Thompson got a small settlement. Occidental's attorney came to Salt Lake City to see me, saying a part of the settlement should be mine since I had a prior agreement with Christopher and Thompson and had financed the attempt to get Occidental a concession. It would have required another suit to get what rightfully was mine, so I said "to hell with it." I had had all I could stand of everyone involved.

CHAPTER 14

UINTA BASIN — THE MATCH
TO THE FUSE

WHEN I RETURNED FROM ARABIA IN 1939, I entered the University of Utah to work on a master's degree in geology. Utah had only four geology professors, and one of them, a former oil company geologist named F. F. Hintze, taught the only class in petroleum geology. In order to fill out the required number of hours for the master's degree, I took several classes in mining and metallurgy. Utah was an important mining state in those days but had no oil production of any consequence. I didn't look forward to going overseas again, where the jobs in petroleum geology were, so my attention was directed toward the mining industry, particularly gold placer mining.

One of my friends, Ferris Andrus, who later became a deputy sheriff, ran a service station in Holladay, the Salt Lake City suburb where we lived, and I frequently gassed up my Mercury convertible there on the way to or from the University. One day Ferris told me that Glen Bird, a mutual friend of ours who was an aircraft mechanic, was friendly with a mixed-blood Indian from the Ute Reservation in the Uinta Basin, Joe Wardell, who had told him of some gold placer land he owned along the Green River, south of Vernal, Utah. While I was studying the techniques in school, Dad had had considerable experience with gold placer prospects on the Colorado River and knew how to pan and evaluate a placer deposit from a practical standpoint. This might just be interesting . . .

I went to the airport to see Bird, and he told me that Wardell lived in a shacky neighborhood out on the city's west side. I went to see him and found that while he had the strong nose and features of an Indian, he "lived Anglo," with a white wife and two kids, and was willing to talk about his placer holdings. How Joe liked to talk about the Uinta Basin and its mining possibilities! He had been born and raised on the Reservation there, and I think he wanted to get out of Salt Lake City and live in the Basin again. The Uinta Basin is a large topographic and geologic basin located south of the Uinta mountain range, the only large range in the country that runs from east to west. It is 120 miles long east-to-west and 100 miles wide north-to-south, and the Green River runs through the middle of it.

Dad and I drove Joe out to the Basin, and he took us down to Horseshoe Bend in the Green to show us the claims. There appeared to have been some placer operations on the land, and we found some river bars that had placer gold showings. The gold was in very fine particles called "flower gold."

I had learned to pan, and in the bottom of a gold pan, which holds ten to fifteen pounds of gravel, after a careful washing there would remain a teaspoonful of black sand, mostly the iron mineral magnetite. Sometimes a one-inch string of very fine gold particles would trail behind this black sand when the water in the bottom of the pan was agitated with a whirling motion. We estimated that some of the gravel might be worth as high as fifty cents to a dollar per cubic yard; at the time, gold was worth thirty-five dollars an ounce. It looked like the deposit had some commercial possibilities but would require large machinery to move the gravel and run it through a sluice box or wilfley tables to recover the gold.

We camped out on the bank of the Green River that night and made a big fire of dead cottonwood logs. Joe dug into his duffle bag and brought out an old Colt single-action Frontier model 45 caliber revolver with a 4-inch barrel. He had taken the trigger out, so it had to be shot by fanning the hammer with the other hand. We all tried our hand at shooting it, but it felt awfully clumsy to me. Joe could get off a string of three or four shots in a hurry, but without much accuracy. I asked him if he had ever shot anything with it, and he said, "No, but a friend of mine has. Drive over onto that hill and I'll show you what it has killed."

We got into the car, and he stopped us at a mound of earth with a crude cross of dead willow wood stuck into it. I said, "What the hell is that? It looks like a grave."

"It is," Joe said. "A friend of mine shot some big, red-headed, bushy-bearded guy who tried to jump his claims. He used this gun."

"Wasn't he arrested?" I asked.

"No," he said, "they called the sheriff and told him what happened."

"And nothing more was done about it?"

"No."

The next day we drove into the town of Vernal. It was Sunday morning, and most everybody was in church. There was hardly anyone on the main street.

Joe was strolling along with his hands thrust through his bib overalls, a typical stance, when he spotted someone across the street. It was an older man, tall and muscular, with a weatherbeaten face. Joe headed right across the street toward him and yelled as he approached, "I can outrun you! I can outwrestle you! I can throw a rock farther than you can! I can ride a meaner horse than you can!"

By this time the man had stopped in his tracks, and Joe went up to him. It looked like a fight was in the making. Instead, the older man took a good look at Joe and said, "What the hell are you doing here, Joe?"

"Just looking around."

They acted like two strange male dogs until Joe shot out his hand and the man took it. They both smiled. Joe said, "This here's Paul Walton and his dad. We're on a little trip. Paul, this is the town sheriff!"

The sheriff said, "Are you staying out of trouble, Joe?" and Joe said, "I sure am, since you gave me my lesson." Then we walked on, but Joe had to tell the story.

One Saturday night he had quite a lot to drink and shot out all the streetlights on the main street of Vernal. The sheriff picked him up and put him in jail overnight. The next day he rousted Joe out early, hangover or not, and had him rake the lawn at the courthouse and clean up the yard. Joe spent the next week working on the road repair crew, until he had earned enough money to buy new bulbs for the streetlights. Then Joe got the big ladder out and personally, without help from anyone, replaced every lamp he had shot out. "I haven't had any trouble with the law since," Joe remarked.

When we got back to Salt Lake City, I talked the prospect over with Kelly Howard, a geology classmate of mine who was currently evaluating gold placer properties for a large mining company. Kelly said he thought it was marginally commercial, but a gold mining company from Denver had the land tied up. When I confronted Joe with this information, he didn't deny that he knew the property was tied up, but said he just wanted to get to know me better and find out if he could trust me before he showed me two other prospects he had in the Uinta Basin.

So we made another trip to the Basin. This time with his wife and kids along. They really filled up the car. We left the family with Joe's brother at Roosevelt, and then he directed me to drive back to Duchesne and up Pigeon Water Creek, about eighty miles from Roosevelt, to see what he called the Caleb Rhodes gold mine.

Much has been written about Caleb Rhodes, a mysterious character who, according to legend, had a placer gold mine he worked by himself and who showed up at various places in Utah during the 1860's and 1870's with gold dust in his possession. Joe claimed to have known him and showed us where he had been killed by Indians near Duchesne, where he said Rhodes was buried.

Later that year I saw Carl Olson, an old friend in Price, 100 miles to the south of Duchesne, whose father ran the first drugstore in town. Carl claimed that Caleb Rhodes used to come in, probably from the Henry Mountains, another 150 miles south of Price, and have his father weigh gold dust on the drugstore scales. This would place Joe Wardell's Caleb Rhodes mine at least 250 miles from Carl Olson's location. Further, Carl said Caleb Rhodes was buried in the Price cemetery. At this point, it all greatly resembled the mystery surrounding Butch Cassidy, as to whether he did or did not die with the Sundance Kid in a gun battle in South America.

It was nearly dark when we got to Pigeon Water in the foothills of the towering east–west Uinta Mountains. We made camp for the night, and Joe regaled us with stories. One was his finding rich gold ore in the Flaming Gorge, where the Green River cuts through the Uintas. Another was finding a black rock in veins nearby on Rock Creek, which, if held next to a radio, would drown out its signal. Still another was finding a ledge of gray rock that held big nodules of lead galena ore in great quantities. That night in our bedrolls, Dad and I wondered about it, and I said, "Do you suppose we can believe *anything* he tells us?"

Next morning we drove down into Rock Creek, where there was a small ranch with irrigated alfalfa fields. Alongside the fields was a terminal glacial moraine consisting mostly of Uinta series quartzite boulders brought down Rock Creek by the glacier. I couldn't believe it, but in these big boulder and rock piles someone had dug two shafts — about twenty feet deep in the rubble — and partially timbered them. We panned the gravel around and found no gold colors at all. I was disgusted and mad at being brought on a wild-goose chase. Joe could see I was unhappy, so he said, "Let's go see the lead mine."

We drove back up out of the Rock Creek canyon and out onto a gravel pediment or terrace that streams flowing out of the Uinta Mountains had built when the surface of the Uinta Basin was at that higher level. Joe said, "This is where the lead mine is." I said, "What do you mean here? This is only a stream deposit. Where is your gray ledge the ore came in?"

It was obvious he had lied, so I didn't press the point. We looked around the gravel terrace. It was possible a few nodules of lead galena ore could have been brought out of the central part of the range by the old stream and left here with the other well-rounded stream pebbles, but it was no lead mine!

I told Dad I would like to take his picture, so I lined him up against the skyline and took it. We stood looking west out over Rock Creek canyon, and I pointed out to Dad the geologic section which was dipping steeply south, away from the mountains and out into the Basin. "There's the Morrison, the Dakota, the gray Mowry shale and the Mancos shale, and there . . . ! Where the hell is the Mesaverde?" On top of the Mancos should have been the thick Mesaverde sandstones and coal beds. Instead, there were red and gray shales and sandstones obviously of Tertiary age.

I said to Dad, "There must be 5,000 feet of beds missing here. All the Mesaverde, the Wasatch, and the Green River formations are gone! This is a tremendous unconformity!"

Well, we never did get Joe to take us to see his black rocks that stopped a radio from working or the gold quartz ore up the Green

River he said he knew about. It's too late for that now, because the Flaming Gorge dam has backed hundreds of feet of water over the spot.

That fall I entered Massachusetts Institute of Technology (MIT) in Cambridge, Massachusetts, and took my required class work. Between my bachelor's and master's credits in Utah, I had been exposed to most of the geology classes they taught at MIT. All I had to do was write my dissertation.

All year during my petroleum geology studies under Dr. Whitehead and my stratigraphy and sedimentation studies under Dr. Robert Shrock, we talked frequently about unconformities and the giant oil fields sometimes associated with them, and I kept thinking about the one I had seen at Rock Creek in the Uinta Basin. There were only very crude maps of the Basin then, and they shed little light on the subject. Geologically, an unconformity occurs where younger strata overlie older strata, usually at an angle, and represents a period of erosion of the older strata followed by deposition of younger strata on this eroded surface.

When it came time to decide on my dissertation problem, I talked the area over with Dr. Shrock and Dr. Whitehead and said I would like to study the oil possibilities of the Cretaceous rocks in the Uinta Basin. They both thought it was a very large area to tackle but approved my doing it. I set out from Boston with an air of great anticipation for the coming geological investigation. Arriving in Salt Lake City, I set about assembling pertinent geological publications, base maps, and camping equipment. I decided I would start with the Cretaceous rock outcrops on the west end of the Basin and work east.

My first camp was at Red Creek, where there were some abandoned coal mines in sandstones of Cretaceous age. I measured the thickness of the various units, collected fossils out of the rocks, and mapped the location of these beds on my map. A thick conglomerate sequence in the area was difficult to work. I named it the Currant Creek conglomerate, and it is still called that in geologic literature.

As I progressed eastward, I moved my camp along the foothills of the mountains. I lived in a tent until it got too cold, then I borrowed a small trailer from my Uncle Sim. The farthest east I worked was the west side of the Rangely anticline, about 105 miles east of my starting point. A few oil wells there were producing from fractures in the Mancos shale. Now this is one of the biggest oil fields in the Rocky Mountains, producing from the deep Weber sand. One of my camps while I worked the Rangely outcrops was at the intersection of the Rangely road and U.S. Highway 40. It was a sagebrush flat then; now it is the location of a town called Artesia, Colorado.

By fall I had pretty well worked out the Cretaceous stratigraphy of the Uinta Basin. But I wanted to tie it into the classical Mesaverde formation section of the Book Cliffs, about fifty miles to the south. I spent some time down there but could make only a tentative correlation. Years later, when wells were drilled between the Uinta Mountains and the Book Cliffs, I wrote a paper for the guidebook of the Intermountain Association of Petroleum Geologists which showed how these two areas were related stratigraphically.

In the course of measuring the thicknesses of the Cretaceous rocks, I followed the giant Tertiary–Cretaceous unconformity I had first seen at Rock Creek clear along the south flank of the Uintas — about ninety miles. Almost everywhere I could get a good look at the contact I could see oil shows in the form of tar sands and asphalt seeps. I just couldn't get over the great number of oil shows in the Uinta Basin — yet no oil field in the whole area! In one particular area north of the town of Lapoint, I found a small anticline in the red surface shale of the youngest Tertiary formation. Just a few miles "up-dip" to the north along the unconformity oil sands appeared.

This area intrigued me from 1941 until 1967, when I finally got it drilled. It was dry — lots of oil shows, but not the commercial kind!

I went back to MIT that winter, studied for my oral exams, and then finished writing my dissertation. I had taken pictures of every outcrop I had measured, so it was easy to combine the data even though I was 2,500 miles from the scene. MIT awarded me a Ph.D. in geology in June 1942.

My first requirement then was a job, but by this time the U.S. had entered World War II. My rheumatic fever attack in Saudi Arabia had left my heart with a murmur, so I was unable to pass the physical exam to pick up the commission as a First Lieutenant in the Field Artillery I had received when I graduated from the University of Utah. A friend at Harvard, Norm Smith, enlisted in the Navy to work on aerial photos. This interested me, since I knew photo work would be used in geological exploration, but I couldn't pass the Naval physical, either. It appeared that the Armed Services didn't want me.

I wanted desperately to go back to work for Standard of California under George Cunningham — who had corresponded with me ever since he hired me to go to Saudi Arabia in 1938 — but their medical department wouldn't allow it. I put out applications to several companies. Finally, Texaco wrote and said to come to New York City for an interview. The chief of Texaco's geophysical department, a Mr. Olson, interviewed me, and he hired me to go to Venezuela to work on a seismograph crew. It was the only offer I had, so I took it. As we walked out of his office afterward, he said, "By the way, you should meet our chief geologist, Mr. C. F. Baker."

We went to Mr. Baker's office and Olson told him about me. Baker inquired about my dissertation, and I described my work in the Uinta Basin. He said, "What the hell are you going to Venezuela for when you have experience in the Rocky Mountains?" I said, "I need a job."

"How would you like to go to Denver? We need a man there." I jumped at the chance, of course, and this changed my whole life. If I had gone to Venezuela, I probably would have spent the rest of my life in foreign work. As it was, I returned to the Rocky Mountains and was able to do further work in the Uinta Basin.

I actually worked in Montana most of the time I was with Texaco, and I got my dissertation published in the *Bulletin of the Geological Society of America*. Then, one day when I came back from breakfast in Stanford, Montana, there was a call for me from Thermopolis, Wyoming. It was from Emil Kluth, chief geologist for Pacific Western Oil Corporation, a Getty company. I met him and Arch Hyden, vice president for Skelly Oil Company, in Billings, Montana, and they hired me to run their Rocky Mountain geological department out of Casper, Wyoming.

Pacific Western was a small company principally interested in the Big Horn Basin of Wyoming. They had been offered farmouts on some drilling prospects there, and they wanted me to evaluate them. I chose the Kirby Creek and Zimmerman Butte structures where I both staked the locations and sat on the discovery wells! Both prospects made small oil fields. Later, I had Pacific Western buy leases on the north end of the Lake Creek and Murphy Dome anticlines. Both structures became oil fields, and Pacific Western's leases were productive.

At the same time, I evaluated and recommended purchase of the Kirk oil properties in the Oregon Basin field and on the Spring Creek anticline. Pacific Western paid $400,000 for these properties, and for the next two decades they made that much profit each year. However, I hankered to get Pacific Western into new areas, so I chose to interest them in the Uinta Basin. My first area of interest was the Ashley Valley anticline, where a few small gas wells that were now depleted had been produced from the Dakota and Morrison sands. I made a surface map of the area, and we tried to get a drilling deal from the lease owners. We failed to do so, but Equity Oil Company got the farmout and made a nice little field in the Weber sandstone at Ashley Valley. In the meantime, they and others had found large production in the Weber at Rangely.

I convinced Emil Kluth that we should do some seismic work in the Basin to evaluate the deeper possibilities on the little structure at Lapoint I had seen during my dissertation work, and that we should also shoot a line across a weak-looking anticline just northeast of the town of Roosevelt. So we moved in a Western Geophysical crew and shot these prospects. Lapoint showed some folding and faulting — not very large. The structure north of Roosevelt had about 500 feet of structural relief, but we had difficulty getting our shot holes down through the thirty to fifty feet of gravel capping most of the area, so we did a minimum of work there. Our shooting showed a long northwest-trending anticline with little closure on the southeast end.

Shortly afterward, Carter Oil (Standard of New Jersey) moved in a seismic crew and cable tool drills to penetrate the gravel deposits. They leased the whole anticline and drilled the discovery well on it. Pacific Western wouldn't even bid at the land lease auction held there by the Indian Agency. Shortly after this frustrating episode, Mr. Getty sent me to Saudi Arabia. When I came home, I started to work again in the Uinta Basin — this time with my new partners, the Morgans. The first block we took was North Bonanza, now part of the Red Wash field. (I have told this story in Chapter 11.)

After I left the Morgan–Walton Oils partnership, I bought aerial photos of the whole Uinta Basin and spent most of a winter working on them. I joined forces with Earl and Howard Colton, geologists from San Antonio, Texas, and together we took a 25,000-acre block in the Rock Creek area — near Joe Wardell's old Caleb Rhodes mine. I made geologic maps and cross sections and finally was able to sell the block to Conoco. These were ten-year leases on land that had been split up so badly that sometimes we had more than a hundred signatures on a single lease! Conoco held the leases until they expired without doing any drilling on them.

After I went into partnership with Tom Kearns in 1955, we had another look at the Uinta Basin and bought federal leases on many different structural anomalies all over it. We sold leases to Shamrock Oil Corporation, and they found a little gas on some lands south of Red Wash and small amounts of oil on some leases south of the town of Myton.

By this time it had become common knowledge that Standard of California's production at the Red Wash field in the eastern end of the Basin was from a river delta deposited by a stream flowing into the old Green River lake — the depositional site of the thick oil shale beds in the Green River formation. I determined that there must have been some streams coming into the old Green River lake on its north side — from the Uinta Mountains. Also, always in the back of my mind, was the possibility of oil occurring somewhere associated with the old Tertiary–Cretaceous unconformity I had seen many years earlier at Rock Creek with Dad and Joe Wardell.

I talked the play over with Tom Kearns, and we hired two landmen to start picking up leases from the landowners on large areas stretching from the Roosevelt field forty miles west to the Rock Creek area. Shell, Amerada, and others had taken most of my old Rock Creek block, but Kearns and I ended up with nearly 90,000 acres scattered throughout the area where I thought there might be oil production.

I knew oil would be deep — 12,000 to 15,000 feet — so we could not keep a working interest; the wells would be too expensive. Green River formation oil was only bringing two dollars a barrel, and it would cost a million dollars to drill a well to test it. So we sold one block to Mobil Oil, keeping a 5 percent overriding royalty interest. In a couple of years they turned the leases back to us. Then I was able to interest Buck Miller of Gulf Oil in the area. He came to see me at my ranch in Jackson, Wyoming, and when I showed him the geology I had worked up on the area, he approved a purchase of leases from us. All told, Gulf finally bought almost all the leases we had. Rentals were eating us up, and we were losing our shirts in Libya at the time, so we sold everything and were able to keep only a 2 percent overriding royalty. Gulf knew we were overextended and cut the price and overriding royalty to the bone.

My partner Tom Kearns died in 1968, and Kearns–Tribune Corporation bought his interest. We renamed the partnership Paul T. Walton and Associates.

Then Shell started drilling on their lands and made one discovery after another to the west of our main lease block. Standard of California drilled to the northeast of us and hit. Our leases were getting close to expiring, so I wrote to Gulf, suggesting that we should unitize and drill at least one or two wells to hold the leases. They answered that they weren't interested. Soon it became clear what they were doing; they were taking so-called "top leases," or extension leases, from the landowners from whom we had taken leases. Then, when our leases expired, they moved rigs in and started to drill on our old leased areas. Of course, they hit one well after another!

We tried to smoke Gulf out on whether they would honor our 2 percent overriding royalty. They gave a mealy-mouthed answer which we thought meant they would. In the meantime, Standard of California top-leased us and immediately wrote that they were honoring our overriding royalty, so we expected Gulf to do the same. But they didn't. So I discussed it with our attorney, and we brought suit against Gulf Oil Corporation. The firm Fabian and Clendenin put Al Colton, a trial lawyer who was also an Episcopal priest, and Scott Clark, a returned Mormon missionary, on it.

We got a court order to examine Gulf's files in Casper, Oklahoma City, and Houston, and Scott Clark and Betty Allen, my land secretary, examined them in detail. They found Gulf had actually started drilling operations on several of our leases before they had expired. While taking Gulf employees' depositions, Colton confronted them with this information. It was sickening to see them lie and squirm — all just to try to do me out of 2 percent overriding royalty. Two weeks before our trial date, Gulf said they wanted to settle. They agreed to pay us the royalty we had coming if we would waive the punitive charges and damages. We felt a poor settlement was better than a good lawsuit. After two years, they fully complied with the court order that they account for all the production and sales from each of the more than thirty oil wells in which we have an interest. Since then, the price of oil has gone from $2.50 a barrel to more than $20.00, with a brief spike to more than $30.00.

Gulf certainly is only paying what they were obligated to pay for in the beginning. And we paid large attorney's fees to force them into paying. It's a tradeoff, I guess. Anyway, the royalty income was a welcome addition to the partnership budget, and the discovery of the huge Altamont-Bluebell oil field certainly confirmed my thoughts about the Tertiary–Cretaceous unconformity I had seen three decades earlier. There *WAS* a giant oil field down-dip from it! The oil seeps along the unconformity were surface indications of its presence. It is nice to be able at long last to have a little share in this geologic discovery I made so many years ago.

It is a shame Tom Kearns did not live to see this area become productive. Timing is so important in exploration. An individual's life span is too short in many cases to see his prospects explored and developed. The ideas one conceives today may take ten to twenty years to bear fruit.

CHAPTER 15

THINGS THAT MIGHT HAVE BEEN

SHORTLY AFTER I WENT INTO PARTNERSHIP with Tom Kearns in the fifties, my uncle Sim Walton was staying with my family in Salt Lake City. In the course of his visit we talked a great deal about his and my father's early life on the family cattle ranch at Woodruff, Utah.

During the summer they ran their cattle east of Woodruff in Wyoming, about ten miles north of Evanston, on a mountain ranch they leased from a family named Rickman (sometimes spelled Ryckman). When my father and five of his brothers came of age, they filed on grazing homesteads in an area known as the Bear River Divide because it was watershed between the Bear River, which drained into the Great Salt Lake, and the Little Muddy–Green River drainage, which found its way into the Colorado River drainage and eventually into the Gulf of California.

Several of the homesteads had groves of pines and Douglas fir. The family bought a small sawmill, run by a wood-fired steam boiler, to utilize the timber for building the cabins and corrals required under the Homestead Law to "prove up" on the homestead claims. I can still remember the summer I was five years old, when my father and mother lived in a sheep camp — a complete bedroom and kitchen mounted on a wagon and covered with a canvas top — set up on top of a ridge above the sawmill.

One day, while Dad and his brother Mark were sawing timber, I went down to the mill with my little sheepdog pup Gypsy. Just as I got close to the sawing area, Dad and Mark came running toward me. Mark grabbed me by my bib overall suspenders and carried me to safety. The blowout valve in the steam boiler had stuck, and the boiler blew up! Fortunately, very little damage was done.

My Uncle Sim said he would like to go take a look at the old sawmill site, because he said he remembered a small oil seep in the stream where they used to fill the steam boiler. I pricked up my ears at the mention of an oil seep, so we left early one morning in my Jeep. All the brothers had sold their homesteads to a cow outfit for a pittance in the early thirties during the Depression, so going back to the area was sort of like visiting a cemetery.

We could not drive all the way to the sawmill site and had to walk about a quarter of a mile more. We found where it had been set up, and the old cabin was still there. However, I couldn't find any sign of an oil seep in the little stream flowing down the canyon. Sim was known for his farfetched yarns, so I ascribed the oil seep story to his imagination. While driving around the area, I could see some evidence of several very low-relief anticlines in the nearly flat-dipping Tertiary Wasatch and Green River formations. The Big Piney area, about sixty miles to the northeast, was just in the process of being developed into a large gas field, so I thought this area might have some possibilities as well.

Returning to the office, I called a broker in Cheyenne to check the federal records to see if any land in the area was under lease. Most of it was open for leasing. I talked the play over with Tom Kearns and J. F. Fitzpatrick, who had an interest in the partnership. Fitzpatrick was strong in his recommendation that we take the whole area, which we did. We filed more than 180,000 acres.

I ordered aerial photos of the whole region and commenced making a photogeologic map. When it was completed, I made an appointment with the exploration manager of El Paso Natural Gas, a large pipeline and gas-producing company which had recently opened an office in Salt Lake City. I made several trips into the field with Keith Hebertson, their district geologist, and he was particularly interested in one of the surface anticlines which lay between Lassell Creek and Ryckman Creek. He recommended that his company perform some detailed photogrammetric work on that fold. They also did a little seismic work. The area was unitized into the largest unit ever proposed in Wyoming to that time, 1957, and we called it the Bridger Hills Unit.

Subsequently, a well was drilled on the Lassell Creek–Ryckman Creek anticline and found no shows in either the Wasatch, Frontier, or Bear River formations — all of which produced gas in the Big Piney area. Tip Top field, immediately west of Big Piney, had just found gas and distillate in a deeper formation, the Nugget sandstone, so Hebertson and I recommended that El Paso deepen the well to the Nugget. It would have required drilling only about 1,500 feet deeper. The company exploration manager was agreeable but, since the present well was encountering dips of over 20 degrees in the strata at the bottom of the hole, he concluded that we were on the west flank of the anticline and said we should drill another well farther east to have a better structural position to test the deeper Nugget sandstone.

The second well, drilled several miles east, also had no shows in the shallow formations, but it encountered fairly steep east dips, so this well was not taken to the Nugget either.

El Paso was going through a reorganization period, and the upper management didn't want to spend any more money on the Bridger Hills Unit, so they let all the leases expire. I could have taken the lease block back and tried to interest some other company, but since neither of the wells had had any oil or gas shows in the Wasatch or Bear River (Dakota) sands, I was discouraged about the possibilities. It was a large block (180,000 acres), and the yearly rentals were $90,000 — more than our budget could afford.

Nineteen years later, in 1976, Chevron did additional seismic work in the area, drilled to the Nugget within a mile of our two early wells, and found a major oil field — now Ryckman Creek. It probably contains more than 100 million barrels of oil. If El Paso had drilled to the Nugget sand in their wells, they would have found the field.

My old Bridger Hills Unit now encompasses the Ryckman Creek and East Ryckman Creek oil fields and parts of the Whitney Canyon, Carter Creek, and Road Hollow gas fields. A gas pipeline has been constructed to take the gas from these fields to California. Kern River Pipeline has built a 48-inch-diameter line with a capacity of over 300 million cubic feet per day. The gas reserves in these three gas fields alone are several trillion cubic feet, and their value is in the hundreds of billions of dollars. Tom Kearns and I had a 25 percent carried working interest in the Bridger Hills leases, which would have been worth several hundred million dollars. And all this was lost because we couldn't persuade El Paso to drill their wells another 1,500 feet deeper.

This is a thumbnail sketch of not only the heartache of missing the discovery of a big oil or gas field, but also the progress which has been made in exploration techniques during that thirty-five-year period — and the geologic motivation and determination to test all possible potentially productive formations, not quitting when the shallower zones are unproductive. In other words, they are now playing the game to the last card. This philosophy is more and more evident, and it is a hopeful sign in America's fight to regain energy independence.

Part IV

GRIZZLIES, CHISELERS, AND POLO PONIES

Margaret Lenore Watts, the author's mother, upon her graduation from the University of Utah in 1906.

The Walton family en route from the Woodruff ranch to the annual summer outing at Bear Lake, Idaho, about 1910. Second from right is Lenore Watts (later Walton), wearing a split riding skirt and a bullet belt; she had prob-

ably shot an antelope or a deer for camp meat. Sixth from right is Paul Walton, the author's father.

The Walton family band, about 1910. Paul Walton, Sr. (right rear, holding cornet), and his brothers entertained many enthusiastic holiday gatherings.

Wesley K. Walton, the author's grandfather, is seated, right.

The hunting trip of a lifetime! *Top:* Paul Walton with his Dall ram on the Chisana River in the Wrangell Mountains, Alaska, 1958. *Bottom:* Betty Walton with her grizzly bear — shot through the heart at 600 yards.

Not to be outdone, Paul Walton, *top*, and *his* grizzly—and the trusty Model 70 Winchester .375 H&H. *Bottom*: Paul with his Boone & Crockett–caliber bull moose, near the end of the expedition, in the White River area, Alaska, 1958.

Top: Mike Muir, left, a good hand, and Paul Walton pause at Mormon Row during the annual cattle drive, about 1980. Every year the herd is driven to the summer range in the Blackrock–Spread Creek Allotment, Bridger Teton National Forest, Teton County, Wyoming. *Bottom:* Looking north toward the Grand Teton (left) during haying season on the Walton Ranch, Jackson Hole, Wyoming. The lower peak on the right is on the ranch.

Top: Paul Walton on Mojo, a Thoroughbred who grew too large for polo but made a good ranch horse. The view is north toward the Tetons. *Bottom:* Paul looking south, from the peak on the Walton Ranch, toward hayfields (center) claimed from swampland near the Snake River (right), August 1992.

Re-establishing polo
at Fort Francis E.
Warren, Cheyenne,
Wyoming, in July 1972.
The Fort was a horse-
drawn field artillery
and cavalry post,
complete with polo
field, until the Army
was motorized in 1939.
Left to right, Warren
Erbe, Jackson, Wy-
oming; Bud and Lyle
Tyler, Pierre, South
Dakota; Paul Walton.
Walton is riding Feisal,
an Arab-Mustang
gelding he raised him-
self and named for
Prince Feisal, later king
of Saudi Arabia.

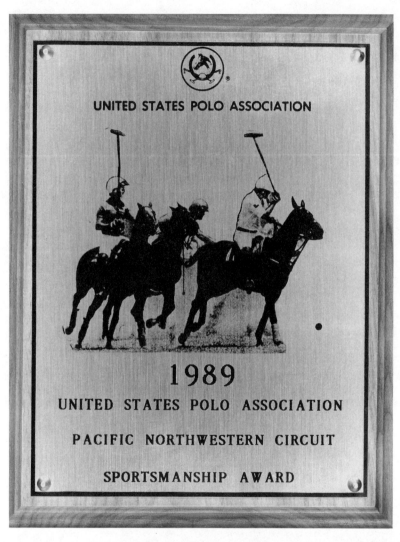

Sportsmanship award presented to Paul Walton by the Pacific Northwestern Circuit of the United States Polo Association, comprising Wyoming, Washington, Oregon, Alberta, and British Columbia, 1989.

Outdoor arena-style polo, played with three men rather than four on a side, a larger ball, and a shorter field than regular polo. Paul Walton, center, Jackson Hole, Wyoming, 1975.

Top: Blackhawk, the greatest horse — a medal winner in his own right! This superb cutting and ranch horse played tournament-winning polo for seventeen years and lived to the age of twenty-seven. Watercolor portrait by Jan Walker-Roenisch. *Bottom:* Winter on the Walton Ranch, described by the Jackson Hole Land Trust as "One of Jackson Hole's unparalleled scenic vistas, . . . admired by millions of travelers from one of the valley's major roads, Wyo. Highway 22. Conservation easements held by the Jackson Hole Land Trust ensure that this land will be protected in perpetuity." Photograph 1989 by Jean Hocker, first executive director of the Jackson Hole Land Trust; Paul Walton served on the Trust's first board of directors.

CHAPTER 16

ALL WORK AND NO PLAY . . .

MY FATHER CAME FROM A BIG FAMILY — ten boys and three girls. They had their own orchestra, brass band, and baseball team. A common Sunday afternoon pastime was to go to the "Farm," my grandmother's place, where Dad and his brothers would bring their families. The brothers would play ball or horseshoes for a while and then get out their musical instruments. My mother and father were both good musicians and wanted me to learn to play the piano, but I wasn't interested.

Games were another matter. It didn't make much difference if the group wanted to play volley ball, kick-the-can, or tennis — I was front and center. Since I was always the youngest in my class at school, having skipped the second and fourth grades, I was never on school teams because I couldn't compete with the older boys. However, when I got into my teens, we had a town baseball team in the village of Holladay, Utah, where I grew up, and I played on it. I played on the church basketball team there too. Being tall and slender, I did well. Later, when I went to the University of Utah, I went out for basketball but had to quit because of a slight murmur in my heart.

My father's parents had a small cattle ranch at Woodruff, Utah, operated by one of Dad's older brothers, Donal Walton. One of my greatest pleasures was going out there to ride horses and hunt jack rabbits and sage hens in the summer and ducks and deer in the fall. In those days hardly anyone else hunted, and we had vast areas to ourselves. At an early age I decided I wanted to own a ranch of my own someday.

[281]

Some summers Dad and Mother and I would drive to the ranch from Salt Lake City in our Model T Ford. It was only a hundred miles, but it took all day over the dirt roads. Then we would pack our camping gear in a horse-drawn buckboard or spring buggy and drive over to Dad's homestead in Wyoming on the Bear River Divide area, another full day's jaunt. They had built a nice one-room log cabin on the homestead, close to a spring. It was a pretty spot with aspen and Douglas fir trees nearby. In 1922 Dad bought some sheep to run, but the bottom fell out of the wool market, necessitating the sale of the herd.

During my last year in high school, Dad sold the 640-acre homestead for six dollars an acre. I was really sick about it. Then he decided to buy some sheep to run on the open range and on a homestead his brother Sim had recently filed on. Dad was going to herd them, and I would be his camp tender for the summer. I hauled the water, chopped the wood, did the cooking, and kept up the camp for him.

We borrowed a cow with a new calf from Uncle Donal, and my cousin Kay, Sim's son, and I drove them to the camp. It took us two days to go the twenty-five miles. The little calf gave out the first day, and I had to rope it and tie it to a big sagebrush for the night. The next day we left the cow, who wouldn't stray from her calf, and rode on to Sim's homestead. When it was nearly dark we could smell their wood campfire, up the canyon more than a mile. Dad and Sim were really tickled to see us. They were afraid something had happened. I was awfully saddle sore. Being thin, I had very little padding between me and the saddle. Next morning we rode back and brought the cow and her calf to camp and enjoyed fresh milk all summer.

We had two tents in the sheep camp, one for the kitchen and the other for sleeping. Dad would get up and leave before daylight to follow the sheep as they left the bed grounds. I would get up a little later, build a fire in the stove, and have breakfast ready when he came back.

After I cleaned up the dishes and made the beds, I would saddle up a horse and go out prospecting. Dad had been around mining a little, and we had a number of laymen's books on geology and minerals. There were some showings of noncommercial copper ore a few miles to the south, and this whetted my appetite to look for something that might be really valuable.

I didn't know it then, but we were camped in the Overthrust Belt, an area of complex faulting and folding not at all favorable for the presence of gold or silver deposits. I would ride my horse to a high point and look the countryside over by the hour, trying to figure out how the hills and valleys were put together and why some of the strata were flat-lying and others steeply dipping. It was frustrating, and I vowed when I went to college I would take a course in geology. Even now, whenever I go to a new area, I'm bothered until I have the basic geologic setting figured out. What a great dawning there was after I had studied geology in college to return to this Overthrust area and see the geologic features I had been completely oblivious to during my "days of ignorance"! You feel almost reborn when you see an old, familiar area with the new eyes of geological knowledge! For a long time I carried two mental pictures of places — one from before I took geology, and the other after.

That summer in the hills of western Wyoming was the determining factor for my professional life. In the fall I entered the University of Utah, enrolling in the School of Mines and Engineering. I knew I was greatly interested in ranching, but I would have to have a profession in order to earn the money to do it. I wanted to be a geological engineer.

When I registered that fall, I also signed up for ROTC. The University had a horse-drawn field artillery unit and about 200 horses stabled on the south part of the campus. They also had a polo field. It was just a dirt field, but it served its purpose. The University had a team, as did the Army post at Fort Douglas, and they played Sundays during the fall and spring. The Ellis brothers, two fellows I knew from a ranch in Woodruff, had taken ROTC at Utah and had played.

Polo was in its heyday nationally and was played from coast to coast. In fact, the opening sequence of "Fox Movietone News," shown in the movie theaters, included a polo player knocking a ball down a field. The game was played mostly by rich people, so it had great snob appeal. I didn't care. I had been riding horseback every day all summer and wanted to give it a try.

When the time came, I bought a 52-inch Meurisse mallet and showed up for practice. There must have been thirty of us freshmen. We were assigned horses and had to ride bareback. They put us in the round bullpen and drilled us on riding. The freshman coach, Captain Murray, said he would cut the group down to ten in about two weeks. He gave us a riding test which consisted of galloping your horse and then making it go around a full 360-degree circle. The tightness of the circle determined who stayed on the squad. About 75 percent of the performance was up to the horse. I was on a grey gelding called Grey Eagle, and he was a good one. He cut the circle beautifully, and I was in.

We didn't get to play at all until spring. When I did finally get in a game, we were all green and did a lot of milling around, but it was such a thrill I have never forgotten it. When school started the next fall, I went out for polo again, but practice started at four o'clock PM and I had a class or a laboratory session every day until five. The School of Engineering schedule was just too demanding. I had to drop out of polo, and it would take me thirty-six years to get back into the game.

Even before the ski lifts were built in the Big and Little Cottonwood canyons east of Salt Lake City, there was some skiing in the valley. At times a foot or more of snow fell on the foothills, and many kids in grade school talked their folks into buying them the usual long wooden skis with a single leather strap binding. I was no exception. We carried our skis over our shoulders to the top of a hill, put them on, and coasted down. We usually made a new track each time, because the toe strap into which we kicked our feet gave insufficient edge control for us to be able to steer or control the skis.

When I moved back to Salt Lake City in the late forties, a T-bar had been built at Brighton in Big Cottonwood Canyon. Then the Collins chair lift at Alta in Little Cottonwood Canyon opened up what was considered the best skiing in the state. So my family wanted to learn to ski, and we got outfitted at a local sporting goods store with long, stiff wooden skis and cable bindings. We took lessons at Alta from Junior Bounous and from K. Smith at Brighton.

After a few years, we were joined by my two secretaries, Betty Allen and Glenna Sorensen. We frequently met at my house, went up to the ski area together, and came back in the evening for drinks and relaxation.

For many years I waited for my kids. Then, when they were in high school, they started entering races and began to wait for me. As time went on, we got shorter metal skis, better bindings, and better instruction, until we would tackle and could handle most any hill anywhere. We skied everything in Utah and then ventured to Aspen, Arapahoe, Winter Park, and Vail in Colorado and to Sun Valley in Idaho. Later we regularly skied the big Rendezvous Mountain at Teton Village in Jackson Hole, Wyoming.

On one of my trips to Libya I spent the Christmas holidays at Zermatt in Switzerland. The facilities were good, the view of the Matterhorn was magnificent, but the skiers and the skiing conditions were definitely inferior to what we enjoyed in the Rocky Mountains.

When I started skiing with my family, I was thirty-eight and thought I was too old to begin. After many years my family had had four broken legs, one broken kneecap, and a multitude of sprains and bruises, but we all kept skiing. Betty and I had mostly switched to cross-country skiing by the mid-seventies, since we disliked the crowds, highly moguled runs, and hot-dogging atmosphere prevalent at the resorts by then. I still got away once in a while to ski the deep powder at Alta or Targhee in Idaho until the early eighties. It was a very satisfying sport for me and relatively safe, since I had only minor bruises and sprains. These days Betty and I spend the cold months in California, where I played polo for fifteen years.

My father's favorite sport was deer hunting, and I grew up sharing that pleasure. But when so many people started hunting after World War II, I no longer enjoyed it and quit. When Tom Kearns, my business partner, had his ranch at the base of the Gros Ventre Mountains in Wyoming, he urged me to come hunting. Tom made arrangements for Bob Strobel to take Betty and me. We hunted with Bob twice and were able to bag several cow elk — but never a bull.

In some hunting magazines I read about the fine hunting in British Columbia. In the fall of 1957 we made arrangements to hunt in the Toby Creek area west of Windermere in the Purcell Mountains. We packed in about twelve miles to a little log cabin, with two young fellows as guides and a Chinese cook named Lim.

Lim was a good cook, but one day Betty asked, "Have you ever seen him wash his hands?" Come to think of it, I hadn't. I wish now we hadn't thought about it, because I started watching and he never did, not even after he caught a pack rat in his trap in the cabin. Of course Lim's "plack lat," as he called him, was probably pretty clean, but it didn't help our digestion any.

The first day out I got a shot at a big bull elk. He fell right over like he had been hit, but when we got to where he had stood in the pine trees, he was gone. We searched vainly for footprints or blood but found neither. We hunted elk for the next few days but saw no more bulls.

Every day we glassed a high mountain where we had spotted some Rocky Mountain goats. We could pretty well predict where they would be every day, so we decided to go after them. Leaving at daylight, the guide and I rode to the bottom of the mountain, where we tied our horses. We climbed steadily through alders and slick grass and rock until afternoon, when we reached a ridge where I could get a shot. When we topped the ridge, the goat saw us and started to run. He didn't have far to go to be out of sight, so I shot in a hurry, right over his back, and missed. Then my Weatherby 300 magnum jammed. I had started having trouble with it when I shot at the elk. Fortunately, I had asked the guide to carry my old Model 70 Winchester .30–06. I called for it and was able to hit the goat before he was out of sight. He dropped onto a long talus slope and rolled and rolled and rolled — nearly to the bottom of the mountain. When we got to him later, most of his bones were broken and his horns had broken off almost to his head.

At that time you could take two goats on a British Columbia license. I asked the guide why two were allowed, and he said, "They're no good eating, and no one here cares enough about getting a trophy to climb this far for a shot." It surely is different now.

We sat and looked around a bit, and I couldn't believe what I saw — another goat about half a mile away just about our elevation. We scrambled across the ledges and talus slopes to the base of a ridge just below him. When I peeked up over the ridge, he was standing on a rock about 150 yards away. I took careful sight and pulled the trigger. The bullet went "whump," but he still stood there. "You missed him," the guide said.

"I don't think so, but I'll try again."

I shot again — the same sound — and still he stood there. Then, gradually, like a rag doll, he collapsed and fell and rolled and rolled and rolled, nearly as far as the first one had. We went down and skinned him out. He had been hit twice, right through the chest. It was dark before we got back to the horses, and I was pretty tired. My rubber-soled hunting boots slipped and slid on the grass and moss. I should have had hobnailed boots like the guides wore. The next day we hiked up and skinned out the other goat as well.

On the last day of the hunt, Betty shot a young bull moose. He had only a very small set of horns, but we thought his meat might be good. We took the goat hides and the quartered moose into Calgary and had the meat processed. It was terrible. The goats came out well, however. We shipped them to Jonas Bros. at Seattle, and they made full-size rugs to hang on a wall. They were beautiful.

Well, we had the hunting bug now, so I made arrangements to hunt in Alaska the next fall. At Vancouver we put our Jeep station wagon on board the *Princess Louise*, a small 2,000-ton ship, and steamed up the Inside Passage to Skagway, making intermediate stops at Ketchikan and Juneau. We put the Jeep on the White Pass railway flatcar and went by rail to Whitehorse, Yukon Territory. What a trip that was — retracing the steps of the stampeders in the Yukon gold rush! And in 1958 even visiting Alaska still amounted to quite an expedition.

We drove from Whitehorse to Chitina on the Copper River, where a pilot for Cordova Airlines flew us into Chisana in a four-place, single-engine Piper Cruiser. We had to traverse the east end of the Wrangell Mountains, and we flew over several glaciers. It was magnificent scenery.

We were met at Chisana by the wife of our guide, Larry Folger. Larry was a former Wyomingite from Laramie who had been a rodeo rider — champion of the world, in fact, in bareback riding. He arrived in camp the next day with two hunters from New

Mexico who had a twin-engine Cessna parked on the landing strip. I could see that he and the hunters, one in particular, were at odds. Larry explained why.

"See these little caribou horns still with the velvet on them. That SOB shot that little caribou calf even though I told him not to do it!"

Larry got the hunters and their trophy heads all packed into their plane, and they took off for Anchorage. Then we sat down in his cabin and proceeded to get acquainted. We were going to spend the next two months with him, so we needed to know how to get along. I marveled at his young, almost boyish-looking face and mentioned it. He said, "The Navy has good surgeons."

"What do you mean by that?"

"I was on the battleship *Arizona* and was blown clear off the top deck when the Japs hit it at Pearl Harbor. My face was completely rebuilt in the naval hospital there."

Early the next day we loaded our guns and duffel bags on Larry's pack horses and headed out for his first hunting camp. We had to cross the Chisana River in a snowstorm, but it let up and we moved into our tent at the camp.

We were after grizzly bears and white Dall sheep at this camp, so we spent the next few days looking the area over. We spotted a beautiful big grizzly one day on top of a timbered river terrace and made a sneak on him. He was gone when we got there. We rode up a main drainage one morning and spotted some Dall sheep high on the hills. We left Betty and Larry's wife in the stream bottom and climbed for an hour to get above the sheep. When we could at last look down on them, the sheep were oblivious to us. All their natural enemies are normally below them, so they didn't look up. We picked out a nice ram, and I shot him with my Weatherby, which I had had repaired. The ram was a beauty. Larry skinned it out, and we carried it back to camp loaded on a pack horse. We enjoyed the meat, which was tender and delicious.

The next day we hunted the same stream drainage and rode up on a ridge to look around. Larry set up his spotting scope and spotted a bear feeding in some low blueberry bushes about two miles away. We all rode down into a canyon, tied up our horses, and worked up the stream bottom until we were close to him. Coming up out of the bottom, we topped a small bank and lay on our stomachs to look over. The bear had seen or heard us and was running away toward a bare hillside. I hurriedly got off one shot at him, and my Weatherby quit me again. It wouldn't stay cocked. I borrowed Larry's .30–06 and fired a few shots but hit way low. Betty stayed prone and, just as the bear was about to disappear from sight, she shot and he fell over like a ton of bricks. I counted my paces over to him, and there were 580. It was the most phenomenal shot I have ever seen! Her little 308 Savage bullet had gone right through his heart, and he was dead as could be. He looked like a big teddy bear.

Fortunately I had anticipated more trouble with the Weatherby, so I had brought along my Model 70 Winchester 375 H&H, with a four-power Weaver scope. I resolved to use this gun from now on while bear hunting. In a couple of days we rode again up the drainage where I had shot the Dall sheep, this time nearly to its head, where a glacier hung down the mountain. It was a six-hour ride just to get there, but it was worth it. We spotted a big grizzly feeding on blueberries in a patch of Arctic willows on a gravel terrace about five feet higher than the flowing stream. Larry and I left the horses with Betty, and we sneaked across the stream to the edge of the terrace. As I raised up to its level, I could see this tremendous silver-tip with his huge humped back at about 125 yards. He was still feeding.

I pulled the cross hairs onto his front shoulders and pulled the trigger. Ordinarily the gun snapped my head and shoulder back and felt like a mule had kicked me; this time I didn't feel a thing. The bear did! He let out an unearthly scream and ran off through the willows. I followed him, and when he stopped again about 200 yards away, I went down on one knee and squeezed off another shot at his shoulders. The bullet went "whump," and he screamed again and ran over into a very thick bunch of willows in a little draw that opened into the main stream. Larry followed me over. We looked at the dark shadows in that willow patch, and I thought, "Boy, I sure don't want to go in after him!"

Larry said, "I'll climb up on top of this little hill and cover you while you go in. When he smells you, he'll come out." I put two more shells in the rifle and threw one into the chamber. I approached the thicket cautiously, watching it intently. All of a sudden there was a noise and here he came, right for me. I threw the gun to my shoulder, looked in the scope, and his head looked three feet wide. I lowered the cross hairs to his huge chest and jerked the trigger. By that time he was about twenty feet from me. He spun around from the shot, and I put another one into his side as he turned. Then he hurtled back into the willow thicket and fell. While I reloaded, Larry threw some rocks at him, but he didn't move.

Larry said, "Stay here and watch him. He could be playing 'possum.' Sometimes they do." Larry had been knocked down and mauled by a big brown bear some years earlier, so he had a healthy regard for a wounded animal. While I watched the bear, Larry went back for Betty and the horses. I noticed he had left his rifle on the ground. It was loaded and cocked and the safety wasn't on; he had really been excited!

It was too late to try to skin the bear out that day, so we left our scent around, with a few pieces of my underwear added; to scare away other bears who might come during the night to feed on the carcass. It was dark long before we got back to camp, and the Aurora Borealis came out in a beautiful big green arch that really lit up the sky. Later on, when it was darker, a satellite, probably Russian, crossed over our heads. It was an elongated object which was tumbling as it shot across our line of sight.

Next morning Larry and I left at daylight. It took us fifteen hours to ride back in, skin out the bear, load it on a pack horse, and bring it back to camp. The grizzly had been hit three times, all within a six-inch circle. His heart was penetrated by the 375 grain bullet. It is no wonder the early explorers had so much fear of these animals. They were very hard to kill. I had been carrying a .357 magnum Ruger revolver for protection in case I ran onto a grizzly when I didn't have my rifle with me. It was apparent the pistol was useless against a grizzly, so I gave up carrying it.

We rested the next day and then packed up and left for Chisana. About five miles out, Betty's horse fell with her, only down to his knees, but she went tumbling off and lay there moaning. I could tell immediately she was badly hurt. We made camp right there and carried her to a bed on a makeshift stretcher. She was in terrible pain. Fortunately, I had brought along some codeine pills, but they didn't help much. She was in great pain all that night. Larry said he would ride back to Chisana, get on the two-way radio, and call for help.

The next morning, just before noon, we heard a helicopter fly over — an Air Force Vertol from Elmendorf Field in Anchorage. They landed and took us aboard. We flew over to Chisana, where they had brought in a Grumman amphibian. They loaded Betty and me on it and flew to Anchorage. At the hospital an orthopedic surgeon x-rayed her and determined that it was a dislocated shoulder which was pinching the nerves and giving her such pain. He gave her an anesthetic, put her shoulder back in place, and put her in a cast. We found a motel where she could stay while I caught the once-a-week Cordova Airlines DC-3 back to Chisana. I was really relieved that we had been able to get her out of the wilderness and into the hospital. I thanked the captain in charge of the rescue operation profusely. When I saw him later in downtown Anchorage, he remarked, "It was nice to rescue someone still alive. Usually they're dead by the time we get there."

When I arrived back in Chisana, Larry was moving the camp equipment back to his base operation. We could go lighter now that no women were along. A few days later we left for the White River drainage, which runs east out of the Wrangells into Yukon Territory. I still had a caribou and a moose to get. We took along a cook, and the three of us camped in a grove of Arctic willows near the drainage divide between the Chisana and White rivers. We saw small herds of caribou running on their huge feet. They reminded me of Wyoming antelope with moose feet. Caribou can run across muskeg that men or horses would sink into up to their knees.

The first night in this camp, Larry spotted a big bull moose about a mile away. We walked out to have a look at him. Larry said, "Watch me call him in."

He proceeded to form a sort of horn with his hands and then made a series of grunting noises. The moose heard him; he threw up his head and started toward us.

"He thinks it's another bull and wants to fight it."

The bull came in close enough for Larry to say, "He's not big enough. There are others here that are much bigger."

He sure looked big to me compared with our smaller Wyoming Shira moose!

We had one tent for cooking and sleeping. About daylight I had to step outside and was surprised to see the bull moose from the night before just a little way from the camp. I thought I would have some fun with Larry, so I stood just outside the tent by a big Arctic willow bush and tried his moose-calling noise. By golly, it worked. The moose came right up to the tent and started to tear up the willow bush with his antlers. The noise woke Larry and the cook, and Larry came boiling out of the tent with his rifle in his hands. By that time, though, the moose had sniffed the man smell and started trotting off. The cook's hands shook for an hour.

It snowed that afternoon, but before dark the storm lifted a little. Just half a mile from the camp, we spotted a caribou bull with a fairly good rack of horns. I had got my Weatherby working again, so I shot him with it. The caribou steaks we had that night tasted much like elk. Next morning we skinned out the bull and packed up. It took us the rest of the day to get to our next destination — a camp in a grove of spruces called First Timber.

Larry trapped wolves and coyotes in the winter, and he had built a cache here to keep meat for his dogsled team — a platform built about ten feet off the ground in the largest tree he could find, a spruce. Since we were near the timberline, none of the trees was very large; they rarely grew more than twenty feet tall. He left most of the caribou meat here to use later in the season.

For the next few days we scouted around for moose. Larry located some about five miles downstream from our camp. The next morning we saddled two pack horses and took them along. We tied the horses in a grove of poplars, where we could look around. There were moose all right. We immediately saw three young bulls. They were cavorting around a large poplar grove in which, we could see as we watched carefully, was a moose cow, apparently in heat, and a huge bull moose. We watched for a while until he became annoyed with the young bulls and came out of the grove to run them off.

He was about 300 yards away. I went down on one knee and got off a good shot for his shoulder. Nothing happened! He just stood there. I couldn't believe I had missed him. I was about ready to fire again when he fell over. I had shot him right through the heart. This moose made my bag limit complete. He was a gigantic animal with a 59-inch spread on his horns. It took several hours to skin out his cape — the skin over the head, neck and part of the front shoulders. His horns were so large they were all one pack horse could carry.

On the way back to camp we met a grizzly sow and her cub on the trail. She stood up and looked at us. Her long, silver-tipped fur rippled in the wind as she strained to see us. What a magnificent sight!

It took two days to ride back to Chisana. When our trophies were packed in sacks, we got on Cordova's two-way radio and called for the plane to pick me up. The weather turned bad, and it was ten days before the plane came. I used the time hunting caribou for Larry's winter meat supply but was unsuccessful.

Since time was obviously heavy on my hands, Larry's wife suggested I pay a visit to Nels Nelson, a former prospector in his late eighties. I did, and it was a remarkable experience.

Mr. Nelson lived in Chisana during the summer and fall and had a nice little bachelor cabin which he kept spic and span. I told him I was a geologist and interested in his experiences. He told me the following story:

"My two brothers and I came from Sweden in 1893. We were sailors there. I enlisted in the U.S. Navy and was in the battle of the Philippines at Manila with Admiral Dewey in 1898. After the war was over, I was discharged at San Francisco, and my brothers came to meet me. I was nineteen years old. They had heard of the gold discovery in the Yukon and wanted to go there.

"We put together an outfit of carpenter tools, nails, shovels, and picks and took a steamer to Skagway. The three of us packed the outfit up over Chilkoot Pass to Lake Bennett. It weighed several thousand pounds. It took lots of short trips, and we took on a partner so one man could guard the supplies at each end while the other two did the carrying.

"We got up to Lake Bennett by early spring. We took our whip-saws and sawed up planks from the spruce trees there and built a boat. We put it in the lake and rowed to where the Yukon River runs out. We floated down the river and through the rapids without capsizing. When we got to Dawson, we looked around a while. We three brothers wanted to stay in the Klondike and try our luck, but the partner wanted to strike out overland to prospect another place. We burned the boat so we could divide up the nails among the partners. They were very valuable."

"Did you prospect or get a claim of your own?" I asked.

"No, we got jobs as carpenters and saved our money. That winter there was a big typhoid epidemic and mining shut down."

"How did you keep from getting it?"

"We moved up on a ridge away from everyone and melted snow for water. Typhoid is carried by water, and the outdoor toilets were polluting the water in Dawson."

I had heard that Mr. Nelson had made a strike near Chisana, so I asked him about it.

"One winter in Dawson an Aleut came to our camp and asked to see what we were mining. I showed him some gold dust, and he said, 'I know where there is a whole mountain of that stuff!'

"He said he could take us to it, but it was a long way. We had a dog team and sled, so we loaded our bedrolls and tools on it and headed out. It was awfully cold — fifty to sixty degrees below zero!"

"How did you keep from freezing?" I asked.

"We would build a fire and put our bed right next to it. Then every hour I would wake up and put more wood on the fire to keep it burning.

"The Indian took us up the canyon east of Chisana — Chisana wasn't there then — and showed me a spot on the stream bank where the ground was gold color. It wasn't gold!"

I had seen this gold-colored outcrop myself. It was volcanic ash that had been altered by hot water so the iron in it had become limonite, a dark yellow to orangish-colored mineral.

Nelson went on. "We had our gold pans, so we thought we would pan the stream anyway. There were some good colors, so I staked a claim. It was a good thing I did, because the next day several other miners arrived. The Indian had talked to other people in Dawson before he came to us, and when we left with him they had followed us."

"What happened then?"

"They all staked claims, and that spring we built sluice boxes and started to mine. That's when I made my stake!"

It must have been a pretty good one, because it had lasted from about 1900 to 1958. He certainly deserved it. He was a fine old man. Larry Folger had shown me the settlement built around this gold discovery. It was called Bonanza, and only one building was left — the brothel, a well-built, two-room log cabin. The miners' cabins had all fallen down.

When I got back to Anchorage, Betty and I spent a few days around town. The Alaska oil boom had just started, and some friends of ours from Salt Lake City, the Swaffords, were there. Jack Swafford had opened an Anchorage office for Mobil Oil Company.

It was now the middle of October, and on the way back to Salt Lake City along the Alcan Highway, we drove on snow-packed roads for 1,500 miles with subzero temperatures all the way. Even with Betty's accident, we both agreed it had been a wonderful two months.

CHAPTER 17

RANCHING — IN THE BLOOD!

ALL DURING THE YEARS I DID GEOLOGICAL FIELD WORK in the Rocky Mountains area, I was looking for the perfect ranch. It had to be in a valley adjoining a timbered rangeland, lie along a stream or river, have good weather, and be within reach of a medium-sized town. Montana was actually my favorite state for my own ranch. I saw one I really liked on the Judith River and another near Choteau. Both had beautiful fields and grasslands adjoining, but the winters were too severe, and Montana was too far from my office in Salt Lake City.

When I became financially able to buy, I looked at a lot of places in Wyoming, Idaho, and Utah. I got quite serious about one in Star Valley, Wyoming, but I'm glad I didn't buy it. Fred Pack, a real estate broker who had shown me several places, called and said he had a ranch in Jackson Hole, Wyoming, that had just been put on the market. He told me where it was — on the Snake River, just west of the town of Jackson. I looked on my aerial photos, and it didn't look like something I would want. However, I thought I should take a look.

It was early July of 1958, and Fred and I and my son, Paul, Jr., drove to Jackson. The 1,100-acre spread was located along the Snake, all right, with about 500 acres of irrigated land and 250 acres of benchland with dryland grain and hay. The ranch put up 350–400 tons of hay a year and had a range permit on Teton Park and Forest lands for 527 head of cattle. The seller was splitting up a larger existing ranch, and this acreage was the least developed part. Some old machinery came with it, but it had no buildings, no corrals, and few fences. The owner wanted $200,000, with one-third down and ten years to pay the balance.

It really wasn't what I was looking for, but it did appeal to me in a peculiar fashion. I guess I am a confirmed do-it-yourselfer, and here was an opportunity to build my own place — sort of like taking up a homestead and doing everything from scratch. There was even a 250-acre swamp which would make a beautiful hay field if it could be drained.

I made the earnest-money down payment. The seller was Mrs. Helen Hancock, a lovely lady, who mentioned an adjoining 630-acre piece of hillside pastureland which could be bought from a local woman. So, I made a down payment on that piece too. That made a total of 1,740 acres. I was immediately faced with hiring a foreman and building corrals, fences, houses, and barns. I was in shock thinking about everything I had to do. In addition, the range permits would expire if I didn't put cattle on the Forest and Park next year. This meant I also had to buy cattle right away!

In the thirty-five years I have owned the ranch, it has taken much more of my time and much, much more of my money than I ever expected. I could write a whole book on building a ranch, developing a good herd of Hereford cows, and establishing a string of saddle and pack horses. Here I will merely mention some highlights of my ranching years.

The first year I operated the ranch we put up 350 tons of hay. It took 1,000 to 1,200 tons to feed the livestock, so I had to buy the rest. Now we put up 1,800 tons. We increased our capacity by draining the swamp and installing flood or sprinkler irrigation on the fields.

The original cattle permit was for 527 head. When Willard Moulton, a rancher running on the same range, sold out, I bought his 125-head permit. Since then, due to our improved range management, the Forest Service has increased my permit to 706 head.

The first year, we built a house for the foreman, and Betty and I and the kids lived in a tent on the ranch. In succeeding years we built a house for the hired married couple, a bunkhouse for the single help, and a two-story mountain-cabin type house for Betty and me. We also built a large series of corrals, a dipping vat, a horse barn with hay and grain storage, weighing scales, and a calving barn. Although the first foreman I hired was incompetent, the

next three — Bill Tanner, Jim Chambers, and Virgil Lowder — all
made great contributions to the building of the ranch. My present
foreman is Bill Cawley, who started right out of college and is the
best yet.

My biggest single project was draining the swamp, which local
people as well as the Soil Conservation Service said couldn't be
done. I contracted for the dragline to dig the drain ditches, then I
plowed it up for the first time with my big crawler tractor. Then I
planted it, and it became prime hayland. This took nearly three
years.

During the middle sixties the oil and gas exploration business in
the Rocky Mountain area slowed way down. This turn of events
gave me time to spend at the ranch making it more productive. It
also gave me a release from the frustrations of the depressed state of
exploration.

Through the years we've certainly had our share of excitement
on the ranch, but the summer of 1992 was particularly dramatic.
We discovered a rogue grizzly bear on our cattle range on the
Bridger Teton National Forest. Terry Schramm, our rangerider,
kept finding calves it had killed, and occasionally a cow or a moose.
He couldn't keep the cattle on the part of the 100-square-mile range
where the Forest's range supervisors wanted them to be. Terry
would take days to scatter the cattle properly, and overnight he
would find they had been stampeded into a drift fence or an area
where the grass was already eaten.

Terry complained to the Forest officials, to the Wyoming Fish
and Game Department, and to the U.S. Fish and Wildlife people,
so, using a dead calf as bait, they trapped the grizzly. He was big —
more than 800 pounds — twelve years old, and obviously a new-
comer to our area. After all, we had lived with grizzly bears on the
range for thirty-four years; but this one was uncontrollable.

So what did they do when he was trapped? They tranquilized
him, took blood samples, weighed him and determined his age,
attached a radio collar, and turned him loose! Within three days
he had killed two more calves and a cow moose, who had put up
quite a battle since she had knocked off his radio collar (later recovered by the rangers).

When we finally got our cattle home in the fall, we were short eighteen calves, and twelve cows were missing. In addition, we had had to hire a second rangerider to help Terry for most of the summer. And when we shipped our steer calves, their average weight was only 466 lbs.; in 1991, the average had been 501 lbs., in 1990, 485, and the average calf for 1989 had weighed 480 lbs. So the bear's stampeding and kills had cost us, at the very least, ten calves, eight cows, an extra hand's pay, and 9,000 pounds of meat (at 95 cents a pound). Pretty expensive!

The response we got from the government people was "Sorry, Charlie, it's your problem, not ours." The only solution proposed was for us to move our thousand head of cattle to get them away from one bear on a rampage. Since the penalty for killing a grizzly is a $10,000 fine and a jail sentence of one year, we did not and do not have many options for solving the problem. The environmental community, with which we have cooperated closely, states that the bear is more important than the food we produce, so they are calling the shots. The Wyoming Stockgrower people, on the other hand, say we should go by the "three S's" — Shoot, Shovel, and Shut-up.

This story almost ended tragically. Terry took some of his friends elk hunting up on Grouse Creek, an area of large open parks and deep timber. He volunteered to try to scare some elk out of a timber grove next to a grassy park, and as he approached the timber, a grizzly bear charged toward him out of the grove, obviously on attack. Terry had left his rifle back in his pickup, but he waved his hands, yelled, and whistled, and the bear quit coming for him. The elk hunters, half a mile off, could hear the bear roaring. Terry backed away carefully, and the bear went back into the timber.

It would have been ironic if the damned bear had killed the man who should have shot it when it started killing cattle, and did not because he thought it would be more appropriate to go through bureaucratic channels to solve the problem — and so spared the rogue's life!

While the ranch has been a terrific drain on my time and monetary resources, and sometimes on my good nature, it has made a big contribution to other facets of my life.

Driving the cattle to the range in the spring and then rounding them up again in the fall requires a month of riding. Finding all the cattle on a hundred or so square miles of range and bringing them home necessitates our maintaining quite a string of saddle horses. Each rider uses two or three horses for the job, and the herd contributed to my getting into polo again.

It was really a fluke — my taking up polo again at the age of fifty-four. Polo is a hard young man's game, and most players in their fifties are thinking of retiring from the game, let alone just starting. I was taking a mare, a Morgan–Thoroughbred cross, to be bred one Sunday morning, when I met Paul von Gontard, a local rancher. He wanted to know about the mare, then he said, "We're having a polo game this afternoon at two o'clock. Why don't you come and see it?"

I had heard that Paul had started a polo club in Jackson Hole, but I hadn't been down to see them play. That afternoon I went to the field and watched. At the end of the game, here came Paul with a horse, helmet, and mallet, saying "Get on."

It was thirty-four years since I had swung a mallet, although I still had the old Meurisse in my closet and thought about the game once in a while. I got on Paul's horse, a small gelding called Little Red, and hitting the ball started to come back to me. My tactics were pretty foggy, but I did get the game back into my mind enough to play a few chukkars (periods) of a practice game before the big tournament of the year. Paul asked me to play on a team half time, using his horse and equipment. I did, and our team won the tournament!

Tony Veen, the pro for California's El Dorado Polo Club, was giving a polo school at Jackson at the time, and I signed up for it. I bought an English saddle in Salt Lake City and tried to use my favorite cutting horse, Fezzan, but he was too wary of the ball and mallet. Ray Chorney had given me an old quarter horse named Spence to keep for him, and I tried him out. Spence did better, and eventually I trained him to play quite well. I enjoyed the polo school, but the season soon ended.

The next year a horse trader from Utah, Floyd Roberts, came to Jackson. He had two good-looking horses. Paul von Gontard said, "Let's buy them. He wants six hundred apiece. Which one do you want?"

I tried them both and took the larger — a bay gelding named Mr. Snip. He was a rambunctious, lunging son-of-a-gun. He had played a little polo, so Roberts said, and wasn't afraid of the mallet or the ball or the other horses. But he was the roughest riding horse I ever sat. The trader told me he came from Central Utah and was just starting to play. Years later I discovered that Mr. Snip had been bred in Oklahoma and sold to Lance Reventlow, Barbara Hutton's son, at the Santa Barbara Polo Club. Mr. Snip frequently threw Reventlow and all his grooms, so he had sold him to Floyd Roberts. Snip threw me off a time or two as well, but he wasn't a mean horse. He just had so much vitality and felt so good he could hardly stand it! After a few years of trailing cattle and rounding them up in the mountains, and with the right kind of bit, he became a very good polo horse. My daughter Ann came in second with him once in a cutting horse contest at the Teton County Fair.

The next year Floyd Roberts showed up again with a whole bunch of horses. I had bought two more from him in Utah in the meantime, but neither worked out. Floyd had a big black, long-legged, mostly Thoroughbred gelding standing tied to his truck. I was struck with his appearance, because he was considerably larger than the average polo horse. When I rode him around the field he allowed me to swing the mallet and hit the ball without flinching, and he was handy and could turn on a dime. I wanted him and traded in the other two horses for him, plus $250 to boot. It was the best deal I ever made in my life. He was only six years old, and I named him Black Hawk. I traced his brand back to his original owner and found he had been trained as a roping horse and then sold to the Mormon Church ranch foreman from whom Roberts had bought him.

Black Hawk became a legend in Jackson Hole polo. In the summer of 1977 he was awarded a medal by Dr. Billy Linfoot, one of America's most revered polo players, for being the horse most responsible for winning the national Sherman Memorial Tournament. I couldn't have been more thrilled. The old pony stuck his head in the air and really looked like a champion when I accepted the medal for him. I was captain of the winning team, and he played beautifully for me. I played Black Hawk seventeen years, and when he got too old to play I retired him; he died at the age of twenty-seven.

In 1979 I attended a dispersion sale held by the Ray Byrne family of Mud Lake, Idaho. Mr. Byrne had about thirty Thoroughbred Jockey Club–papered mares and two stallions. I ended up, not with one or two, but with seven horses — four mares and three geldings, all one or two years old and only halter broke! In addition I had a two-year-old gelding out of my own Thoroughbred mare Lady. Barlee Davies was working for me then, so together we started all of them in their training.

First we fitted a rawhide bosal on their noses and tied a rope to it about twenty feet long. Then we used a long whip and longed (pronounced "lunged") them in a small circle inside our big horse corral. Then we lengthened the rope to thirty-five feet and longed them in a larger circle in a pole-fenced training ring. When they would start and stop and go around a circle on command, we put on a bridle with a snaffle bit; when they got used to the bit in the mouth, I put a saddle on them and drove them around the corral with the reins running back from the bridle through the stirrups to about six feet behind the horses' rear ends. When they learned to start, stop, and go around a circle and their heads dropped down to a proper driving stance, I took the next step. I tied them to a corral pole and got on and off the saddle from both sides until they paid no attention to me.

Then I fitted the bosal and bridle with short reins and got on. Using a small riding crop, I rode them around the corral and then the ring. When they were used to this, I rode them out into the pasture and up on the mountain on the north side of the ranch. After a few days of this I rode them while swinging a polo mallet on all sides until they accepted it, too.

During the fall and spring, while moving our cattle herd to and from the summer range, I spent long hours with each of the nine colts, driving or sorting the cattle. After two or three years of this, I started hitting the polo ball while riding them and then putting them into a slow polo game.

I was fortunate that all nine horses learned to play — some much better than others, however. Two of the geldings grew to sixteen hands high and were too big to be agile enough to play polo well. But they did make very good ranch horses. I lost one mare to a hoof injury; otherwise, they are all still part of my polo string and ranch "using" horses.

Polo has been the great bonus of my ranching experience. Our local club has expanded its membership and brought in world-famous players to school us in the game. Dr. Billy Linfoot has joined us three times. Together with the Sheridan, Wyoming, club, we had Bob Skeen, America's only recent ten-goal player, give a polo clinic. Our Jackson Hole club team on which I played has traveled many times to Denver, Cheyenne, Sheridan, Spokane, and Calgary to play in tournaments. And we have brought home many trophies.

I also joined the El Dorado Polo Club in Palm Desert, California, with my fellow Jackson Hole players Paul von Gontard, Skip Wright-Clark, and Bark Hickox. Later the club moved to Indio, and I played there seventeen different winters. One year the team I played on won the coveted Governor's Cup, and another year I was on the runnerup team. Anywhere from eleven to forty teams compete in this tournament.

To illustrate what a sport like this can do for a middle-aged man, I was sitting in the Calgary polo clubhouse one evening, having a drink with Charles Hetherington. He too is in the oil and gas exploration business and is president of Pan Arctic, a consortium exploring the Arctic Islands of northern Canada. The subject of polo came up and how it had enriched our individual lives. He said polo had been a major factor in his life and that of his family. He was raised in Oklahoma, where two of his brothers play, and both his sons play in Calgary. He occasionally goes to England to play.

My son, Paul, Jr., a California architect, has never played, but my son-in-law, David Brinton, plays in Jackson — and we have been on the same winning team several times. Another time, Willis Allen, a player from La Jolla, California, declared to a group of us, "My polo horses have really made money for me." Henry Trione, president of El Dorado, exploded! "Oh, come off it, Willis, polo horses always cost money — *never* make it!"

"Not so," said Willis. "I had to move to the outskirts of town and buy a place for my horses. Then the town moved against me, and I had to sell the land at a big profit and move farther out. Every time I sold I made money. This has happened three times."

I will have to admit that my horses have never made any money for me, but they don't owe me a dime. They are all honest, hard-playing, good, kind horses on the polo field. No matter what it costs to keep them, they more than pay their way by being used to take the cattle to and from the range each year. I am now raising, breaking, and training my own horses, and this is a very satisfying endeavor.

In the late 1980's, England's Prince Charles came to the El Dorado Polo Club to play a tournament. He is a beautiful player — has a classic swing with his mallet and rides very well. His team won the tournament, and the Club owners had a cocktail party for them after the game. All the Club owners were introduced to Prince Charles, and each was expected to carry on a short conversation with him.

On being introduced, I commented on his classic swing. The prince asked if I played, and I replied that I did and added that I had won a tournament that day as well.

"My God, how old *are* you?" he exclaimed.

"Seventy," I replied. "I got a late start; I started to play when I was fifty-four."

He shook his head and said, "My dad quit when he turned fifty!"

I contracted giardia — a protozoan parasite found in some streams on our cattle range — and never fully recovered, so I quit polo in my seventy-fifth year. But I had twenty-five years of excellent fun and I knew I couldn't play forever. I was lucky and suffered only some minor injuries — a broken collar bone, a broken ankle, and a separated shoulder — none life-threatening!

Some people have asked me why I took up polo at an age when most players are giving it up — and played for twenty-five years. The following is my response:

What Is Polo?

It's going out to the horse pasture in the morning while the dew is still on the grass and before the mosquitoes and flies are awake.

It's catching the horses, using a bucket of oats, and leading them into the hitching rail by the tack room. It's brushing the dirt and dust off while they eat their pans of oats.

Then, it's tacking them up — English saddle, four-rein bridle with gag bit, together with tie-down. Then placing the halter over the bridle and feathering the reins back to the saddle over the stirrup irons.

It's loading them, usually six or seven horses and mares, into the truck or trailer, where they are tied crosswise of the bed. Black Hawk is in first, then Feisal, Clover, Pebbles, Mintea, Pronto, and Snip last. The order is important; otherwise, they bite and kick each other. The biting is minimized by tying them alternately head-to-tail.

It's unloading the horses on the loading ramp at the field, then tying them to the sides of the truck next to the polo ground. It's wrapping their legs with protective bandages while Betty ties up their tails so the swish of a tail won't block the swing of a mallet.

It's putting on spurs, riding belt, and helmet, picking up a mallet, and warming up the horse before the game by knocking a ball around the end zone of the field.

It's riding out onto the field as a team, when called, and being introduced to the crowd in the stands.

It's lining up for the throw-in and taking a deep breath before the ball is put into play.

It's riding hell-for-leather, giving all you have for the full game. It's reveling in a good shot, a hard-to-make goal, a last-minute hook of an opponent's mallet that prevents his scoring a goal.

It's getting ridden off, riding off an opponent, getting banged, being bumped, but feeling little pain until the game is over.

It's loving your horse for a good move and cursing him for failing to perform as you expect.

It's like war, but its exhilaration makes it pleasure.

At the ending whistle, it's riding off the field, crestfallen if you lose, after congratulating and shaking the hands of all the other players. Or, if you win, it's riding to the sideboard, dismounting, and receiving the winner's trophy and a kiss from the lady awarding the silver.

It's receiving the good wishes of your friends in the stands, win or lose, and the warm feeling that you did your best. It's going to the clubhouse for a drink with your team and your opponents.

It's trucking the horses home, where your groom untacks and feeds them, then turns them out so they can roll.

It's the end of a polo day — you're tired, sore-muscled, and warmly satisfied with yourself.

It's a feeling akin to what a world-famous baseball player once said — that he would give up all his honors, trophies, and public acclaim if he could just put on his uniform again and play one more game.

Ranching, with its ancillary benefits, becomes a way of life. It is unfortunate that it is usually an economic failure as well. A pertinent story concerns an old rancher who, after selling his mineral rights for a million dollars, was asked what he was going to do now. He replied, "Just keep on ranching until it is all gone!"

CHAPTER 18

ENERGY: PHANTOMS AND STEAM CLOUDS

In 1946, while I was working for Getty's Pacific Western Company in Casper, Wyoming — and before my Saudi Arabian sojourn on Getty's behalf — a friend of Frank Leonard, our division landman, came to the office one day. The friend's name was Joe Juhan, and he lived in Glenwood Springs, Colorado. Frank had met Joe while he was working in the nearby Wilson Creek oil field. Now Joe was active as a promoter of oil leases and oil shale claims in the Piceance Creek basin.

The three of us talked about the future of the tremendous oil shale deposits of the Piceance Basin, and Joe showed us a map of his holdings. He and Mike Dougan of Equity Oil had assembled several thousand acres of oil shale claims and were looking for someone to buy them. Frank and I got a plat of Joe's holdings and submitted it to Pacific Western's executive committee with our recommendation that we ought to get a position in oil shale.

Some parts of the central Piceance Basin have oil shale beds more than a thousand feet thick. Around the Basin's edge, where Joe's claims were located, the shale was still 200 to 300 feet thick. If a commercial process could be worked out for mining and retorting the shale, trillions of barrels of oil could be recovered — a productivity equal to oil recoveries from the new Saudi Arabian oil fields, as well as those not yet discovered!

Of course, there was always the intriguing possibility that someone might someday invent a way to recover the oil with an *in situ* process, eliminating the extensive mining and retorting necessary for a large operation.

[307]

During the 1920's, when it appeared (again) that the United States was running out of oil, the Piceance Basin had seen great activity. Thousands of acres of mining claims were staked and never patented because President Franklin Roosevelt had placed a moratorium on the assessment work required to keep claims active. Consequently, these unpatented claims had not been forfeited by the owners and could still be patented.

The company's executive committee turned Frank and me down on our proposal to buy a position in the oil shale area, saying it was a "manufacturing process," and they wanted to stick to conventional exploration for oil and gas.

In about a year, however, I got a letter from Emil Kluth, chief geologist for Pacific Western, saying Mr. Getty had requested that the company acquire some oil shale lands. I never did learn whether my earlier recommendation had been seen by Mr. Getty or whether he had conceived the idea himself. Anyway, I was told to evaluate the oil shale potential of the Piceance Basin and recommend areas for acquisition. This I did.

We also had ownership maps of the Basin prepared and found that major oil companies like Standard of California (Chevron), Ohio (Marathon), Texaco, and others had bought oil shale claims many years earlier, but that there were a lot of gaps between their ownerships. One gap in particular, near the head of Parachute Creek, where the richest oil shale bed — the Mahogany Ledge — was several hundred feet thick, was covered by unpatented mining claims controlled by an old gentleman named Potter who lived in Denver.

Ray Chorney, my assistant, and our district landman, Jerry Bishop, looked Mr. Potter up, and we found he could deliver a solid block of about 24,000 acres of unpatented mining claims which he would patent for us for $20 per acre. I got approval from Pacific Western, and we made that purchase — which made Mr. Getty's company a major oil shale owner.

Some years later, in 1956, after I had moved to Salt Lake City, El Paso Natural Gas Company got interested in oil shale land, and I did a consulting job for them, re-evaluating the oil shale potential of the Piceance Basin. By then more wells had been drilled, so the presence of the oil shale strata was better known. I was able to recommend several areas for their purchase — notably some holdings of United States Senator Millikin of Colorado. However, the price had gone up to $500 per acre, and El Paso chose not to buy any lands. Since then, public sales of U.S. government lands have been held, and Gulf and other companies have paid several thousand dollars an acre for shale land. By the late seventies, Getty's $20-per-acre purchase had become a hundred times more valuable.

In about 1965 I was approached by a lawyer in Salt Lake City by the name of Rod Dixon. He had applied for patents on a process to recover the oil from oil shale using sequential nuclear blasts to fracture the dense rock and apply heat to it. The resulting liquefied oil generated from the rock's kerogen would be recovered by conventional wells and would constitute an *in situ* process. He called his company Nuclear Processing Company. In addition, Dixon had several leases from the State of Utah on lands in the Uinta Basin where oil drilling had revealed a 3,000-foot oil shale bed near the town of Roosevelt. His nuclear process required an overburden of 5,000 to 6,000 feet above the oil shale bed to contain the nuclear energy used to fracture the shale. This area near Roosevelt had the necessary overburden.

I was intrigued with the idea, and so was my partner, Tom Kearns, so we put up $7,500 for a half interest in the company. It had been apparent to many oil analysts since 1958 that, due to the influx of cheap foreign oil and the consequent decline in exploration drilling, the United States was no longer discovering as much oil as was already being produced domestically. The time seemed ripe to try a new approach to finding oil reserves by using the vast potential of oil shale and a new technology — that of nuclear fusion.

As our original investment was expended, Dixon brought in other Salt Lake City people — notably John Wallace, Sr., and his son Walker. In the meantime, Dixon's patents were granted, and he endeavored to sell the idea to many companies. I accompanied him on several exploratory trips to talk to potential investors, as did Walker Wallace.

The major oil companies weren't interested. They had cheap overseas oil they were importing and selling much more cheaply than they could find and produce domestic oil. Other companies were wary of entering an unfamiliar area of endeavor, either as service companies utilizing the technology of Dixon's patents or directly exploiting oil shale land.

So, with funds depleted, Dixon sought other means to keep the company alive. He solicited various underwriting firms to raise money through a stock sale. He was fortunate in meeting Milton Fisher of A. D. Gilhart Company in New York City. Mr. Fisher, a lawyer as well as an underwriter, agreed to do a $500,000 stock offering. Dixon hired Alec Keller of Denver to do the Securities and Exchange Commission work. The SEC was not at all receptive to the use of "Nuclear" in the company's name, and a confrontation with the SEC by Fisher, Dixon, Keller, Walker Wallace, and me was required.

The SEC insisted that we change the name of the company to American Oil Shale Corporation and stress the oil shale holdings rather than the nuclear technology. Then Milton Fisher successfully concluded the underwriting, which, for the first time, gave the company financial stability.

We still needed someone to carry the ball for us in developing the nuclear oil shale technology. Through a contact of Walker Wallace, we had Battelle's Northwest Institute of Washington do a study of the costs involved in extracting oil from oil shale. Their figure was close to one dollar a barrel. Crude oil was selling in the Uinta Basin of Utah for two dollars a barrel! This appeared to be a real breakthrough, but oil shale's time had not yet come.

Don Stewart, an engineer for Battelle, presented a new approach to the use of the company's nuclear patents. He suggested they might be used in the so-called "dry geothermal" process, which would entail fracturing a dry hot rock and then drilling wells — some for injection and others for producing the resulting steam. His preliminary study indicated that electric power companies in Nevada, California, Oregon, and Washington would prefer this type of steam electric generation to that of coal-fired plants (coal having to be hauled in for hundreds of miles from Utah, Arizona, and Wyoming), and it was pollution-free!

Battelle proposed a joint study between American Oil Shale Corporation, the Atomic Energy Commission, and Battelle to study this "dry hot rock" approach to geothermal production, and the company put up $80,000 for it.

While the study was under way, Battelle held numerous meetings and seminars with power companies, trying to line them up for further work after the study was completed. The Atomic Energy Commission sponsored two trips to the Yucca Flat Proving Grounds for investors to see the results of both surface and subsurface nuclear blasts. The extent of fracturing in the Rainier blast was encouraging. The granite plug in which the blast was located was fractured more than 1,000 feet away from the bore hole. These fractures would allow steam from water injected by a nearby well to flow to the bore hole. A surface plant would generate electricity using steam from this well.

Battelle seemed assured that this study would bring the power companies in on the project and that they would want to make a test of the dry geothermal concept. They asked that I study Utah for a possible site for the test. Dixon hired me as a geologic consultant for this work, since I was neither an employee nor an officer of the company — only a stockholder.

I soon discovered that all the really interesting sites for a test were on federally owned land not available for leasing. Senator Bible of Nevada had introduced a bill in the U.S. Senate to provide for geothermal leasing on federal land. Stewart of Battelle and I appeared as witnesses for the bill at hearings in Washington, D.C.

My testimony was that a cubic mile of 300-degree Centigrade rock had as much energy as a 300-million-barrel oil field. Senator Bellmon of Oklahoma really pricked up his ears at that. He asked, "Does that mean geothermal would eliminate the need for oil and gas?"

"Not at all. We will need every drop of oil and gas we can produce," I replied.

He appeared satisfied that we were no threat to his state's oil and gas production.

The Bible bill made slow progress through the Senate procedures. A like measure, the Hosmer bill, was slow in getting through U.S. House of Representatives hearings. It appeared that it would be years before United States land could be leased. Therefore, if we wanted a spot to try a dry geothermal test, it would have to be on privately or state-owned lands.

Finding a dry hot rock buried at sufficient depth to prevent a nuclear blast from venting to the surface and also on patented land appeared very difficult. Dixon said we had to have a site, so I selected one on farmland near Kanosh, Utah, where a line of recent volcanic necks, hot springs, and warm-water wells occurred. We decided to lease these lands, but first we needed a lease form, since none existed for leasing geothermal lands.

Betty Allen and I decided we would make our own, and it would be a total mineral lease — oil and gas, metals, geothermal, everything! We sent Barr Smedley, a broker, out and leased the Kanosh area. Now we had a site, I hoped, where we could try a dry geothermal nuclear stimulation test.

But when the joint Atomic Energy Commission–Battelle–American Oil Shale study was completed, not a single power company was interested in pursuing the matter further. Either they didn't believe the AEC, or they lacked confidence in the credibility of Battelle Institute. I will never know.

One thing the study did, however, was to bring together a lot of people who were interested in geothermal energy. We met the Magma Power, Thermal Power, and Union Oil Company people who were currently producing geothermal steam at the Geysers, north of San Francisco. It appeared to me that conventional geothermal steam production was an energy source for which the time had come — not just dry geothermal rock requiring a nuclear blast to get it started.

I discussed this with Dixon, Fisher, and Walker Wallace, and we decided to acquire leases where there would be possibilities for conventional geothermal power.

Four other areas in Utah had intrigued me when I made my initial dry geothermal study. They were the Dog Valley–Cove Fort area, where two boiling-water stock-watering wells occur; the Roosevelt Hot Springs area, where highly siliceous sinter was being deposited, indicating high subsurface temperatures; the Thermo area, where other siliceous springs occur; and Fumarole Butte, where an extinct volcano still occasionally shows plumes of steam.

We hired land brokers and were able to get a large spread of leases at Roosevelt Hot Springs and smaller blocks at Dog Valley and Thermo.

Unfortunately, these lease acquisitions strained the company's funds and, with Rod Dixon's salary and expenses as president, the company was clearly going to go broke if something were not done. Milton Fisher, the underwriter, came to Salt Lake City and held a series of meetings with Dixon and the board of directors. It was concluded that the company would be bankrupt in a year if all expenditures were not chopped off. Rod Dixon resigned as president; Milton Fisher became chairman of the board, and I — who loathed being an officer of a public company — became president. All officers were to work without compensation.

At about this time we were approached by Jack Von Hoene, who, with a Dr. Davey of Milford, Utah, had taken a lot of patented land geothermal leases in the Roosevelt Springs–Milford area. They offered to do some shallow thermal gradient hole drilling for an option to drill some deep wells for an interest in our leases at Roosevelt Hot Springs. We entered into a farmout agreement with them, and they drilled a few holes on or near our leases. Some had high thermal gradients, indicating the possibility of geothermal energy at depth. Dr. Davey was killed in the crash of his airplane, however, and his and Von Hoene's company, Thermal Power of Utah, went into limbo, choosing not to go any further on our joint farmout agreement.

At long last, the federal lands in the Roosevelt Hot Springs area became available for leasing and were put up for public bid. Phillips Petroleum Company was the successful bidder on much of the area adjoining our leases. Union and Getty also won tracts.

Phillips unitized an area near the Roosevelt Hot Springs and has since drilled several wells capable of producing very large amounts of steam and water — much larger amounts than those at the Geysers in California. Some of our company's leases were included in the Roosevelt Hot Springs Unit Area, a Bureau of Land Management–administered lease block. Phillips sold out to Chevron Resources, and California Energy purchased Chevron's interest. Our leasehold interest in the participating area brings in a six-figure share of the steam production each year.

I have already related how the Securities and Exchange Commission forced us to change the company name from Nuclear Processing Company to American Oil Shale Corporation.

Now that our principal assets were thousands of acres of geothermal leases in Utah, Idaho, and Nevada, we decided to rename the company American Geothermal Energy, Inc. — with AGE as a logo. However, when we went back to our stockholders for a rights offering, the SEC balked again at our name and refused to allow us to retain the word "geothermal" because we were not yet in production. Never mind that we held thousands of acres of geothermal leases issued by the federal government — or that we held leases in a federal unit in which six producing geothermal wells had been drilled! So we were forced to change our name again — this time to American Geological Enterprises, Inc., still retaining the AGE logo. How the SEC could construe this name change to be a protection for the stockholders is a mystery known only to some federal bureaucrat.

CHAPTER 19

POOR NO MORE

One day in 1973 I got a call from G. W. (Andy) Anderson, a landman and independent operator in Salt Lake City. He had been located in Salt Lake for more than twenty years and had originally been associated with Dorsey Hager, the first geologist in the United States to write a book on petroleum geology.

Andy said he had several blocks of acreage in Central Utah, and he needed some geological work done to put them in shape to sell to oil companies. He wondered if I would be willing to do the work for an interest in the profits from the leases.

We looked over his lease blocks, and I told him the type of geological report I could prepare for him on each play. He thought that would be sufficient for his purposes, so I commenced preparing maps, cross sections, and reports.

Before I could complete the work on a big block in the south end of the Uinta Basin, he was offered a good price for the acreage and sold it. He wanted to pay me for my time, but I declined, saying, "Let's put together some more blocks and turn them."

He leased about 50,000 acres in the Clark Valley area near Price, Utah, which I thought had gas possibilities. We planned to submit the block to a large California–based gas transmission company which had recently opened an exploration office in the Rocky Mountains. Gas pipeline companies from California, as well as the Texas and midcontinent areas, were streaming into the Rocky Mountains at this time, looking for reserves to keep their pipelines full. They were feeling the pinch of the energy crisis long before the problem became a political football and were trying to do something about it.

[315]

By the time I had completed my geologic studies and report on the Clark Valley prospect, Andy had lined up a drilling contractor who would drill four shallow tests for gas for a half interest in the block.

We took the play to a gas company's office in San Francisco, where they had their staff and consultants review it. It took them about six weeks, but they bought the play. We retained a small working interest and an overriding royalty. Andy was encouraged with this sale and said we should get some more prospects.

American Quasar had recently made a discovery in the Overthrust Belt in northern Utah, so I got to thinking about the southeast Idaho portion of the Overthrust Belt. Back in the early fifties, Sinclair had leased a number of big textbook-type anticlines in the Caribou Mountain area of Bonneville County. Then Sun drilled a well on Big Elk anticline as a farmout from Sinclair. They found carbon dioxide gas in the Weber sand, with no oil shows. The Weber was highly porous and permeable, however, and was an excellent reservoir rock.

During the mid-sixties I had spent a lot of time in the area and had made a photogeologic map of the region. I took some leases then and had held them for years, thinking there would be renewed interest in the area. But there wasn't, and the leases expired.

I discussed southeast Idaho with Andy, and he liked the idea. He checked the records and found almost all the structures to be open for leasing. There were eleven anticlines I wanted to lease.

This was a big play. Andy had to borrow the money to take the leases, but he filed on all the structures. The U.S. Geological Survey had made some new topographic maps in the area, and, incorporating my aerial photos, I was able to come up with a pretty good structure contour map of all the major anticlines. When I completed the report on the area, with the maps and cross sections, we took it to the gas transmission company in California. Their vice president liked it, and I took their new exploration manager, Jack Wroble, out in the field several times to see the structures.

As a result, the company took a seismic option on the play by paying us just a little more than Andy had in lease costs. It wasn't much of a deal, but if they exercised their option, they would be obligated to pay more money and drill several wells.

The company did a little shooting and was at the point where they had to decide whether or not to exercise their option. Their vice president came to my ranch in Jackson Hole, Wyoming, for a short vacation and to talk to me about the play. The next morning he was making a call to his office when he was stricken with a massive heart attack and died on the spot. I brought his widow and daughter out to the ranch for the night until a company plane could fly them back to San Francisco. This event threw the company into a tailspin. As a result, they did not exercise their option, and we were faced with massive rentals and lease expenses.

But Andy Anderson sure lit on his feet. He set up meetings with other companies, and I presented the plays all over again. We sold two of the structures outright to a major oil company. Then we sold a quarter interest in another one to another major company. Then we farmed out the rest of the structures to American Quasar for two free wells.

Andy put the remaining leasehold interests in a company of his own, A A Minerals. He used the money from the sales of the other structures in his company to buy more leases in Utah and Nevada. Then he was able to merge his company into the producing subsidiary of a large Texas-based gas transmission company.

So, in the end, we came out with sizable blocks of stock in a well-heeled oil and gas exploration company called Supron. Allied–Signal, a conglomerate, got interested in buying Supron for its gas production. Allied started buying Supron stock, and its price escalated nearly 500 percent, at which time they made a tender offer for all the stock. Most of Andy's partners in his A A Minerals Company sold their stock for dollar amounts in six and seven figures — mine included.

Since then, almost all of the Idaho prospects have been drilled, and they were dry. One small property in Utah was productive. I find it ironic that all my life I have made money only out of finding oil and gas production, but on this project the money came from the sale of the stock.

I guess the answer is that the oil and gas business is a game, and they keep score with dollar bills.

AFTERWORD:
A LOOK BACK

I HAVE SPENT MOST OF MY LIFE looking for oil and gas production, and the principal reason that, as an under-financed individual, I have been able to succeed to some degree is the thoughtful provisions of our U.S. Constitution. The framers gave the mineral rights as well as the surface rights to the original farmers and homesteaders as their property.

In the West, where only part of the land was homesteaded, land still held by the federal government or ceded to the individual states was made available to individuals or companies either through filing claims or leasing the rights subject to a basic royalty. Federal lands were originally acquired through filing oil placer claims but were later made available for lease applications. A lease was once limited to four sections, or 2,560 acres, but multiple leases could be taken to cover a large prospect. And both federal and state governments were anxious to lease land, because if it was proven productive, they received one-eighth, or 12.5 percent, of the value of the oil and gas sold. In states in which the federal government owned most of the land (such as Wyoming and Utah), the state was given a considerable portion of the royalties paid to the federal government. Wyoming's schools and highways were built with oil royalty money, as were Utah's, Colorado's, and Montana's, to a lesser extent.

This is how, with the help of partners, I was able to lease thousands of acres on the Wasatch Plateau, in the Uinta Basin in Utah, and in various areas of Wyoming on geologic prospects I had worked out through aerial photography, geologic field work, and geophysical and well-log research. Wells drilled on these prospects found gas at Clear Creek and Flat Canyon, Utah — which for many years heated much of Salt Lake City — oil at Red Wash in Utah, gas at Desert Springs, and oil at Grass Creek, Wyoming. The money from federal and state royalties, severance taxes, county ad valorem taxes, etc., was funneled into various government agencies and paid a lot of bureaucrats' and teachers' salaries.

Similarly, privately owned lands taken up by homesteaders included mineral rights, and when they were leased, drilled, and made productive, these lands brought great income to the owners through their retained royalties. In the Uinta Basin area of Utah, I leased more than 90,000 "fee land" acres — and much of this area is now in the greater Altamont–Bluebell field; the landowners' royalties have amounted to millions of dollars. A lot of new pickups, tractors, barns AND houses, as well as shopping centers in the towns of Roosevelt, Vernal, and Duchesne, show that the farmers and ranchers spread their royalty money around locally for many people's good.

Sure, I have made a lot of money, but I made a hell of a lot more for OTHER people, my lessors as well as my partners, and I take pleasure in that.

Where else in the world but the United States could personal initiative, knowledge, industry, drive, and good luck make so many people fortunate? The answer, to a small extent, is Canada, but for the most part, the rest of the world is like Saudi Arabia: the sovereign owns the oil and gas, and it takes a major company or a consortium to negotiate a concession agreement and to carry it out. If there is production, the profit funnels to the sovereign's bureaucrats or the stockholders of the major company, and not much goes to the little guys on the ground who would probably spread the largesse further.

I am proud that I helped to spread the wealth of the energy business, particularly since a little of it rubbed off on me. My own experience further emphasizes the point that my partner N. G. Morgan Senior used to make: "The most glorious adventure in life is making your own way in the world."

Amen.

P.T.W.

INDEX OF NAMES

From Prospect to Prosperity
by PAUL T. WALTON
was produced for Utah State University Press by
McMURRIN–HENRIKSEN BOOKS.
This is one of the last volumes to be set completely in hot metal.
The typeface is Intertype Baskerville, with handset foundry
and Monotype display types.
Editing and project direction by Trudy McMurrin.
Design, hot metal typography, and composition by Donald M. Henriksen.
Jacket/cover design by Richard Firmage.
Maps by DIGIT Lab, University of Utah.
Photo pages and interior pasteup by Richard G. Howe.